LIFE
LESSONS
FROM THE
BOOK OF
MORMON

LIFE
LESSONS
FROM THE
BOOK OF
MORMON

JACK R. CHRISTIANSON & K. DOUGLAS BASSETT

DESERET
BOOK

SALT LAKE CITY, UTAH

Library of Congress Cataloging-in-Publication Data

Christianson, Jack R.
    Life lessons from the Book of Mormon / Jack R. Christianson, K. Douglas Bassett.
        p.   cm.
    Includes bibliographical references and indexes.
    ISBN 1-59038-171-8 (alk. paper)
        1. Christian life—Mormon authors.   2. Church of Jesus Christ of Latter-day Saints—Doctrines.   3. Book of Mormon.   I. Bassett, K. Douglas.   II. Title.
BX8656.C4956 2003
289.3'22—dc22   2003015360

Printed in the United States of America   18961-7129
R. R. Donnelley and Sons, Crawfordsville, IN

10   9   8   7   6   5   4   3   2   1

CONTENTS

CONTENTS

ACKNOWLEDGMENTS

No book on the Book of Mormon can adequately portray the depth and power of its life-changing doctrines and principles. However, with the loving help of many, this attempt to help readers drink deeply from its living waters has come to fruition.

We wish to thank Cory Maxwell at Deseret Book for his patience and faith in us, as well as Janna DeVore for her marvelous editing skills and helpful suggestions. We generously thank Katie and Mike McDonald. Acknowledgments and gratitude for our wives, Arlene Bassett and Melanie Christianson, are without measure. Without their kind critiques, patience, and continual encouragement, we could not have done it.

Most of all we thank the Lord for letting us be on the earth in a time when this glorious testament of Christ, the Book of Mormon, is on the earth.

THAT EVERYONE
MIGHT HEAR

JACK R. CHRISTIANSON

An event in the fall of 1976 changed me forever. Memories of what happened have become more sacred and humbling with each passing year. At that time I was the only returned missionary on my Weber State College football team. Being the only returned missionary was not always easy, but it was exciting and rewarding.

One weekend we flew to St. Louis, Missouri, and then took a bus to Macomb, Illinois, where we were scheduled to play Western Illinois University. The game would not be played until Saturday evening, which allowed much of the day for preparation. After our Saturday morning meeting, I returned to the hotel room and began my preparations.

A knock came at the door. It was Ralph Hunter, one of our coaches. Coach Hunter and his dear wife, Shirley, were like parents to my wife and me. They were active members of the Church and understood some of my feelings about being the only returned missionary on a major college football team.

Coach Hunter stood at the door with a brown paper bag in his hand. He said he wanted me to go with him for a couple of hours. I was somewhat hesitant because of the chiding of my roommates. They knew that Coach Hunter was a Latter-day Saint, and they often teased me about being his "pet" and always getting favors from him.

Coach Hunter said he wanted me to come with him because I would understand what I would see—I was married and had served a mission. I had no idea where we were going or what was in the paper bag; I just knew I should go, no matter what harassment I had to take from my teammates. That one decision forever influenced me. It was one of those milestone experiences that don't necessarily change a person but become an anchor, a reference point, allowing the person, in times of doubt or discouragement, to cast his mind back upon the time when God so willingly spoke peace to his mind and gave him a witness. (See D&C 6:23–24.)

We walked through the rolling hills of Macomb and made our way through an old cemetery. As we journeyed, Coach Hunter told me we were taking the Book of Mormon on cassette tape to a twenty-three-year-old man whom Coach Hunter's son had taught and baptized. His son had served as a missionary in Macomb some months prior to our visit. The paper bag contained the cassettes. He didn't share much more about the young man or his conversion because he said I would better understand once I met him.

As we approached the young man's home, we saw an older gentleman sitting in a rocking chair inside a screened porch, smoking a cigarette. He saw us on his walkway and arose to greet us. When he recognized Coach Hunter, he crushed the cigarette under his foot and extended his arms to hug him. Tears trickled down his cheeks as the two men hugged and exchanged warm greetings. I was introduced as a returned missionary football player.

The man called for his wife to come and see who was at the door. When she arrived, she was not nearly so warm and friendly to Coach Hunter as was her husband. When I was introduced as a former missionary, she looked at me and grunted, "Huh, huh, huh," and walked away. I remember wondering what on earth I had done to receive such a cold reception. The husband encouraged me not to be offended and then said, "Brian would love to meet you."

Who is Brian? I silently wondered. Then we entered the home. The smell of cleaning solution and antiseptic filled my nostrils. Everything in the room was meticulously clean. As I looked around the room, my eyes beheld Brian Foster for the first time.

To describe what Brian looked like is difficult. I was shocked at his appearance! It hadn't occurred to me that he would be disabled. He was lying on a covering of sheepskin to prevent bedsores. He was approximately three feet long and weighed at most sixty pounds. His arms and legs were terribly disfigured, and his skin was stretched tightly over his bones like a tight-fitting rubber glove on a hand. There was no muscle tissue that I could detect, just rough, leathery skin stretched over his completely disfigured body. His abdomen looked much like an oversized football or rugby ball, and his head was narrow, like two dinner plates face down on one another. His teeth stuck almost straight out, and his eyes were sunk deep into dark sockets. To my knowledge he could not move any part of his body on his own other than his mouth and eyes.

He could read and talk with a low, gruff voice. A large-print edition of *Reader's Digest* and the Bible were sitting on a music stand next to his bed. His dad had to turn the pages for him, and reading tired him easily. That was the major reason Coach Hunter wanted to bring the Book of Mormon on cassette tape. Then, instead of laboring to read the scriptures or having someone read them to him, Brian could just listen. After our introduction, Brian looked at me and said, "Pretty sad, huh?" I didn't know exactly what he was referring to, but then he put me at ease by saying something funny.

At that time, Coach Hunter explained that we were in town to play a game that night and that his son had asked him to bring a special gift for Brian. Brian asked what it was, and Coach Hunter pulled the tapes from the paper bag. What happened next was incredible.

Coach Hunter handed Brian the tapes and then said a few words on behalf of his son. Brian said nothing; he couldn't talk. I watched as a small pool of tears gathered above the bridge of his nose and then burst over. As the tears dripped from his nose to his pillow, it was all I could do to keep my composure. After minutes of teary silence, Brian said the only thing he could muster. In a quiet, raspy whisper he said, "Thank you, thank you, thank you. Now I can be a missionary! Thank you."

After composing himself somewhat, he said, "I'll play these tapes every day, all day, on full blast! Anyone who comes to our home will hear the message of the Book of Mormon."

All Brian could think about was sharing the truth of the Book of Mormon message and being a missionary. I almost shrank in shame as I experienced being in the presence of this near-perfect young man.

For the next two hours or so, Brian and his dad shared with us his story of finding and joining the Church. His mother never entered the room or said a word to us. From what Coach Hunter had told me, I understood that she was very bitter and angry with God for sending her a "freak" for a son.

Brian told us that after his birth he had needed constant attention. His dad stayed with him full-time while his mother worked to support the three of them. Brian also suffered from an immune system deficiency so he was not allowed to leave his room, nor was he allowed visitors often, especially if they had been ill with anything. I then understood why everything smelled and looked so meticulously clean. Even our being there was a risk. However, it was a risk Brian was willing to take.

He continued with the story of how he and his dad had become so disillusioned with various preachers and ministers not being able to answer his difficult questions about life that they concluded the answers were not found in organized religion. Shortly after that, my coach's son and his companion approached the Foster home and knocked on the door. They were turned away and told never to come back. However, a couple of months later, they came back anyway. They checked their tracting record for details of what had happened. They read the "don't come back" message but felt that they should try again. They were scared but felt inspired. When they knocked on the door, Mr. Foster answered. He went through the same routine and again told them not to return. The two dejected missionaries walked away, wondering whey they had felt inspired to knock on the door.

After they left, Brian asked who had been at the door. His dad responded, "Those blankety-blank Mormons again!"

Brian told him they had never heard the Mormons' message and asked his dad to go get them and invite them in. Reluctantly, Mr. Foster returned to the door, opened it, and yelled for the missionaries to return.

The elders were understandably hesitant to come back. Mr. Foster assured them it was okay. He and his son just wanted to hear their message.

When they entered the room and sat down, Brian asked them the same questions he had asked all the others: "Why did God make me this way? How come my mother will have nothing to do with me and thinks I'm a freak of nature?"

I don't remember how Brian said the elders answered, but he said that when they shared the plan of salvation and the Joseph Smith story and bore simple, humble testimonies of Christ, he knew the Church was true.

It took several weeks to teach Brian because the missionaries could come only once a week. By this time, my coach's son had been transferred, and new missionaries began teaching Brian. Eventually, the day arrived when he was ready to be baptized. The only problem was that Brian, because of his illness, had not been outside in twenty-three years. He asked the elders if he could be baptized in his bathtub. They called the mission president and were told to find another way.

When they told Brian the news, they were discouraged and frus-trated. Then Brian became the teacher rather than the student. He stunned the elders with a bold question: "Elders, don't you have any faith? You've been teaching me about faith all these weeks, and you don't have any! Don't you believe that we can pray and fast for a per-fect day so I can go outside without getting sick and be baptized into the Lord's true church?"

How would you have answered such a direct, bold question? The elders didn't know what to say. With faith they set a date for the bap-tism and, following Brian's orders, they all prayed and fasted for a per-fect day.

The day arrived, and the elders wrapped Brian in blankets, laid him down in the backseat of the car, and headed for the baptism.

Brian then told me how wonderful it was to look up through the window and see limbs of trees passing by. He said it was magnificent to hear all the sounds that he had heard previously only on a television.

Never in his life had he experienced the common things that you and I take for granted. He had never run on the grass with bare feet, never thrown a snowball, never been to a movie, a dance, or a ball game. He had never seen or smelled the ocean or the mountains. This day in the car was like being "born again."

He told me that one of his favorite things was seeing telephone lines stretched from pole to pole. "I always wondered how a phone worked." We laughed many times as he told his story.

He continued with how he felt when the elders wrapped him in a white sheet because no clothes would fit his disfigured body. Four elders went into the water with him, and one offered the baptismal prayer. Then all four lowered him into the water. After coming up out of the water, the missionaries quickly took the wet sheet from his body, wrapped him up again in blankets, and rushed him home to confirm him and confer upon him the Aaronic Priesthood.

As he finished telling me the story, he said, "So, here I am. And now you guys have given me an opportunity to be a missionary. Thank you, thank you, thank you."

As this story is being written, even now, nearly twenty-five years later, my heart swells with emotion as I ponder what happened just before Coach Hunter and I had to leave to prepare for our ball game that night.

Brian quietly asked me to place my hand on his shoulder so he could feel my touch as he bore his testimony. I did so with some apprehension. He rolled his eyes in my direction, looked me squarely in the eye, and said, "You and I will probably never see each other again in this life. However, hopefully we will up there," motioning with eyes toward heaven. I then made some comment about teaching him how to play ball in the next life, when his body was whole. His eyes then filled up with tears. "Thanks, my friend, for allowing me to be a missionary and share the Book of Mormon."

I left Brian's home a new man. I hardly remember anything about the game that night. All I could think about was Brian's testimony and his desire to be a missionary by sharing the Book of Mormon with anyone who came into earshot of the sound of his tape recorder.

Time passed quickly, and that season of football ended. School was difficult, and I was so busy that I didn't think a great deal about Brian. Then one day I received a message to meet with Coach Hunter in his office. I had no idea what he wanted, so my mind did crazy things as I walked toward the stadium. I wondered if I was going to lose my scholarship for some reason. It didn't help when I walked in and Coach Hunter was very serious. After asking me to sit down, he looked at me as tears filled his eyes.

"Jack," he said, "I received a call from Brian's dad yesterday and thought you would like to know that Brian passed away yesterday. You should also know that the Book of Mormon was playing on his recorder when he died."

I cried hard that day. Brian had been right. We would never see each other or talk with each other again in this life. Our ball game would have to be in another life. But it would sure be fun to play basketball with Brian having a perfect body. I realized that day in Coach Hunter's office how much I loved and admired Brian.

As the school year was coming to a close, Coach Hunter asked me to speak in his sacrament meeting before I left for the summer. Just before the meeting, he told me that he had received a call from Brian's mother that afternoon, and Brian's mom and dad had been baptized the day before. Words cannot describe the excitement that rushed through me as he told me what had happened.

Day after day, Brian's mother kept hearing the powerful messages of the Book of Mormon as Brian played the tapes. When Brian died, his mother finally realized what she had done to her son by barely acknowledging him. The pain of rarely having held him in her arms and never having told him that she loved him was haunting. I couldn't believe the coach was talking about the same woman who had smugly said at our meeting, "Huh, huh, huh," and walked away.

He said she had felt so bad that she called the mission president and told him her story. She told him she felt something she couldn't describe when she heard the words of the Book of Mormon. She wanted to know if she could be forgiven, and if there was any possibility of her ever seeing or being with her son again. She wanted to make it up to him.

I'll bet the mission president nearly fell out of his chair! He sent his two assistants to teach Mrs. Foster, and she gained a testimony and desired baptism. Her husband was now the one who balked at the idea. He felt that Brian's death was the fault of the missionaries because they took him outside to baptize him. Mrs. Foster simply said, "I'm going to be with our son again, with or without you!" Her mighty change of heart must have stirred him somehow, because he was baptized with her.

I have no idea what has happened to the Fosters since then, but I

know that Brian received his wish—he was a missiona
direct converts were his parents. It is my hope that h
some of the readers of this book enough to want to join the
become active again, stay strong in the Church, or study the glorious
Book of Mormon! That book can and *will* change lives!

President Ezra Taft Benson testified of this truth when he taught,
"There is a power in the book which will begin to flow into your lives
the moment you begin a serious study of the book. You will find greater
power to resist temptation. You will find the power to avoid deception.
You will find the power to stay on the strait and narrow path. The scriptures are called 'the words of life' (see D&C 84:85), and nowhere is that
more true than it is of the Book of Mormon. When you begin to hunger
and thirst after those words, you will find life in greater and greater
abundance." (*Ensign*, Nov. 1986, p. 7.) Brian Foster experienced this
miracle, this "mighty change" (see Alma 5:12), and so can we!

Perhaps his story can help us use the Book of Mormon properly so
that the entire Church can begin to get out from under the condemnation we are under for not using the Book of Mormon properly. (See
D&C 84:54–57.)

President Ezra Taft Benson wisely asked this question: "Are we
using the messages and the method of teaching found in the Book of
Mormon and other scriptures of the Restoration to teach this great
plan of the Eternal God?" (*A Witness and a Warning*, p. 32.) The Book
of Mormon is not only the message; it is also the method by which we
can teach the true gospel to our families and to all the world.

Hopefully Brian's story will help us appreciate what we have in our
lives and inspire us to use it to bless the lives of others. Hopefully his
example of bravery and faith will help all of us want to be brave sons
and daughters of Almighty God. It will be difficult, but we can do it. I
know we can!

The words of Elder Neal A. Maxwell put this entire story—and the
reason for all the stories in this book—into perspective. He said, "The

special spirits who have been reserved to live in this time of challenges and who overcome will one day be praised for their stamina by those who pulled handcarts." (*Notwithstanding My Weakness*, p. 18.)

I believe that someday I will not only greet "those who pulled handcarts" but will have the chance to meet Brian Foster as well. And maybe, just maybe, we will be able to shoot a few baskets or throw a football or two together!

CHAPTER 1

A Prelude to
Understanding

JACK R. CHRISTIANSON

Have you ever tried to negotiate a southern California freeway system without a map? It's quite a frustrating experience. In fact, even with a map it can be not only difficult and aggravating but also downright intimidating. You have various highways: the 5, the 405, the 57, the 10, the 15, and numerous others. Without a map or an in-car navigation system, it is nearly impossible to get where you want to go. You may eventually get there, but not without losing precious time and possibly the companionship of the Spirit!

The Prophet Joseph Smith said, "I told the brethren that the Book of Mormon was the most correct of any book on earth, and the keystone of our religion, and a man would get nearer to God by abiding by its precepts, than by any other book." (*History of the Church*, 4:461.) Is it possible to negotiate our way through the "most correct of any book on earth" without some sort of guidance system? Are we in such a hurry to get to 1 Nephi 1:1 (the most-read verse in all Mormondom) that we skip the very road map that will open up and better our understanding of not only that verse but also the entire book? That road map is the title page of the Book of Mormon. Do we become what Elder Neal A. Maxwell described as "hurried tourists?" He explained: "The Book of

Mormon will be with us 'as long as the earth shall stand.' We need all that time to explore it, for the book is like a vast mansion with gardens, towers, courtyards, and wings. There are rooms yet to be entered, with flaming fireplaces waiting to warm us. The rooms glimpsed so far contain further furnishings and rich detail yet to be savored, but décor dating from Eden is evident. There are panels inlaid with incredible insights. . . . Yet we as Church members sometimes behave like hurried tourists, scarcely venturing beyond the entry hall." (*Not My Will, But Thine*, p. 33.)

Are we in such a hurry that we scarcely venture beyond the entry hall and don't take the time to carefully wander through the gardens, the towers, the courtyards, and the wings? Are we in such a hurry that we don't come inside the "vast mansion" of the Book of Mormon, sit by the glowing fire, and let it warm us? The Prophet Joseph Smith declared, "The title-page of the Book of Mormon is a literal translation, taken from the very last leaf, on the left hand side of the collection or book of plates." (*History of the Church*, 1:71.) Since it was the last leaf, or page, of the record, and the title page itself says that the Book of Mormon was "sealed by the hand of Moroni," it is believed that the title page was written by Moroni himself. Thus, the title page becomes a guide or a road map to help us understand the major purposes of the book, and because it was part of the plates, it too is scripture.

Taking the time to study the title page will illuminate our understanding of such significant topics as (1) for whom the book was written; (2) the role of the house of Israel; (3) how and by what spirit the book was written; (4) various purposes for the book; and (5) why every man, woman, and child needs a Savior. With the direction given by the title page, we not only have a road map to help us negotiate through the pages of the book but also several "flaming fireplaces . . . to warm us" and some incredibly beautiful "gardens, towers, courtyards, and wings."

FOR WHOM THE BOOK WAS WRITTEN

The title page begins with the phrase, "The Book of Mormon, an account written by the hand of Mormon upon plates taken from the plates of Nephi." The first sentence, which is the entire first paragraph, begins, "Wherefore, it is an abridgement [in other words, an edited version] of the record of the people of Nephi, and also of the Lamanites— Written to the Lamanites, who are a remnant of the house of Israel; and also to Jew and Gentile." These opening lines raise several questions: To whom was the book written? What is a "remnant of the house of Israel"? Who belongs to the house of Israel? Who are the "Jew and Gentile"?

First, the Book of Mormon is written to everyone! The Lamanites, who are a remnant (a piece or a part of something left over from the original) of the house of Israel, are a major audience but certainly not the only audience. The Jews, who of course include other members of the house of Israel, are another audience. The Gentiles make up yet another audience. Merriam-Webster's Tenth Collegiate Dictionary describes a Gentile as "a person of a non-Jewish nation or non-Jewish faith: a Christian as distinguished from a Jew . . . [or] . . . a non-Mormon." This means that a large number of the world's population can be categorized as Gentiles.

Understanding where we fit in and learning how we are a part of the house of Israel is central to understanding who the Book of Mormon is written for. So, where do we fit in? And why is that so significant to us? Many of us have received, or are preparing to receive, a patriarchal blessing, but we may have little or no idea what it means when our lineage is declared in that blessing. What does it mean when we are told that we are descended from Ephraim, Manasseh, or one of the other tribes? Why are Joseph, Ephraim, and Manasseh distinguished as being different? Perhaps the best way to understand it all is to go back to the Old Testament and review the outline of the entire house of Israel from Abraham, Isaac, and Jacob (Israel) and his twelve sons.

A careful study of all the tribes of the house of Israel grants us an understanding that the story of Israel is the story of a family and their central role and destiny in taking the gospel to the entire world. Learning through our patriarchal blessings that we are descendants of that family demonstrates to us that we are a part of the story recorded in the Old Testament. We are members of the house of Israel on earth today—the Book of Mormon was written for us and our posterity.

Elder Bruce R. McConkie taught, "The greatest and most important talent or capacity that any of the spirit children of the Father could gain is the talent of spirituality. Most of those who gain this talent were chosen, before they were born, to come to earth as members of the house of Israel. They were foreordained to receive the blessings that the Lord promised to Abraham and to his seed in all their generations. This foreordination is an election, Paul tells us, and truly it is so, for those so chosen, selected, or elected become, in this life, the favored people." (A New Witness for the Articles of Faith, p. 512.) Of course, being favored does not mean that they are better than others; these spirits are favored because they are of the seed of Abraham, of the house of Israel, and they have an obligation to the world. The Lord's blessing to Abraham in Genesis 12:2–3 is powerful and falls upon each member of the house of Israel: "I will make of thee a great nation, and I will bless thee, and make thy name great; and thou shalt be a blessing: and I will bless them that bless thee, and curse him that curseth thee: and in thee shall all families of the earth be blessed."

Part of the role of young people in the Church today is to take the gospel to all the world. I believe with all my heart that if young people understand the house of Israel and their role in it, they will know why they should serve missions, why they should marry in the temple, why they should live the gospel at school and everywhere else, and why studying the Book of Mormon is so significant: Because it is for them. This is their book. It's not written just to those who are Lamanites, Jews, or Gentiles. It's to all of us. President Joseph Fielding Smith said, "Every person who embraces the gospel becomes of the house of Israel. In other words, they become members of the chosen lineage, or Abraham's children through Isaac and Jacob unto whom the promises were made." (*Doctrines of Salvation*, 3:246.) Again, that should give young people motivation—motivation to live and share the gospel, because they understand how important it is to influence for good those among us who are not of our faith.

Elder Bruce R. McConkie said, "Every living being is a descendant of Adam. Now we of the Church are also the children of Abraham; we are his seed. We are natural inheritors by blood lineage or by adoption of all the blessings that God gave Abraham—the blessings of glory and immortality and eternal life. We are the children of the prophets. We are a select and favored group known as the house of Israel. We have been gathered in from the ends of the earth so that God can fulfill the covenants made with our fathers and offer to us again, as he offered to them, the fullness of every great, glorious gospel principle. And the summation of these is to have the family unit continue eternally." (*Ensign*, Apr. 1971, p. 4.)

In teaching my students, I sometimes take two or three days to explain the Book of Mormon's title page so that my students can understand where they fit in. Hopefully by the time they get to 1 Nephi 1:4, they understand pretty much what's happening in the house of Israel, the division of the kingdoms, what happened to Israel, why they were scattered, what's happening in Jerusalem, why Lehi is being dealt with the way he is, why Zedekiah is king—how all of the puzzle pieces fit together. When they've had a good overview of the title page and understand the scattering and the gathering of Israel and the division of the kingdoms, then suddenly it makes sense that the ten tribes were not in Jerusalem; only *remnants* of those tribes were there, which is where Lehi fits in. They understand why Jeremiah played such a prominent role, and why Jeremiah and the other prophets were so upset with the way the people were living. The students then have an overview, an understanding and a basis for understanding why things were the way they were in 600 B.C. when the Book of Mormon begins.

In the July 24 Celebration Fireside of 2001, President Gordon B. Hinckley pled with us to be good neighbors and to respect and honor the religious beliefs of those around us. Wouldn't understanding the role of the house of Israel, that the Book of Mormon was written to Jews, Gentiles, Lamanites, and everyone who becomes part of the house of Israel help in this regard? The first two lines of the title page now become very significant in our lives.

This also helps us understand, as Elder Melvin J. Ballard said, that "there was a group of souls tested, tried, and proven before they were born into the world, and the Lord provided a lineage for them. That lineage is the house of Israel, the lineage of Abraham, Isaac and Jacob and their posterity. Through this lineage were to come the true and tried souls that had demonstrated their righteousness in the spirit world before they came here." (*Melvin J. Ballard—Crusader for Righteousness,* pp. 218–19.)

This truth can give each of us great strength when we know we've already been valiant once and that we can call upon that and use it again in this life. Oh, brothers and sisters, the title page begins to be so exciting as we understand for whom it was written.

HOW AND BY WHAT SPIRIT THE BOOK WAS WRITTEN

As we read on in the title page, we learn that the Book of Mormon was "written by way of commandment, and also by the spirit of prophecy and of revelation." If the book was written "by the spirit of prophecy and of revelation," then how must it be studied? Of course, it should be read by the same spirit—the spirit of prophecy and revelation. Do we as members of The Church of Jesus Christ of Latter-day

Saints have an idea or an understanding of what the spirit of prophecy and revelation is and why it is so significant? Unfortunately, if we just read the book as we would a John Grisham thriller or an Agatha Christie novel, then it will be just as Mark Twain reportedly said it was when he read the book. Not reading it, to my understanding, as a humble seeker of truth but as a nineteenth-century novelist, he said it was "chloroform in print." If that is true, then of course the book of Ether would be named appropriately. But if we read with the spirit of prophecy and revelation, it can be like going beyond the entry hall and being warmed by a glowing fire. In fact, the book can not only warm us but forever change our lives. What, then, is that spirit of prophecy and revelation? Revelation 19:10 says that "the testimony of Jesus is the spirit of prophecy."

Elder Bruce R. McConkie added greater explanation to this scripture when he taught, "Chiefly the gift of prophecy is to know by revelation from the Holy Ghost of the divine Sonship of our Lord. . . . [It is] the greatest of all the gifts of the Spirit. Prophecy is revelation; it is testimony; it is Spirit speaking to spirit." (*Doctrinal New Testament Commentary*, 2:384–86.)

President Joseph Fielding Smith counseled us, "All members of the Church should seek for the gift of prophecy, for their own guidance, which is the spirit by which the word of the Lord is understood and his purposes made known." (*Church History and Modern Revelation*, 1:184.)

Do we as parents, teachers, leaders, and students pray for the spirit of prophecy and revelation before we teach, before we study, before we give a talk in sacrament meeting? All members of the Church should pray for the spirit of prophecy and revelation; then, in time, we can understand and know what the Lord knows. Then we would be able to teach what the Lord wants us to teach; we would be able to teach with power and authority.

Many of us are familiar with the story in Alma 17 when the sons of Mosiah meet up with Alma the younger after being separated for several years. Mormon writes of them, "They had searched the scriptures diligently, that they might know the word of God." (Alma 17:2.) But that wasn't all. You will remember that "they had given themselves to much prayer, and fasting; therefore they had the spirit of prophecy, and the spirit of revelation, and when they taught, they taught with power and authority of God." (Alma 17:3.)

Not only was the spirit of prophecy and revelation the key to understanding, but it was also the key to teaching. Again, if the Book of Mormon is written by the spirit of prophecy and revelation, it must be read the same way. Could it be that this is where most of us as students and teachers fall short—in reading it just to read and not, as Elder Dallin H. Oaks has said, "to become"? (*Esnign*, Nov. 2000, p. 32.) To become like what? Like Christ. The Savior in 3 Nephi asks and then answers a question: "What manner of men ought ye to be? . . . Even as I am." (3 Nephi 27:27.)

As we study and teach with the spirit of prophecy and revelation, we will understand what the scriptures mean. Spirit will speak to spirit. Mormon's message, Moroni's message, the other writers' messages will come through to us by the gift and power of the Holy Ghost. Alma described it well when he said, "This is not all. Do ye not suppose that I know of these things myself? Behold, I testify unto you that I do know that these things whereof I have spoken are true. And how do ye suppose that I know of their surety?

"Behold, I say unto you they are made known unto me by the Holy Spirit of God. Behold, I have fasted and prayed many days that I might know these things of myself. And now I do know of myself that they are true; for the Lord God hath made them manifest unto me by his Holy Spirit; and this is the spirit of revelation which is in me.

"And moreover, I say unto you that it has thus been revealed unto me, that the words which have been spoken by our fathers are true, even so according to the spirit of prophecy which is in me, which is also by the manifestation of the Spirit of God." (Alma 5:45–47.)

Again, when we learn by what spirit the book was written and then study the book with the same spirit, it will begin to make sense as never before.

The second paragraph of the title page begins with the line, "An abridgment taken from the Book of Ether also, which is a record of the people of Jared." It goes on to talk about Jared's people being scattered and about the confounding of their languages. The book of Ether, of course, is a second witness of everything in the Book of Mormon. As we learn in 2 Corinthians 13:1, "In the mouth of two or three witnesses shall every word be established."

VARIOUS PURPOSES FOR THE BOOK OF MORMON

There are various major purposes of the Book of Mormon as outlined in the title page. The fourth line of the second paragraph states, "Which is to show unto the remnant of the House of Israel what great things the Lord hath done for their fathers." One of the major purposes of the book is to teach us what the God of heaven has done for our forefathers.

President Hinckley has suggested that we must never forget the pioneers. He has instituted an annual fireside in remembrance of the pioneers coming into the Salt Lake Valley. It's not just a celebration for Latter-day Saints, but it is to be a celebration of all pioneers. We cannot forget the pioneers. In Helaman 5, the word *remember* is mentioned fifteen times in ten verses. Verse 14 begins, "And they did remember his words." One of the major reasons Satan doesn't want us to study the scriptures is because we will then remember the blessings of our fathers. We will remember the covenants made to Abraham, Isaac, and Jacob and all the great Book of Mormon prophets. We will remember who we are and why we are here. We will remember how the Lord delivered so many people from bondage, heartache, and sorrow.

Satan does not want us to read the Book of Mormon because then we will be "reminded" every day. Remember what King Benjamin taught: "I would that ye should remember that were it not for these plates, which contain these records and these commandments, we must have suffered in ignorance, even at this present time, not knowing the mysteries of God.

"For it were not possible that our father, Lehi, could have remembered all these things, . . . except it were for the help of these plates. . . . [W]ere it not for these things, which have been kept and preserved by the hand of God, that we might read and understand of his mysteries, and have his commandments always before our eyes, that even our fathers would have dwindled in unbelief." (Mosiah 1:3–5.) The first major purpose of the book, then, is to help us remember what the Lord has done for our fathers.

Another major purpose of the book, as stated on the title page, is "that they may know the covenants of the Lord." If we don't know the covenants of the Lord, how can we keep them? Because again, there's nothing Satan wants more than to have us forget our covenants and not be reminded of them, to not know about the covenant made with Abraham, Isaac, Jacob, and all the righteous ancients. These covenants are still in effect today. Some of the great, plain, and precious truths taken out of the other scriptures are the covenants of eternal marriage, the sealings of families one to another, and the oath and covenant of the priesthood. All of these marvelous things will be forgotten if we don't regularly study the Book of Mormon.

A third major purpose of the book that is too often overlooked follows the statement on the title page about the covenants of the Lord. The line continues, ". . . that they are not cast off forever." I believe this is one of the most significant purposes of the book. It's not the central purpose—we'll talk about that later—but if a person reads every day, and doesn't just read but studies, trying to "become," that person will learn that no matter what his or her past has been like, the future can be spotless. The person is not cast off forever. People quit trying to live the gospel because they believe they've gone too far. Perhaps they believe the Satanic lie that there is no forgiveness, that the Atonement applies to everyone else, not to them.

If we study the book every day, we'll learn that we're not cast off forever, that there is hope for us. We'll begin to understand what the scriptures mean when we get to Alma 22:15, where King Lamoni's father asks Aaron, "What shall I do that I may be born of God, having this wicked spirit rooted out of my breast, and receive his Spirit, that I may be filled with joy, that I may not be cast off at the last day?" We'll learn to rely upon the merits of Jesus Christ. We'll learn that the major purpose of the book is to show that Jesus *is* the Christ, and that as long as there's a Savior, everything will work out. We will learn that Captain Moroni is not the focus of Alma 48:17–18, although those verses are about him. But really, those verses describe the effects of the Atonement, its cleansing influence, and how it keeps us from being cast off forever when we truly repent and exercise our faith in the Lord Jesus Christ.

I had the privilege of being in a training meeting with Elder Richard G. Scott a short time ago where he taught this marvelous principle. His insights taught me to look at this passage in ways I had never considered. Here, Mormon likens Captain Moroni to Ammon and the sons of Mosiah, as well as to Alma and his sons. Many of us are familiar with verse 17, where Mormon writes of Captain Moroni, "If all men had been, and were, and ever would be, like unto Moroni, behold, the very powers of hell would have been shaken forever; yea, the devil would never have power over the hearts of the children of men."

Then he says, "Behold, he was a man like unto Ammon, the son of Mosiah. . . ." Well, what do we know about Ammon? In the book of Mosiah, we learn that he was one of the "vilest of sinners" (Mosiah 28:4), but now he's being compared to Captain Moroni! Mormon continues, ". . . yea, and even the other sons of Mosiah." What do we know about them? Again, "they were the very vilest of sinners." (Mosiah

28:4.) ". . . yea, and also Alma and his sons." And what do we know about Alma the younger? He was the worst of the lot! What about Corianton, the immoral missionary? He too is included with the group described by Mormon as being "all men of God." (Alma 48:18.) How could that be? When the atoning blood of Christ, the blood of the Lamb, cleanses us, we are no longer, as Elder Scott says, "second-class citizen[s] in the kingdom of God." (*Ensign*, Nov. 2000, p. 26.) We are cleansed and made whole through the holy blood of the Lamb. This is one of the greatest passages in all of holy writ about the atonement of Christ.

Do you see why Satan doesn't want my sweet mother to read the Book of Mormon? If she reads and studies the Book of Mormon every day, she will know that her other son, who isn't the religion teacher, is not cast off forever. But if she quits studying, she may give up on her other son, whom we all pray will come back to the fold and be washed and cleansed through the holy blood of Christ.

It is easy to understand why Satan doesn't want a young man who is involved with drugs to read the Book of Mormon, because he'll realize that if Alma and the sons of Mosiah could be forgiven, then so can he. We can see why Satan doesn't want a young woman who has had a baby out of wedlock to read the Book of Mormon, because then she too will learn that she's not "cast off forever" (Mosiah 28:4); if Corianton can be forgiven and become a man of God, then she can be forgiven and become a woman of God.

We do ourselves a major injustice if we don't take the time to discover what the purposes of the Book of Mormon are. Of course there are other purposes, but now we come to the most important purpose of the entire book. Toward the end of the title page we are plainly taught, "And also to the convincing of the Jew and Gentile that Jesus is the Christ, the Eternal God, manifesting himself unto all nations." Of course, the major purpose of the book is to testify that Jesus is the Christ. We know the word *Christ* in Greek means "the anointed one"—not the anointed two, not the anointed few, the anointed *One*. And then of course in Hebrew it means "the Messiah, the Redeemer, the Savior of the world." If we study this book, we will know that Jesus is the Christ.

Elder L. Aldin Porter made a marvelous statement in a recent general conference. He said, "As Moroni concluded the immense work of his father and others, he made a promise that has been shared widely in a multitude of languages. But I fear it has become too commonplace among us. We learn about it in Sunday School, in seminary, in family home evenings, and we even memorize it as missionaries. But today I would ask that you listen as I read this promise as if you have never heard of it. 'And when ye shall receive these things, I would exhort you that ye would ask God, the Eternal Father, in the name of Christ, if these things are not true; and if ye shall ask with a sincere heart, with real intent, having faith in Christ, he will manifest the truth of it unto you, by the power of the Holy Ghost.' (Moroni 10:4.) This is the promise, that our Eternal Father will give us a manifestation of truth—a personal revelation of eternal consequence."

Elder Porter then mentioned that the Book of Mormon was given for the convincing of the Jew and Gentile that Jesus is the Christ, manifesting himself to all nations. "Do not treat lightly the revelations of God. Do not treat lightly this astonishing promise. I bear a solemn testimony to you that this promise has been fulfilled not only in my life but in the lives of hundreds of thousands, even millions, of people. You will find that when Moroni's promise is fulfilled and you are given the knowledge that the Book of Mormon is truly the word of God, there will come with it a witness that Jesus is the Christ, the Redeemer and Savior of the world. I have never known an instance where this did not occur. Moreover, I do not believe a violation of this principle will ever take place. A spiritual witness of the Nephite scripture will always bring the certainty of the Savior's existence." (*Ensign*, May 2001, pp. 30–31.)

Again, why does Satan not want us to read this glorious book?

Because by doing so, we will come to know Christ. We will come to know *who* he is and *why* he is. As President Ezra Taft Benson stated, "Just as a man [or a woman] does not really desire food until he [or she] is hungry, so he [or she] does not desire the salvation of Christ until he [or she] knows why he [or she] needs Christ." (A *Witness and a Warning*, p. 33.) And no other book in the world tells us why we need Christ better than the Book of Mormon.

Elder Russell M. Nelson, speaking of various aspects of the book, says, "Interesting as these matters may be, study of the Book of Mormon is most rewarding when one focuses on its *primary* purpose—to testify of Jesus Christ. By comparison, all other issues are incidental. When you read the Book of Mormon, concentrate on the principal figure in the book—from its first chapter to the last—the Lord Jesus Christ, Son of the Living God. And look for a second undergirding theme: God will keep His covenants with the remnants of the house of Israel. The Book of Mormon is a crucial component of that covenant." And then as he concludes that marvelous address, he makes a promise that is absolutely remarkable: "Each individual who prayerfully studies the Book of Mormon can also receive a testimony of its divinity. In addition, this book can help with personal problems in a very real way. Do you want to get rid of a bad habit? Do you want to improve relationships in your family? Do you want to increase your spiritual capacity? Read the Book of Mormon! It will bring you closer to the Lord and His loving power. He who fed a multitude with five loaves and two fishes—He who helped the blind to see and the lame to walk—can also bless you! He has promised that those who live by the precepts of this book 'shall receive a crown of eternal life.'" (*Ensign*, Nov. 1999, pp. 69–71.)

Could anything help us more in that great quest to receive a crown of eternal life than to absolutely know that Jesus is the Christ, the eternal God, manifesting himself to all nations? As we read, teach, or testify, we should look for Christ in everything. If the major purpose of the book is to testify of him, then I suggest that every single story, including those in the war chapters, is about him. The book is about him.

Let's look at one brief example. It really wouldn't matter what chapter we chose to talk about because almost every chapter is about him. In fact, Susan Easton Black, a professor at Brigham Young University, did a marvelous study in which she concluded that the Book of Mormon has 6,607 verses, of which 3,925 verses refer to Jesus Christ, employing more than 100 titles. "The Book of Mormon prophets mentioned some form of Christ's name on an average of once for every 1.7 verses." (*Finding Christ through the Book of Mormon*, pp. 15–16.) Think of it—every 1.7 verses of this book is about Christ. There is no other book in all the world where every 1.7 verses testify of Christ, and of his divine role as the living Son of the living God. Why would Satan not want us to teach from this book and to read it with the spirit of prophecy and revelation, to understand to whom it is written, and by what spirit it is written? Because if we do, every 1.7 verses we'll be reminded of Christ, and we will become true followers of Christ as we apply the book's teachings.

President Boyd K. Packer has taught us that 1 Nephi chapter 8, the vision of the tree of life, is the central message of the Book of Mormon. Why? Because the chapter is about Christ. In verse 10 we read, "I beheld a tree, whose fruit was desirable to make one happy." What is the tree? We learn from 1 Nephi 11 that it is the love of God. It's wonderful to know *what* the tree is, but *who* is the tree? *Who* is the love of God? John 3:16 says, "God so loved the world, that he gave his only begotten Son." Hence we know that the tree is Christ. We learn that the fruit of the tree is "desirable to make one happy." What then is the fruit? We know it's the love of God also, but again, *who* is it? It is Christ; it is his atonement; it is everything associated with him. It is vast and broad, and when you pluck the fruit of the tree it will make you happy.

Now I ask a question: How does fruit hang from a tree? By a stem.

In Isaiah chapter 11, a chapter that was given by the angel Moroni to Joseph Smith, Isaiah describes Christ as the *stem* of Jesse. Elder Jeffrey R. Holland suggests in his writings that "the tree of life as a symbol includes the tree on which he would be slain for the sins of the world." (*Christ and the New Covenant*, p. 90.) And when we pluck the fruit of that tree, it will make us happy, because it is the fruit of the Atonement, of the Resurrection, of forgiveness of sins, of anything that is involved with Christ, which is infinite and eternal.

As we prayerfully and seriously study the Book of Mormon, let's include the title page as part of that study. To neglect it would be like trying to negotiate that Southern California freeway without a map. It would be like not going beyond the entry hall but just opening the door, peeking in, and then closing it, not going in and sitting down by the inviting fire and letting it warm us. Let's allow this glorious book not only to warm us but also to fill our souls with a burning testimony of its principal character, the Lord Jesus Christ.

CHAPTER 2

WHY WE NEED
THE BOOK OF MORMON

JACK R. CHRISTIANSON

As we strive to live the gospel of Jesus Christ, our roots will grow deep and take hold. (See Alma 32.) Our foundation will become a "sure foundation." (Helaman 5:12.) Then, with a secure root system and a sure foundation, when the storms of life descend, as they do in each of our lives, and "when the devil shall send forth his mighty winds, yea, his shafts in the whirlwind, yea, when all his hail and his mighty storm shall beat upon you, it shall have no power over you to drag you down to the gulf of misery and endless wo, because of the rock upon which you are built, which is a sure foundation, a foundation whereon if men build they cannot fall." (Helaman 5:12.) In other words, when the heat of the day falls upon us, we will not wither and die. (See Matthew 13:1–9.) The sure foundation is, of course, Christ, our Savior and our Redeemer. As was mentioned in a previous chapter, he is not only the rock upon which we must build, but he is also "the way, the truth, and the life." (John 14:6.) He is the light and the life of the world. (See John 8:12.) He is the Messiah, the "Holy One of Israel." (2 Nephi 9:41.)

Elder M. Russell Ballard taught it this way: "By focusing on and living the principles of Heavenly Father's plan for our eternal happiness, we can separate ourselves from the wickedness of the world. If we are anchored to the correct understanding of who we are, why we are here on earth, and where we can go after this mortal life, Satan cannot threaten our happiness through any form of temptation. If we are determined to live by Heavenly Father's plan, we will use our God-given moral agency to make decisions based on revealed truth, not on the opinions of others or on the current thinking of the world." (*Ensign*, May 1995, p. 24.)

What, then, happens to us as we move through our lives? Why does the innocence of our childhood leave? Why do we so often become hardened to the finer sensitivities of the Spirit? As we mature, shouldn't we increase in faith and righteousness rather than decrease? In our childlike innocence we are meek; we love Jesus, and we love to hear stories about him. What happens to that faith? Do we, in our "intelligence" and wisdom, lose sight of why we need him so desperately? Or is it that disappointment and reality slap us so hard in the face that we question not only our need for him but also his very existence? If he exists, and if his gospel is one of gladness, happiness, and joy, why then is there so much suffering, pain, and sorrow in the world around us?

The answers to these and other questions are the essence of why we need Christ. Let me illustrate. Many years ago when our oldest children were small, I took the opportunity to tuck our second daughter into bed one night. She asked me to tell her many stories. Her five-year-old mind was intensely inquisitive. She asked if I would turn on the light and read her a story from the *Friend*. As we thumbed through the magazine together, she noticed a picture of Nephi standing over Laban's drunken body with his sword raised to cut off Laban's head. She let out a cry: "Daddy! Read that one. I love this story."

I remember thinking how strange it seemed for a five-year-old girl to be excited about Nephi cutting off Laban's head. Nevertheless, I read the story. When I finished, there was a long pause. You could almost see a video going on in her head. She looked at me as if she were embarrassed. She said, "Dad, I really like this story out of the *Friend*, but I like it a lot better out of the Book of Mormon."

I didn't quite know how to respond. After holding her in my arms and secretly praying that she would feel that way when she was a teenager, I asked her why she felt the way she did. All she said was that it felt different when it was read from the Book of Mormon. Though she didn't understand everything when we read from the scriptures, in her innocence and childlike faith she could feel the Spirit. She knew that the Lord had commanded Nephi to slay Laban; therefore, it was okay to do it. Her faith was sweet and profoundly simple. She was experiencing what all may experience if they will spend sufficient time "feast[ing] upon the words of Christ." (2 Nephi 32:3.) She understood what the Lord has said: "These words [the scriptures] are not of men nor of man, but of me; wherefore, you shall testify they are of me and not of man; for it is my voice which speaketh them unto you; for they are given by my Spirit unto you, and by my power you can read them one to another; and save it were by my power you could not have them; wherefore, you can testify that you have heard my voice, and know my words." (D&C 18:34–36.)

I believe that my daughter, in her innocence and purity, could recognize the voice of the Savior when the scriptures were read to her. That's why it was "better" when we read from the scriptures themselves.

Since then, I have often thought of Parley P. Pratt's experience with reading the Book of Mormon for the first time. He wrote, "I read all day; eating was a burden, I had no desire for food; sleep was a burden when the night came, for I preferred reading to sleep.

"As I read, the spirit of the Lord was upon me, and I knew and comprehended that the book was true, as plainly and manifestly as a man comprehends and knows that he exists. My joy was now full, as it were, and I rejoiced sufficiently to more than pay me for all the sorrows, sacrifices and toils of my life. I soon determined to see the young man who had been the instrument of its discovery and translation." (*Autobiography of Parley P. Pratt*, p. 32.)

Perhaps our problem as we grow older is that we try to think, to intellectualize, so much in our approach to spiritual matters that we become "past feeling." (1 Nephi 17:45.) We then begin to rely on ourselves and forget why we need Christ. Remember President Benson's teaching: "Just as a man does not really desire food until he is hungry, so he does not desire the salvation of Christ until he knows why he needs Christ.

"No one adequately and properly knows why he needs Christ until he understands and accepts the doctrine of the Fall and its effect upon all mankind. And no other book in the world explains this vital doctrine nearly as well as the Book of Mormon." (*A Witness and a Warning*, p. 33.)

One major reason for studying the Book of Mormon daily is so we can learn why we need Christ! As we learn why we need him, we will desire to follow him and be even as he is. (See 3 Nephi 27:27.) President Harold B. Lee said, "If one wants to get close to God, he can do it by reading the Book of Mormon.

"You . . . can do nothing better to whet your spiritual appetites and to maintain your spiritual tone than to read and reread year by year the precious things as taught in the Book of Mormon.

"If you want to fortify students (children and families) against the apostate teachings, the so-called higher critics that are going to challenge their faith in the Bible, give them a fundamental understanding of the teachings of the Book of Mormon. Review it again and again." (*Teachings of Presidents of the Church: Harold B. Lee*, pp. 62–63.)

Remember, the title page of the Book of Mormon testifies that one of the book's major purposes is "to the convincing of the Jew and Gentile that Jesus is the Christ, the Eternal God, manifesting himself unto all nations." There is a power that comes from daily searching in the Book of Mormon that can come in no other way. It not only gets us nearer to God and teaches us why we need Christ, but as President Benson taught, there is something more: "There is a power in the book which will begin to flow into your lives the moment you begin a serious study of the book. You will find greater power to resist temptation. You will find the power to avoid deception. You will find the power to stay on the strait and narrow path. The scriptures are called 'the words of life' (see D&C 84:85), and nowhere is that more true than it is of the Book of Mormon. When you begin to hunger and thirst after those words, you will find life in greater and greater abundance." (*Ensign*, Nov. 1986, p. 7.)

When Nephi had heard his father's teachings concerning the tree of life, his desire was great not only to see what his father saw but also to hear and know these teachings for himself. He was not satisfied just to hear his father speak of these things, because he knew that he could have the same testimony as Lehi: "After I, Nephi, having heard all the words of my father, concerning the things which he saw in a vision, and also the things which he spake by the power of the Holy Ghost, which power he received by faith on the Son of God—and the Son of God was the Messiah who should come—I, Nephi, was desirous also that I might see, and hear, and know of these things, by the power of the Holy Ghost, which is the gift of God unto all those who diligently seek him." (1 Nephi 10:17.)

Nephi then put his faith to work in order to fulfill his great desire to "see," "hear," and "know." He did the three things each of us can do to have the same type of experience: "After I had *desired* to know the things that my father had seen, and *believing* that the Lord was able to make them known unto me, as I sat *pondering* in mine heart I was caught away in the Spirit of the Lord." (1 Nephi 11: 1, italics added.)

Nephi *desired*, he *believed*, and he took the time to sit *pondering* in his heart! He paid the price to find out for himself what his father, who was also his priesthood leader, was trying to teach and get his people to understand! Have we caught the vision of what the Lord's messengers in our day are trying to teach us? Do we feel what they feel? Do we see what they see? Do we know what they know? Are we following Nephi's example? Do we desire to know? Do we believe we can know? Do we take the time to ponder in our hearts, not only their words but also the words of the holy scriptures, particularly the Book of Mormon?

President Gordon B. Hinckley, in sharing his vision of the importance and truthfulness of the Book of Mormon, has taught us this:

> As if [the First Vision] were not enough to certify to the personality and the reality of the Redeemer of mankind, there followed the coming forth of the Book of Mormon. Here is something that a man could hold in his hands, could "heft," as it were. He could read it. He could pray about it, for it contained a promise that the Holy Ghost would declare its truth if that witness were sought in prayer.
>
> This remarkable book stands as a testimonial to the living reality of the Son of God. The Bible declares that "in the mouth of two or three witnesses every word may be established" (Matthew 18:16). The Bible, the testament of the Old World, is one witness. The Book of Mormon, the testament of the New World, is another witness.
>
> I cannot understand why the Christian world does not accept this book. I would think they would be looking for anything and everything that would establish without question the reality and the divinity of the Savior of the world. (*Ensign*, Nov. 2002, pp. 80–81.)

And I cannot understand why we as members of the Church, for the most part, do not take full advantage of having this glorious second witness of Christ by drinking deeply from its living waters every day of our lives. How can we catch the vision? Do we have the same vision as President Ezra Taft Benson when he taught:

> The Book of Mormon is the instrument that God designed

to "sweep the earth as with a flood, to gather out [His] elect." (Moses 7:62.) This sacred volume of scripture needs to become more central in our preaching, our teaching, and our missionary work. . . .

The time is long overdue for a massive flooding of the earth with the Book of Mormon for the many reasons which the Lord has given. In this age of electronic media and mass distribution of the printed word, God will hold us accountable if we do not now move the Book of Mormon in a monumental way.

We have the Book of Mormon, we have the members, we have the missionaries, we have the resources, and the world has the need. The time is now!

My beloved brothers and sisters, we hardly fathom the power of the Book of Mormon, nor the divine role it must play, nor the extent to which it must be moved.

"Few men on the earth," said Elder Bruce R. McConkie, "either in or out of the Church, have caught the vision of what the Book of Mormon is all about. Few are they among men who know the part it has played and will yet play in preparing the way for the coming of Him of whom it is a new witness. . . . The Book of Mormon shall so affect men that the whole earth and all its peoples will have been influenced and governed by it. . . . There is no greater issue ever to confront mankind in modern times than this: Is the Book of Mormon the mind and will and voice of God to all men?" (*Millennial Messiah*, pp. 159, 170, 179.) We testify that it is. (Ezra Taft Benson, *Ensign*, Nov. 1988, pp. 4–5.)

President Benson also suggested that because we have not been using the Book of Mormon as we should, our homes are not as strong as they could be, our families may be corrupted by worldly trends and teachings, our missionaries are not as effective, our church classes are not as Spirit filled, and our nation will continue to degenerate. He further counseled, "Every Latter-day Saint should make the study of this book a lifetime pursuit. Otherwise he is placing his soul in jeopardy and neglecting that which could give spiritual and intellectual unity to his whole life. There is a difference between a convert who is built on the rock of Christ through the Book of Mormon and stays hold of that iron rod, and one who is not." (*Ensign*, May 1975, p. 65.)

These statements leave us asking some serious questions as to whether we are using the Book of Mormon as it was intended. Each of us must resolve really only two questions when it comes to religion, whether we are Church members or not. Is there a God? Is the Book of Mormon true? Upon those two questions hangs the balance of religious truth. Elder Bruce R. McConkie said it this way:

"These are deep and solemn and ponderous matters. We need not think we can trifle with sacred things and escape the wrath of a just God.

"Either the Book of Mormon is true, or it is false; either it came from God, or it was spawned in the infernal realms. It declares plainly that all men must accept it as pure scripture or they will lose their souls. It is not and cannot be simply another treatise on religion; it either came from heaven or from hell. And it is time for all those seeking salvation to find out for themselves whether it is of the Lord or of Lucifer." (*Ensign*, Nov. 1983, p. 73.)

We must find out for ourselves! In order to do that, we must read it with a sincere heart, ponder its pages, and ask the Lord if it is true. (See Moroni 10:4–5.) He will let us know. I am convinced that he wants us to know the truth. He knows that life eternal is to know the true nature of God and his Son whom he has sent. (See John 17:3.)

As President Benson has suggested, "We must flood the earth with the Book of Mormon—and get out from under God's condemnation for having treated it lightly." (*Ensign*, Nov. 1988, p. 5.)

What is this condemnation that the entire Church is under? Why did the Lord use such powerful language as the Brethren returned from their missions in 1832? He said: "Your minds in times past have been darkened because of unbelief, and because you have treated lightly the things you have received—which vanity and unbelief have brought the whole church under condemnation. And this condemnation resteth upon the children of Zion, even all. And they shall remain under this condemnation until they repent and remember the new covenant, even the Book of Mormon and the former commandments which I have given them, not only to say, but to do according to that which I have written." (D&C 84:54–57.)

Concerning these verses Elder Russell M. Nelson of the Quorum of the Twelve Apostles tells the story of being called into President Ezra Taft Benson's office shortly after Elder Nelson's call to the Quorum of the Twelve. The prophet expressed his deep concern to Elder Nelson that members of the Church did not fully appreciate the value of the Book of Mormon, and he quoted the preceding verses from section 84 with emotion in his voice. Elder Nelson then related, "I shall never forget that lesson. Since then, President Howard W. Hunter, President Gordon B. Hinckley, and many other leaders of the Church have continued to extol the Book of Mormon to people throughout the world. I would like to add my testimony of the divinity of this book." (*Ensign*, Nov. 1999, p. 69.)

Certainly we must do better in sharing the Book of Mormon with the world. Certainly part of the condemnation is that our families are not as strong as they could be. It also includes a loss of spiritual light. But is this all that the condemnation consists of? I think not. Robert Millet, former dean of the College of Religious Instruction at Brigham Young University, said this of the condemnation we are under:

In a broader sense, I believe the condemnation that rests upon the Latter-day Saints is a loss of spiritual power, a loss of blessings, a loss of perspective about eternal possibilities. Perhaps we have not enjoyed the revelations, the divine direction, the sweet promptings of the Spirit, that might have been ours. We have not been the recipients of the fruit of the Spirit—"love, joy, peace, longsuffering, gentleness, goodness, faith, meekness, temperance" (Galatians 5:22–23)—as we could have been. Surely we have not enjoyed the understanding, the light and truth, the lens of pure intelligence, that is so readily accessible. In too many cases our minds and hearts have not been shaped and prepared by the Book of Mormon, by its lessons and logic, testimony and transforming power, and thus too often the judgment and discernment so essential to perceiving the false doctrines of the world, and even the irrelevant, have not been as strong as they might have been. Because we have not immersed and washed ourselves in those living waters that flow from the Book of Mormon, we have not enjoyed faith like the ancients, that faith which strengthens resolve and provides courage and peace in a time of unrest. So much of the stress and fear and apprehension and exhaustion that now exist in society is so very unnecessary; ours could be the right to that lifting and liberating Spirit that produces hope and peace and rest. Though the light of the fulness of the everlasting gospel has begun to break forth into a world of darkness (see D&C 45:28), yet too often we walk in darkness at noonday, or at least we traverse the path of life in twilight when we might bask in the bright light of the Son. (*The Power of the Word: Saving Doctrines from the Book of Mormon*, p. 303)

The lack of "faith like the ancients." "Much of the stress and fear and apprehension and exhaustion that now exist in society!" Could drenching ourselves in the living waters of the Book of Mormon actually do all that? Could it help with such practical matters? Of course!

Could part of the condemnation we are under also be that we do not have all the scriptures the Lord would like to bless us with? Could many if not all of the difficult questions that trouble so many be answered if we had the sealed portion of the Book of Mormon, the records of the lost tribes of the house of Israel, or the record of the vision of the Brother of Jared? Remember, Mormon wrote that he did not even write "a hundredth part of the things which Jesus did truly teach unto the people." (3 Nephi 26:6.)

Each year of teaching usually brings with it the same questions raised by inquiring students. They generally want to know about the Creation, organic evolution, the Second Coming, and, of course, where the dinosaurs came from if there was no death of any living creature before the fall of Adam and Eve. They generally believe they can find answers about the Creation, evolution, and the Second Coming in the Book of Mormon, but they're certain there is nothing about dinosaurs. Now, I'm not sure about all the theories concerning dinosaurs, but I know dinosaurs were on the the earth, and I know that they're old! I've been to Vernal, Utah. I've seen that evidence. So, I tell the students, "Let's turn to the Book of Mormon to answer your inquiries about dinosaurs and other difficult questions." Looks of surprise cover their faces. Many have read the book previously, and their questioning looks reveal that they do not remember reading about dinosaurs.

We first turn to 2 Nephi 27:6–8, 10, a teaching from the prophet Isaiah. It reads, "The Lord God shall bring forth unto you the words of a book, and they shall be the words of them which have slumbered.

"And behold the book shall be sealed; and in the book shall be a revelation from God, from the beginning of the world to the ending thereof.

"Wherefore, because of the things which are sealed up, the things which are sealed shall not be delivered in the day of the wickedness and abominations of the people. Wherefore the book shall be kept from them. . . .

"But the words which are sealed he shall not deliver, neither shall he deliver the book. For the book shall be sealed by the power of God, and the revelation which was sealed shall be kept in the book until the own due time of the Lord, that they may come forth; for behold, they reveal all things from the foundation of the world unto the end thereof."

Evidently the sealed portion of the Book of Mormon contains a history of "all things from the foundation of the world unto the end thereof"—even the answer to the nagging question about where the dinosaurs came from! Again, all the questions can be answered if we can lift the condemnation and receive all the teachings the Lord desires us to have.

Elder Bruce R. McConkie taught a group of religious educators this:

> When, during the Millennium, the sealed portion of the Book of Mormon is translated, it will give an account of life in pre-existence; of the creation of all things; of the Fall and the Atonement and the Second Coming; of temple ordinances in their fulness; of the ministry and mission of translated beings; of life in the spirit world, in both paradise and hell; of the kingdoms of glory to be inhabited by resurrected beings; and many such things (see, e.g., Ether 1:3–5).
>
> As of now, the world is not ready to receive these truths. For one thing, these added doctrines will completely destroy the whole theory of organic evolution as it is now almost universally taught in the halls of academia. For another they will set forth an entirely different concept and time frame of the Creation, both of this earth and all forms of life, and of the sidereal heavens themselves, than is postulated in all the theories of men. And sadly, there are those who, if forced to make a choice at this time, would select Darwin over Deity. (*Sermons and Writings of Bruce R. McConkie*, p. 277.)

After this stunning statement by an apostle of the Lord Jesus Christ, the students are doing some thinking that most have not done previously. Interest is piqued, and a desire to learn more generally settles on the class. We then turn to 3 Nephi 26:3. The Savior, as a resurrected being while visiting the Americas, "did expound all things, even from the beginning until the time that he should come in his glory—yea, even all things which should come upon the face of the earth, even until the elements should melt with fervent heat, and the earth should be wrapt together as a scroll, and the heavens and the earth should pass away."

The Nephites and the Lamanites of A.D. 34 knew everything about the Creation! They knew everything from the beginning to the end of the earth. Then Mormon makes a comment that he has written only the lesser part of the things Jesus taught the people, declaring that he has written them "to the intent that they may be brought again unto this people, from the Gentiles . . .

"And when they shall have received this [the Book of Mormon], which is expedient that they should have first, to try their faith, and if it shall so be that they shall believe these things then shall the greater things be made manifest unto them.

"And if it so be that they will not believe these things, then shall the greater things be withheld from them, unto their condemnation." (3 Nephi 26:8–10.)

If we do not use the portions of the Book of Mormon that are now in our possession, it will be "unto [our] condemnation!"

Mormon desired to make everything available to us that Jesus taught. He said, "Behold, I was about to write them, all which were engraven upon the plates of Nephi, but the Lord forbade it, saying: I will try the faith of my people." (3 Nephi 26:11.) Mormon knew the answers to my students' questions, and he made it clear that we of the latter days would not know until we use the Book of Mormon properly! Perhaps this is one of the reasons the prophets continually ask us to read and reread the book and to flood the earth with it!

Of the return of these records, Elder Neal A. Maxwell wrote,

"Today we carry convenient quadruple combinations of the scriptures, but one day, since more scriptures are coming, we may need to pull little red wagons brimful with books." (A *Wonderful Flood of Light*, p. 18.)

How exciting! With the invention of laptop computers, Palm Pilots®, and other technological devices, perhaps we won't need the wagons after all. As memory in these devices increases, regardless of the number of pages contained in the writings, all the records will be instantly brought up on a screen before our very eyes.

It's also fun, if time permits, to take the students to Ether 3:25–26 and Ether 4:7 as a third witness of all the truths we've just covered. As we use the Book of Mormon as the Lord intended, the day will come when we receive these other records. Then, certainly, the condemnation will begin to be lifted, and we will begin to know all things.

The Book of Mormon, this glorious treasure, has changed my life forever. I read it in seminary in the ninth grade; however, I did so only to fulfill my assignment and didn't give it much thought. At age eighteen, I left home to enter the world of college football. At the time I hadn't decided whether I would serve a mission. I wanted to play football. I thought of little else.

One night after a home game, I went with some of my teammates to an activity in a nearby city. We arrived home about 8:30 the following morning. It was Sunday, and priesthood meeting started at 9:00. I showered and walked to church at the institute of religion across the street from our dormitory. As I walked in, the bishop greeted me. He asked me a few questions, and then we went to his office to talk. I don't remember all we talked about, but I remember going back to the dorm determined to read the Book of Mormon, pray, and find out if it was true!

When I arrived back at the dorm, I pulled my scriptures from the shelf. The scriptures were a high school graduation gift from my parents.

The previous year in seminary I had not missed a day of reading the Doctrine of Covenants, but I had not read for the entire summer.

I opened the Book of Mormon and began reading. Before long some of my teammates walked in and began giving me a hard time. After that, I decided to read in private. Every morning I got up early to read and pray. To this day I can remember finishing Moroni 10 and applying the magnificent promise found in verses 4 and 5.

That day I discovered that the book is true, and I needed to share that knowledge with others. Doing so, however, was not easy. I was on scholarship and was committed to play football. I felt that my decision had been made. I would stay and play football and be a missionary by my actions.

Thanksgiving vacation came, and I returned home. After talking with my family, I went to visit my good friend Taylor Manning. Again, I thought my decision was made—that is, until I walked into Taylor's kitchen and saw him, with a missionary haircut, sitting at the table eating a bowl of cereal. "What happened to you?" I asked.

He responded, "I'm going on a mission, Ed!" (He always called me Ed for some reason.) He told me that he knew the Book of Mormon was true, and he wanted to serve his Father in Heaven. I knew it was true as well. But give up a football scholarship? I was stunned. However, it didn't take long before my testimony of the book, and Taylor's testimony, won the battle.

When I went back to school, I talked with my coach, and we worked out arrangements for my return in two years. I served in the New Mexico and Arizona Mission. Taylor went to the Netherlands. Neither of us would be where we are today had we not read and prayed about the Book of Mormon.

After coming home, I was able to play football for three more seasons. However, these last three seasons were focused on far more than just how far or how accurately I could throw a football. I had found out, to some extent, why I needed Christ. I had come to realize that the

Book of Mormon and the message of the restored gospel of Jesus Christ was the answer to the world's problems. I have since learned that what President Boyd K. Packer has taught is true: "The Book of Mormon: Another Testament of Jesus Christ has the nourishing power to heal starving spirits of the world." (*Ensign*, Nov. 2001, p. 64.) I have also learned that this healing power of the scriptures is taught in the Book of Mormon by Jacob the brother of Nephi. He taught, "It supposeth me that they have come up hither to hear the pleasing word of God, yea, the word which healeth the wounded soul." (Jacob 2:8.)

We all need to learn why we need Christ, to become more like little children, and to feel the power of the word. By doing so, we can bring our lives under the infinite reaches of the Atonement and become not only alive in Christ but also *consumed* in Christ. This can happen if we will use the Book of Mormon properly and help lift the condemnation. We can't read the book as if it were a novel. We must use consistency and intensity to uncover its treasures.

CHAPTER 3

The Great Plan of Happiness

JACK R. CHRISTIANSON

You may have heard of Elder Alma Sonne, a former Assistant to the Twelve Apostles, but you may not be familiar with his life. He was a magnificent General Authority for many years and a great preacher of righteousness. Back in the early 1900s he went on a mission to the British Isles. He left behind a dear friend named Fred Dahle, whom Elder Sonne was later able to persuade to serve a mission. Fred then had the opportunity to serve in the British Isles at the same time Elder Sonne served.

Elder Sonne, as a young missionary, kept writing his friend, Fred Dahle, and pleading with him to come on a mission, but Brother Dahle expressed little interest. Eventually, however, he gave in to Elder Sonne's pleading and, as was mentioned, he was called to serve in the British Isles. He later wrote to Elder Sonne, "Thank God, you were on the map when I was supposed to be a missionary." Think of that. Elder Dahle's gratitude knew no bounds because Elder Sonne helped him be on a mission when the Lord wanted him to be there.

One of Elder Sonne's principal responsibilities on his mission was to plan travel arrangements for new converts traveling to America and the missionaries as they arrived and left the mission field. At the conclusion of his mission Elder Sonne was able to secure passage for himself, Elder Dahle, and other missionaries on a brand new ocean liner that was scheduled to make its maiden voyage from England to New York City. The year was 1912. The new ocean liner was the *Titanic*. Arrangements were made for a train to pick them up in New York, and they would travel across the United States on their way back to Cache Valley, Utah.

A few days before the great trip across the ocean and then across the United States, Elder Dahle sent a wire indicating that he could not make the scheduled departure and suggesting that the elders go on without him. However, Elder Sonne, for some inexplicable reason that would be known only later, cancelled their bookings on the *Titanic* and rebooked them all on another ship, the *Maurentania*, leaving a day later. The others in the group manifested resentment because they were not sailing on the *Titanic*.

While they were en route, the purser of the *Maurentania* told Alma in confidence that the *Titanic* had struck an iceberg and sunk on the 15th of April, with the loss of 1,517 passengers and crew and only 705 survivors. The elders were stunned by the news. As Elder Sonne and Elder Dahle walked on the deck, gazing into the dark waters of the Atlantic, Alma remembered Fred's letter. He turned to Elder Dahle and said, "Thank God, Fred, you were on the map when I was supposed to be on the *Titanic*." (Galyn Hopkins, Presentation to the Alma Sonne Family Reunion and a Faculty Inservice Meeting, Orem Institute of Religion.)

One thanked God that the other was alive when he was supposed to be on a mission. And the other thanked God that the other was alive when he was supposed to be on the *Titanic*. What would have happened had Fred Dahle not wired Elder Sonne? What if Elder Sonne had not followed the promptings of the Spirit? We don't know. But this we do know: Alma Sonne lived and became a General Authority of the Church and a great preacher of righteousness. It's easy to understand when teaching the Book of Mormon what Elder Sonne meant when he said, "Thank God Fred Dahle was on the map when I was supposed to be on the *Titanic*." And I say, "Thank God the Book of Mormon is on the earth when I have a chance to live, when I'm supposed to be a son of righteousness. And you're supposed to be a faithful son or daughter of God and to be strong and of good courage." Can we thank Heavenly Father every day of our lives that the Book of Mormon is on the earth when you and I are privileged to be here, and need to know how to navigate our course across some very stormy waters?

We should consider a word that is difficult for some. The word is *truth*. When Jesus stood before Pilate, Pilate asked, "What is truth?" (John 18:38.) The Savior did not answer at that time. However, many hundreds of years later the Savior told the Prophet Joseph Smith the answer to Pilate's question. In Doctrine and Covenants 93:24 we learn the definition of truth: "Truth is knowledge of things as they are, and as they were, and as they are to come." What truth is, then, is a knowledge of things past, present, and future.

Do you remember the diagram of the plan of salvation that many of us saw in our youth? Although the diagram is not found in the scriptures, it gives us a mental picture of the different stages of our eternal existence. You will remember there's a circle representing the premortal life, a veil, and a circle that represents Earth. The diagram is informative, but there can be a problem with it. If we're not careful, we can begin to compartmentalize everything. Joseph Smith explained that everything is constantly before the Lord; "the past, present, and the future were and are, with Him, in one eternal now." (*Teachings of the Prophet Joseph Smith*, p. 220.) With the Lord, everything exists in one eternal now! Everything is before him, past, present, and future.

The diagram also shows that there is a veil of death, a resurrection, and the judgment. We are sent to one of four places: the celestial kingdom, the terrestrial kingdom, the telestial kingdom, or outer darkness. Section 76 of the Doctrine and Covenants teaches that the only people who qualify for outer darkness are those who have a full knowledge of the truth and then turn away from it, who have received all the ordinances and then become enemies to righteousness and would kill the Savior if he were here, or consent to his death.

As you consider the beautiful diagram of the plan of salvation, are you aware that there are several different names for that plan in the scriptures? Most of them are found in the Book of Mormon. Two are found in the Pearl of Great Price. The great plan of truth is described by Alma to his son Corianton as, of course, "the great plan of happiness." (Alma 42:8.) There are many other names for the plan, such as "the plan of salvation" (Jarom 1:2), "the plan of redemption" (Alma 42:11), "the merciful plan of the great Creator" (2 Nephi 9:6), and on and on.

What is the world's understanding when it comes to this plan? Without the Book of Mormon and the Pearl of Great Price, people have little or no understanding. People don't have access to the Book of Mormon or the Pearl of Great Price unless we give it to them! They could do better if we would give it to them. Of course, we can't force anything spiritual, so we must allow people the agency to choose for themselves. But we can at least give them the opportunity to choose. As I understand it, truth is a knowledge of things as they were (meaning premortal life), as they are (meaning mortality), and as they will be (meaning the spirit world or postmortal life). Somehow we tend to get caught up in Act 2 of a three-act play. We sometimes fail to consider what took place before we came to earth (Act 1) and what will take place after we leave this earth (Act 3). As Act 2, or mortality, begins to take its toll, because of its difficulty, we sometimes forget all about Acts 1 and 3. If we're just thinking of truth as knowledge of things in the past, present, and future of Act 2, we've missed it, because not all of the difficulties, challenges, and inequities associated with mortality are going to be worked out in this life. We will need to move into Act 3 to understand answers to many of the perplexing questions posed in

Act 2. I suppose there *are* answers if we could see all of Act 1 and all of Act 3 and know how things will turn out. That surely would be a lot easier, wouldn't it? But the Lord says, "No, just trust me. I'll send you my word." (See Boyd K. Packer, *Our Father's Plan*, pp. 60–61.)

The words of Christ are found in the scriptures and in the words of the apostles and prophets. That's *what* the word is. But *who* is the Word? Remember what John 1:1 says? "In the beginning was the Word, and the Word was with God, and the Word was God." Verse 14 goes on to say, "And the Word was made flesh, and dwelt among us." Christ is the Word. Yes, the iron rod is the word of God and will safely guide us through. (See *Hymns*, no. 274.) The iron rod is the scriptures. It is the words of the modern prophets. But it is also Christ. He is the Word.

Again, what is truth? Truth is a knowledge of the plan: past, present, future; premortal, mortal, postmortal. But who is truth? Jesus said in John 14:6, "I am the way, the truth, and the life." When one comes to a knowledge of the truth, it's not just a knowledge of the plan but also a knowledge of who makes the plan possible. It is a knowledge of the Savior himself. He is the Truth. He is the Life. He is the Word.

We learned in our chapter on the title page of the Book of Mormon that Christ is also the tree of life. Therefore, in order to get to the tree of life, we must hold fast to the iron rod through the mists of darkness, the temptations of the world. That will allow us to stay on the strait and narrow path, continually holding fast to the rod of iron, until we can fall down and partake of the fruit of the tree. (see 1 Nephi 8:30.)

"I . . . beheld a strait and narrow path, which came along by the rod of iron, even to the tree by which I stood; and it also led by the head of the fountain, unto a large and spacious field, as if it had been a world." (1 Nephi 8:20.) How do we get to the tree? Where does the path go? It goes right through the world (the field). It doesn't go under it. It doesn't go around it. It doesn't go over it. There is only one way to get to the Savior and to the fruit that is "desirable to make one happy," and that is to be in the world but not of the world. The only way to stay on the path is to hold fast to the scriptures, to the prophets, and to the Savior.

In fact, Elder Neal A. Maxwell has taught, "The strait and narrow path, though clearly marked, is a path, not a freeway nor an escalator. Indeed, there are times when the only way the strait and narrow path can be followed is on one's knees! And we are to help each other along the path." (*Ensign*, May 1982, p. 38.) There is no other way. As we go through the world, it can be very difficult to obtain the fruit that is "desirable to make one happy." (1 Nephi 8:10.)

HAPPINESS IN LIFE AND DEATH

Alma wrote at length about some of the more difficult matters of this great plan of happiness, namely, that physical death is a part of Heavenly Father's plan for each of us. "Behold, it was appointed unto man to die—therefore, as [Adam and Eve] were cut off from the tree of life they should be cut off from the face of the earth—and man became lost forever, yea, they became fallen man.

"And now, ye see by this that our first parents were cut off both temporally and spiritually from the presence of the Lord; and thus we see they became subjects to follow after their own will.

"Now behold, it was not expedient that man should be reclaimed from this temporal death, for that would destroy the great plan of happiness." (Alma 42:6–8.) How can you have happiness in death? How is it possible that taking away death would take away happiness? Let me share a personal story that may shed some light on this question.

Years ago, some dear friends of mine lost their little boy named Tyler. He was killed in a tragic house fire just before Christmas. This story is shared with the father's permission.

It was less than a week before Christmas. Most of the family was away shopping. Three-year-old Tyler was being taken care of by his grandpa. While Tyler was sleeping in a bedroom upstairs, the Christmas tree somehow caught fire. His grandfather tried to climb the stairs on his hands and knees, hoping to avoid the heavy smoke and fumes. The heat was so intense, however, that it melted the carpet to his hands and knees, causing him to stick to the searing carpet. When the firemen finally arrived, they were able to save Tyler's grandpa, but it was too late for Tyler.

I had the unenviable task of being asked by his parents to speak at the funeral. The speaker that preceded me was Tyler's nursery teacher. I currently serve as a stake president and have kidded occasionally that I would love to serve as a nursery teacher when I'm released because it would be such good duty. But as I listened to Tyler's teacher, my heart-strings were wrenched. I don't know if I could have done what she did. She gave a marvelous talk about the great plan of happiness. Then as I stood to speak about the very things we have been discussing in this chapter, Tyler's grandpa, who had just been released from the hospital, was brought in, in a wheelchair. His hands, feet, arms, and legs were in bandages. They wheeled him down to the front row, placing him at the end of a bench. I almost lost control of my emotions. I'm not trying to be dramatic or emotional but simply to illustrate a significant point. Going back again to Alma's statement to his son Corianton, Alma taught us that if we take away death, we take away the plan of happiness. This whole plan is a plan of happiness in spite of pain that, at times, seems unbearable. Of course, after the funeral Tyler was buried. It was a horrible Christmas for the family and a somewhat melancholy one for me.

Then, as life would have it, the day after Christmas one of my dearest friends and colleagues, with whom I have taught for a number of years, was on his way to Cache Valley for a family Christmas party. He, his wife, and some of their children were in one car, and four more of their children were in another. A group of four teenagers from Logan, coming from the opposite direction, hit a piece of ice in Sardine Canyon and spun out of control, smashing into the car that was driven by my colleague's children, killing two of his daughters and critically injuring another daughter and son. Two of the young people in the car that hit them were also killed. Elder Richard G. Scott of the Quorum of the Twelve Apostles went to the hospital to give blessings to my friend's injured children. A few days later Elder Scott presided at the funeral for the two girls. The other two children, who had been released from the hospital, were able to attend the funeral.

At the viewing the night before, as I stood with this father next to the caskets of his sweet girls, he took me in his arms. He told me, "Just go home and call your children around you and hold them! Don't ever let them go, Jack. Just love them. Tell them how much you love them." I was heartbroken for my friend. I was heartbroken for little Tyler's family. Things seemed very dark at that point. Driving home was difficult.

My wife and I are the parents of four daughters. When we arrived home that night, I called our married daughter and said, "Please come over here as soon as you can." I located another daughter at work and said to her, "I don't care what you're doing, please come home now." We also found our seventeen- and eleven-year-old daughters and gathered all of them together in our living room and knelt in prayer. I wanted them never to leave my presence.

In Alma 42:16 we learn, "Repentance could not come unto men except there were a punishment, which also was eternal as the life of the soul should be, affixed opposite to the plan of happiness, which was as eternal also as the life of the soul." So how old is this plan? It's as eternal as the life of the soul. It has no beginning. It has no end. To comprehend it seems beyond our grasp. All I know is that it is a plan of happiness. As we live it, as we understand the plan, as we learn of the premortal, mortal, and postmortal truth, we come to the knowledge of him who is the Truth. Then the plan is truly one of happiness even in times of deepest sorrow and trial.

Do you think my friend who lost his two children doesn't still suffer? I have sat with him in faculty meetings. He's come to my door and the doors of others on our faculty just to talk. Because my wife and I lost a son in 1989, my colleague asked me one day in my office, "Does it ever get better, Jack? Do you ever stop hurting?" I cried. Does knowing the plan always take away the pain? Of course it doesn't! So how could it be a plan of happiness if we can't eliminate death or sin? It becomes a plan of happiness when we more fully understand the meaning of the plan and who is the central figure of the plan. It becomes a plan of happiness when we understand who and what the truth is. We know the Atonement is real. We know we can overcome death. We know that the words of Alma are true: "Behold, I say unto you there be many things to come; and behold, there is one thing which is of more importance than they all—for behold, the time is not far distant that the Redeemer liveth and cometh among his people." (Alma 7:7.) Before we go on, keep in mind the diagram of the plan with its circles, veils, and all the little lines going everywhere. But remember that in reality these things are not all compartmentalized. In fact, Brigham Young said, "Where is the spirit world? It is right here." (*Journal of Discourses*, 3:369.) We need to remember all this and in our mind's eye picture a clothesline, to represent the plan, strung from post to post, so to speak, and then hang on that clothesline of the plan every single thing that happens to us, good or bad, everything we learn, temporally and spiritually, and see where it fits in. Then as we begin to ache and grieve and go through trying times—and we will all go through them— we can ask ourselves, "Where does it fit in the plan? How is it covered by the Atonement? What am I to learn?" Then it is easier to keep things in perspective.

Is it going to take all the pain away? No! If you take all the pain out of mortality, there's very little to learn. Remember what Abraham was told, "We will prove them herewith, to see if they will do all things whatsoever the Lord their God shall command them." (Abraham 3:25.) Sometimes, we think it would be nice to live a cushy, earthly existence. In reality, without opposition there would be no growth.

How would we ever gain strength? We wouldn't. If we can just take life's experiences and hang them on the clothesline of the plan, I testify that we will begin to see life differently, no matter what it throws at us. Does it throw us some curve balls? Yes, it does, because we live in a fallen world.

President Boyd K. Packer made this marvelous statement: "There are many things that cannot be understood or taught or explained unless it is in terms of the plan of redemption. Unless you understand the basic plan—the premortal existence, the purpose of life, the Fall, the Atonement, the Resurrection—unless you understand that, the unmarried, the abused, the handicapped, the abandoned, the addicted, the disappointed, those with gender disorientation, or the intellectuals will find no enduring comfort. You will not think life is fair unless you know the plan of redemption.

"Some say they are born with some tendency. Whether you are born with them or you acquired them or you got them through over-medication, addiction, or any other way, what should you do? Resist them! You resist them and push them away. How long? As long as you live. There are some things that are a life-long battle." (CES Fireside for Young Adults, Feb. 2, 2003, p. 6.)

To understand the plan we have to know the words, and before we know the words we need to know where they are found: in the scriptures, the words of the prophets, the iron rod, in the teachings of the Savior. If we're not conversant with the scriptures, then we struggle.

Elder Packer said this: "True doctrine understood changes attitudes and behavior. The study of the doctrines of the gospel will improve behavior quicker than a study of behavior will improve behavior. Preoccupation with unworthy behavior can lead to unworthy behavior. That is why we stress so forcefully the study of the doctrines of the gospel." (*Ensign,* Nov. 1986, p. 17.)

Again, in order to understand the plan, we must understand and be familiar with the words of the plan. Let me give you a few of them:

creation, fall, atonement, faith, repentance, baptism, Holy Ghost, Father in Heaven, Christ, Savior, Redeemer, Advocate, mercy, justice, sanctification, justification, redemption, premortal existence, agency, opposition, death, mortality, patience, obedience, law, covenants, ordinances, dispensation, postmortal existence, celestial, terrestrial, telestial, temple, rebirth, earth, punishment, temptation, Lucifer, Satan, resurrection, gratitude, service, scriptures, prayers, prophets, apostles, priesthood, plan, worth of souls, family, procreation, sin, sorrow, children, probation, first and second estates, pain, suffering, happiness, and on and on. Where will we find them? They will be found in the very path that leads us to the tree that is desirable to make one happy.

Now, may I just give you one of the bylines of my life? It is "scriptures, prayer, prophets, service, and temples." If you will be involved in these five sacred activities, I am certain you can make it to the tree.

Recently while I was at our stake Young Women camp, a fellow priesthood leader taught me a great truth. He said, "May I ask you a question? Have you ever noticed that the other thing that is there at the end of the iron rod is a father, standing at the tree and beckoning to his family to come and partake?" (see 1 Nephi 8:15.) I had read that passage numerous times but never with that insight. Could it be our Father in Heaven standing next to his Son and beckoning all of his children to come unto them by holding fast to the iron rod as we experience "the mist of darkness" (1 Nephi 8:23) or "the temptations of the devil" (1 Nephi 12:17)? He is standing there beckoning to us. What are we as earthly fathers doing? Are we following the example of Lehi and our Heavenly Father? Are we beckoning our children to come and partake of the fruit of the tree of life?

President Packer has taught, "If you are reverent and prayerful and obedient, the day will come when there will be revealed to you why the God of heaven has commanded us to address him as *Father*, and the Lord of the Universe as *Son*. Then you will have discovered the Pearl of Great Price spoken of in the scriptures and willingly go and sell all that you have that you might obtain it." And then he says, "The great plan of happiness (see Alma 42:8, 16) revealed to prophets is the plan for a happy family. It is the love story between husband and wife, parents and children, that renews itself through the ages." (*Ensign*, May 1995, p. 8.) That is the plan!

But what of you that are single? Please don't you ever forget that there is a Father beckoning you to come home, and if you are righteous, no blessing will ever be taken from you. You will have it all. Some of you say, "But that's like telling starving children you'll feed them next week." All I can say to that is, be patient and wait on the Lord and give thanks in all things. (See D&C 98:1–2.) God knows your life and your future. Remember, with him it is one eternal now.

Being mortals, we have difficulty prioritizing our lives to keep the plan at the forefront of our thoughts. Elder Richard G. Scott has taught, "Part of that testing here is to have so many seemingly interesting things to do that we can forget the main purposes for being here. Satan works very hard so that the essential things won't happen. The plan is really very simple when considered in its essence. The Lord has told us that we are here to be tried—to be proven, to see whether we will be valiant and be obedient to His teachings. You among all of the people on earth have the best possibility of doing that because you have access to the fulness of the restored gospel and the teachings of the Savior. In quiet moments when you think about it, you recognize what is critically important in life and what isn't. Be wise and don't let good things crowd out those that are essential."

Many of the major choices in life really aren't between good and evil, they are between good and good. Don't let the good things crowd out that which is essential. Elder Scott continues, "Whether you intend to or not, when you live as though the Savior and His teachings are only one of many other important priorities in your life you are clearly on the road to disappointment and likely on the path to tragedy." (*Ensign*, May 1997, pp. 53–54.) If our getting on the strait and narrow path and our study of the scriptures and the prophets is just another thing on our to-do list in our planners, we're on the path to tragedy rather than on the path that leads to the tree whose fruit is desirable to make one happy.

Alma 7:11 gives us great insight into the Savior's mission: "He shall go forth, suffering pains and afflictions and temptations of every kind; and this that the word might be fulfilled which saith he shall take upon him the pains and the sicknesses of his people." What kind of sicknesses? I read it as any kind of sickness, not just physical maladies. Notice, no reference has been made to sin yet.

"And he will take upon him death. . . ." Don't you think that Tyler's family and the family of my colleague are grateful for the Atonement? That's what makes possible the plan of happiness: ". . . that he may loose the bands of death which bind his people; and he will take upon him their infirmities, that his bowels may be filled with mercy, according to the flesh, that he may know according to the flesh how to succor his people according to their infirmities." (Alma 7:12.) The word *succor* means "to run quickly to." He knows how to run quickly to us.

"Now the Spirit knoweth all things; nevertheless the Son of God suffereth according to the flesh that he might take upon him the sins of his people, that he might blot out their transgressions according to the power of his deliverance; and now behold, this is the testimony which is in me." (Alma 7:13.) May I add to Alma's testimony that this is the testimony that is also in me! The reason the plan of salvation is a great plan of happiness is because of the Savior, because of the Tree (who he is), because of the Truth (who he is), because of the life that he gives to us. He is everything!

May I plead with you concerning one thing? Although I'm not your priesthood leader, I'm just asking you to consider something as a fellow member of the Church. May we please look at him as more than just our elder brother who loves us? He's far more than that. He is our

God, our King, our Savior, and our Redeemer. He is the Holy One of Israel. He is everything, and his gospel is a plan of happiness.

If you are ever feeling discouraged and want to be lifted by the scriptures, 2 Nephi 9 is filled with wonderful and encouraging truths that teach about the Savior and his power to lift and redeem us.

Jacob the brother of Nephi expresses his feelings about the plan in this marvelous chapter: "As death hath passed upon all men, to fulfil the merciful plan of the great Creator, there must needs be a power of resurrection, and the resurrection must needs come unto man by reason of the fall; and the fall came by reason of transgression; and because man became fallen they were cut off from the presence of the Lord.

"Wherefore, it must needs be an infinite atonement—save it should be an infinite atonement this corruption could not put on incorruption." (2 Nephi 9:6–7.) "O the wisdom of God, his mercy and grace!" (2 Nephi 9:8.) "O how great the goodness of our God." (2 Nephi 9:10.) "O how great the plan of our God!" (2 Nephi 9:13.) "O the greatness and the justice of our God!" (2 Nephi 9:17.) "O the greatness of the mercy of our God, the Holy One of Israel!" (2 Nephi 9:19.) "O how great the holiness of our God! For he knoweth all things, and there is not anything save he knows it." (2 Nephi 9:20.)

Do we truly believe this? Do we put our trust in him, believing that he really does know the end from the beginning, and then let him do with us whatever he desires? "And he cometh into the world that he may save all men if they will hearken unto his voice; for behold, he suffereth the pains of all men, yea, the pains of every living creature, both men, women, and children, who belong to the family of Adam." (2 Nephi 9:21.)

If there is a plan of happiness, what must there also be? Jacob answers our question: "O that cunning plan of the evil one!" (2 Nephi 9:28.) Satan's plan is a plan of misery and sorrow. If we follow him in any way, it will lead to unhappiness, sorrow, and suffering. In fact, we learn from verses 28 and 29 that the cunning plan of the evil one is to get people to believe they know more than the prophets of God: "O the vainness, and the frailties, and the foolishness of men! When they are learned they think they are wise, and they hearken not unto the counsel of God, for they set it aside, supposing they know of themselves, wherefore, their wisdom is foolishness and it profiteth them not. And they shall perish. But to be learned is good if they hearken unto the counsels of God."

Elder Dallin H. Oaks made a magnificent statement in general conference of 1993. He said this about Satan's plan: "Although Satan and his followers have lost their opportunity to have a physical body, they are permitted to use their spirit powers to try to frustrate God's plan. This provides the opposition necessary to test how mortals will use their freedom to choose. Satan's most strenuous opposition is directed at whatever is most important to the Father's plan." What are some of the most important elements of the Father's plan? Things like marriage and family, sexual relations (because that's how families are created), and anything that would take away freedom—drugs, alcohol, and pornography. Elder Oaks continued, "Satan seeks to discredit the Savior and divine authority, to nullify the effects of the Atonement, to counterfeit revelation, to lead people away from the truth, to contradict individual accountability, to confuse gender, to undermine marriage, and to discourage childbearing (especially by parents who will raise children in righteousness)." (*Ensign*, Nov. 1993, p. 72.) In this talk he takes on each one of those challenging issues, everything from confusion in gender to not having children because we want to pursue other interests. That's Satan's plan.

President Boyd K. Packer has taught us this:

> If we have come to know our Father's plan, we are never completely lost. We know something of how it was before our mortal birth. We know much of what lies beyond the horizon on either side, and which path will be safe for us to follow.

With a knowledge of the plan comes also the determination to live the principles leading to eternal life.

With that knowledge comes testimony. For we find along the way spiritual provisions of insight, courage, and direction. There are experiences that convince us that we are never alone.

We come to know through our feelings the presence of a divine providence watching over us as we move through mortality.

When we know the plan, we understand why mortality must be a test. We know why so much must be taken on faith alone. We develop patience with the unanswered questions of life and face with greater resolution the trials and tribulations that are the lot of humankind.

When we know the plan, we know who we are, we know why we are, and we know where we are. We know that each is a son or daughter of God. One day, if we will, we may return to His presence. For this is the grand purpose of the Father and of the Son, who spoke to Moses saying, "Behold, this is my work and my glory—to bring to pass the immortality and eternal life of man." (Moses 1:39.) (*Our Father's Plan*, pp. 60–61.)

That is true. May each of us be found doing our Father's business, which is bringing to pass the immortality and eternal life of man, and I promise you that the great plan of happiness will bring much joy into each of our lives.

fINDING HAPPINESS AMID AffLICTION

JACK R. CHRISTIANSON

On the east end of Parley Street in Nauvoo, Illinois, sits one of my favorite locations in all of Church history. A short distance off the road, back in the trees at the end of a dirt path, lies the Nauvoo burial ground. It looks very similar to how it would have looked in the 1840s. It is not a popular tourist attraction. There is no visitors' center there. Other than the headstone of Edward Partridge, the first bishop of the Church, and a small covered gazebo with a list of the names of those buried there, the only structure is a life-sized statue of a family coming to the grounds to bury their child. Eighty percent of the people buried in this hallowed place are children. It is hard to describe the sacred feeling that comes while wandering through the grassy knolls with small, mostly unidentifiable headstones dotting the landscape.

One of the children buried there is the first son of the Barlow family. Israel Barlow, the father, was one of those who went up the Mississippi from Quincy and helped scout out the area that later became Nauvoo. He and his family lived in Nauvoo and came west with the Saints as some of the early pioneers.

Elder Loren C. Dunn related the events surrounding Israel Barlow's

call to serve a mission to Great Britain and the sacred event that
occurred as a result of that call:

In the early 1850s he was attending a general conference
of the Church.

It was in that meeting that Israel Barlow heard his name
mentioned from the pulpit. In those days, this was how the
brethren were called on missions. Israel Barlow was called on a
mission to Great Britain. He didn't have to have an interview.
He didn't have to have a medical examination. He was called
to go on a mission. He had a family and was just getting started
in his new area, so it was no small sacrifice to answer the call
from the presidency of the church. But he had enough faith
that this was what he knew he must do. His wife was support-
ive of him, but she asked him for one favor on his way to the
mission field. Would he stop at their old farm in Nauvoo and
find where they had buried their firstborn child and remove
the grave to the Old Nauvoo Burial Ground? He said he would
do this, and he made his way back across the Mississippi River
and came up to Nauvoo. He went to the farm and got the permission of the people who lived there to look for and move the
grave. He said that at first he could not find it, but then he
located it because his wife had planted ground cover around it.
When he dug down, he felt that the grave was in such a condition that it couldn't be moved. According to his journal, he
said to himself that he would leave it to the morning of the
first resurrection and hoped his wife would understand. As he
turned away to continue his journey up the river and on to
Great Britain, he turned back one more time just to be sure he
had made the right decision. He again felt that nothing more
could be done, and as he turned away again he said that words
came into his mind so clear that he knew he had not put them
there. These words were, "Daddy, don't leave me here!" He

said he stopped and took the necessary time and effort to move the grave of his firstborn child to the Nauvoo burial ground.

After he had completed the work, he said that he spent some time by the grave feeling this bond between himself and his firstborn child before he left, not knowing if he would return. To our knowledge, he never did return to the site. (See Ora H. Barlow, *The Israel Barlow Story and Mormon Mores*, pp. 300–8.)

There is a message in the expression, "Daddy, don't leave me here." That message is, don't leave the great characters, stories, doctrines, and principles with their saving and healing powers on the pages of the book. How do we get what is in the scriptures off of the pages and into our heads, and then transfer it into our hearts so it becomes a part of us? I can almost hear Nephi, Alma, Mormon, and Moroni pleading with us, their readers, "Brian, Ricky, Emily, Mandi, Molly, Kevin, Rebecca, don't leave me here!" Don't let what happened, don't let what is taught, don't let what the writers of scripture and what the Lord intended for us to gain stay within the pages. Rather, let it be as Paul declared to the Corinthians: "Ye are our epistle written in our hearts, known and read of all men: forasmuch as ye are manifestly declared to be the epistle of Christ ministered by us, written not with ink, but with the Spirit of the living God; not in tables of stone, but in fleshy tables of the heart." (2 Corinthians 3:2–3.)

Somehow as the power of the scriptures is written in our hearts, we will become what Elder M. Russell Ballard of the Quorum of the Twelve Apostles describes as *believing* and *behaving* Latter-day Saints. (Conference Report, Oct. 1999, p. 79.)

When this occurs, we won't just be studying, praying, and holding family home evening because that's what Latter-day Saints do, but we'll do it because that is what we have *become*. The gospel then becomes what we are, not just a social or cultural organization. Then our eye will be "single to the glory of God" (D&C 4:5), and the Father and the Son will become the center of our lives. Then the "mighty change" spoken of by Alma (Alma 5:12) will take place within our hearts, and happiness can be a part of our lives no matter what trials and afflictions we are required to pass through. We will all go through them. No one is exempt. Each person's trials are tailored to his or her need for individual growth.

Elder Richard G. Scott has wisely counseled us:

> The Lord is intent on your personal growth and development. That progress is accelerated when you willingly allow Him to lead you through every growth experience you encounter, whether initially it be to your individual liking or not. When you trust in the Lord, when you are willing to let your heart and your mind be centered in His will, when you ask to be led by the Spirit to do His will, you are assured of the greatest happiness along the way and the most fulfilling attainment from this mortal experience. If you question everything you are asked to do, or dig in your heels at every unpleasant challenge, you make it harder for the Lord to bless you.
>
> Your agency, the right to make choices, is not given so that you can get what you want. This divine gift is provided so that you will choose what your Father in Heaven wants for you. That way He can lead you to become all that He intends you to be. That path leads to glorious joy and happiness. (Conference Report, Apr. 1996, p. 33.)

Some time ago while traveling home from a distant city, I sat next to a woman on a plane whose tears were flowing freely. I asked her if she was all right and if there was anything I could do to assist her. She replied that she was on her way to Florida to attend to her dying father. Through her tears she explained how he was severely suffering from cancer and she simply wanted his suffering to end. She couldn't understand why God would allow such suffering to take place for so long. As I listened, some words of Elder Orson F. Whitney came into my mind:

"No pain that we suffer, no trial that we experience is wasted. It ministers to our education, to the development of such qualities as patience, faith, fortitude and humility. All that we suffer and all that we endure, especially when we endure it patiently, builds up our characters, purifies our hearts, expands our souls, and makes us more tender and charitable, more worthy to be called the children of God . . . and it is through sorrow and suffering, toil and tribulation, that we gain the education that we come here to acquire and which will make us more like our Father and Mother in heaven." (cited in Spencer W. Kimball, *Faith Precedes the Miracle*, p. 98.)

She looked at me with wonder and said that she had never thought of suffering as a learning experience. She had felt that God was punishing them. Why would he not deliver them from their anguish? Why would he allow her father, whom she loved so dearly, to suffer so desperately? The hearing of true doctrine changed her entire attitude. She began to ask meaningful doctrinal questions that I was able to answer through the scriptures and the teachings of apostles and prophets. She asked if I had something she could read as she flew from Salt Lake City to Florida. I was able to provide her with some reading materials, and she provided me with an address so the missionaries could call on her after returning from Florida. Though she continued to suffer, she began to feel there was hope, and she realized there can be purpose in suffering.

As we talked, I shared with her the truth that we live in a fallen world and that difficult and painful things often happen to good, innocent people. I paraphrased the teaching of the Prophet Joseph Smith, who said, "Happiness is the object and design of our existence; and will be the end thereof, if we pursue the path that leads to it; and this path is virtue, uprightness, faithfulness, holiness, and keeping all the commandments of God." (*Teachings of the Prophet Joseph Smith*, pp. 255–56.)

I also mentioned the teaching of Lehi, who also taught that our purpose here is to be happy: "Adam fell that men might be; and men are, that they might have joy." (2 Nephi 2:25.)

If one of our principal purposes for being on this earth is to have happiness and joy, then why do so many people, like the woman who sat beside me, experience sorrow, sadness, and disappointment in their lives?

Mortality was not meant to be easy or free from pain and suffering. Elder Boyd K. Packer explained, "It was meant to be that life would be a challenge. To suffer some anxiety, some depression, some disappointment, even some failure is normal. Teach our members that if they have a good, miserable day once in a while, or several in a row, to stand steady and face them. Things will straighten out. There is great purpose in our struggle in life!" (*Ensign*, May 1978, p. 93.)

Often, when I speak on this subject of happiness amid affliction, there are generally a few in the audience who have difficulty believing that any lasting happiness is possible in their lives. Some will say, "But Brother Christianson, I do all the things that you talk about; I read and pray daily, I fulfill my church responsibilities, I love my children, and yet I never feel happy." Perhaps those people suffer from a chemical imbalance or clinical depression and need medical attention to bring into balance their chemical makeup. The Lord has given a pattern through his prophets for happiness: "He who doeth the works of righteousness shall receive his reward, even peace in this world, and eternal life in the world to come. I, the Lord, have spoken it, and the Spirit beareth record." (D&C 59:23–24.) When we follow that pattern and happiness and peace do not materialize, obviously something out of our control is happening. Remember, Enos and the brother of Jared taught us that God cannot lie: "I, Enos, knew that God could not lie; wherefore, my guilt was swept away." (Enos 1:6.) "Yea, Lord, I know that thou speakest the truth, for thou art a God of truth, and canst not lie." (Ether 3:12.)

Elder Marvin J. Ashton, a member of the Quorum of the Twelve

Apostles, made a marvelous analogy concerning faith and medicine that adds understanding to this concept: "Our relationship with the Lord and the role of information are very important and neither must be slighted. Perhaps an appropriate analogy here is the relationship between healing by faith and the doctor's remedy. We encourage both with the expectation that they complement each other. I would suggest that acting on information without accompanying inspiration would be folly to the Lord's eyes. Likewise, however, it would appear that seeking out inspiration without having sought out the best information available would be considered equal folly. Information and inspiration work together as the blades of a pair of scissors." (From remarks given at the All-Church Coordinating Council, Nov. 1991.) We must use our faith and medical treatment as the blades of a pair of scissors. Some people need both blades.

We must remember that we cannot force anything spiritual, or we leave ourselves open to being deceived. (See *Ensign*, Jan. 1983, pp. 53, 55–56.) Happiness, or joy, is a fruit of the Spirit (see Galatians 5:22) and cannot be forced, coerced, or mandated. Elder Richard G. Scott taught it this way: "Now, the most important principle I can share: Anchor your life in Jesus Christ, your Redeemer. Make your Eternal Father and his Beloved Son the most important priority in your life— more important than life itself, more important than a beloved companion or children or anyone on earth. Make their will your central desire. Then all that you need for happiness will come to you." (*Ensign*, May 1993, p. 34.)

Happiness will come to you! But you cannot force it. Some people try so desperately to find and keep happiness that they are miserable! They seek happiness with drugs, alcohol, pornography, money, fame, or sexual impropriety. In the end, however, they find only sorrow, heart-break, and emptiness. Genuine, lasting happiness is a by-product of sincerely following the Father and his Son and of making and keeping sacred covenants. Happiness cannot be forced any more than a plant can be forced to grow.

We can do all we can, and then we must wait for the Savior (the tree of life) (see 1 Nephi 11:21–24) and our Father to bring forth fruit unto us. Alma said it this way: "Then, my brethren, ye shall reap the rewards of your faith, and your diligence, and patience, and long-suffering, waiting for the tree to bring forth fruit unto you." (Alma 32:43.)

We must not forget that in the vision of the tree of life, the fruit of the tree was "desirable to make one happy." (1 Nephi 8:10.) We must let happiness, the Spirit, and spiritual gifts come as God grants them to us. When we put our Father and his Son at the center of our lives, these gifts will flow unto us "without compulsory means . . . forever and ever." (D&C 121:46.)

The Book of Mormon teaches some incredible principles about happiness amid affliction, principles with great relevance in our troubled world. The family of Lehi and Nephi experienced every kind of heartache, hardship, trial, and suffering that you and I face today, and yet Nephi was still able to write, "We lived after the manner of happiness." (2 Nephi 5:27.)

They lost their home (see 1 Nephi 2:4), their country (see 1 Nephi 17:20), their money and possessions (see 1 Nephi 3:25). They went on an extended "campout" with all of their brothers and sisters and their families for eight years in a tent! (see 1 Nephi 17:4.) In their family they experienced domestic violence (see 1 Nephi 3:28), attempted murder (see 1 Nephi 17:48), the breakup of the family (see 2 Nephi 5:5–6), abuse (see 2 Nephi 2:1–3), and death (see 2 Nephi 4:12). And you think your family has problems!

Let us explore how they experienced all of these challenges and still kept the spirit of happiness and peace. Our understanding begins in the very first verse as Nephi begins telling the story of his family: "I, Nephi, having been born of goodly parents, therefore I was taught somewhat in all the learning of my father; and having seen many afflictions in the course of my days . . ." Before the very first sentence of the first verse of the first chapter ends, Nephi declares that life is difficult and that he has experienced many afflictions, particularly referring to those mentioned in the preceding paragraph. However, in that same sentence he writes, ". . . nevertheless, having been highly favored of the Lord in all my days; yea, having had a great knowledge of the goodness and the mysteries of God . . ." (1 Nephi 1:1.) The thing that allowed him to consider himself favored in the midst of affliction was his great "knowledge of the goodness and the mysteries of God." He kept the Father and the Son at the center of his life.

He closes the chapter with these words: "But behold, I, Nephi, will show unto you that the tender mercies of the Lord are over all those whom he hath chosen, because of their faith, to make them mighty even unto the power of deliverance." (1 Nephi 1:20.) Nephi teaches us that, yes, life is difficult, but that God will deliver us from our afflictions, in his own due time, if we but have faith in him.

After an eight-year journey, they arrived at a land they called Bountiful. Nephi writes, "We did again take our journey in the wilderness; and did travel nearly eastward from that time forth. And we did travel and wade through much affliction in the wilderness; and our women did bear children in the wilderness." (1 Nephi 17:1.) How would you like that? No birthing rooms, no comfortable hospitals, simply a tent in the middle of the windswept Arabian Desert. Yet in the very next line Nephi says, "And so great were the blessings of the Lord upon us. . . ." (1 Nephi 17:2.)

Nephi then describes a little of the difficulty of the eight-year journey: "We did pitch our tents by the seashore; and notwithstanding we had suffered many afflictions and much difficulty, yea, even so much that we cannot write them all, we were exceedingly rejoiced when we came to the seashore; and we called the place Bountiful, because of its much fruit." (1 Nephi 17:6.) Their afflictions were so great that they could not write them all, and yet they rejoiced and were grateful for the fruit and the temporary end of their journey. They were happy!

Have you ever wondered why 2 Nephi 2, the great chapter on the necessity of opposition in all things, comes where it does in the record? In this chapter, Lehi is approaching his death, which will take place in chapter 4, and he desires to speak to his son Jacob, who has experienced much stress and abuse as a result of some of his elder brothers. Lehi states, "Jacob, I speak unto you: Thou art my first-born in the days of my tribulation in the wilderness. And behold, in thy childhood thou hast suffered afflictions and much sorrow, because of the rudeness of thy brethren. Nevertheless, Jacob, my first-born in the wilderness, thou knowest the greatness of God; and he shall consecrate thine afflictions for thy gain. Wherefore, thy soul shall be blessed." (2 Nephi 2:1–3.)

Jacob suffered from the rudeness of his brethren. The word *rude* means harsh, coarse, crude, or vulgar. In our vernacular we would call that abuse. Lehi lamented the fact that his tender son had to endure such a difficult life, and yet he assured Jacob that his soul would be blessed and his afflictions would be for his gain. Jacob could still be happy in spite of his difficulties because of the "tender mercies of the Lord." (1 Nephi 1:20.) We can be happy, regardless of what we are called to pass through, when we keep the Father and the Son at the center of our lives. Jacob had learned what you and I learn from the proclamation on the family: "Happiness in family life is most likely to be achieved when founded upon the teachings of the Lord Jesus Christ." ("The Family: A Proclamation to the World," 1995.)

Have you ever prayed for something to get better and it just got worse? Join the club. Nephi had the same experience after the death of his father: "I, Nephi, did cry much unto the Lord my God, because of the anger of my brethren. But behold, their anger did increase against me, insomuch that they did seek to take away my life." (2 Nephi 5:1–2.) Though Nephi prayed in faith, the behavior of his brothers and others was no reflection on Nephi's righteousness or faithfulness.

People have their agency to choose how they will respond to truth. In fact, without Lehi to influence Laman and Lemuel, Nephi was in danger. He wrote, "The Lord did warn me, that I, Nephi, should depart from them and flee into the wilderness, and all those who would go with me. Wherefore, it came to pass that I, Nephi, did take my family, and also Zoram and his family, and Sam, mine elder brother and his family, and Jacob and Joseph, my younger brethren, and also my sisters, and all those who would go with me. And all those who would go with me were those who believed in the warnings and the revelations of God; wherefore, they did hearken unto my words." (2 Nephi 5:5–6.)

There was a breakup in the family of a prophet! Though it was not the breakup of a husband and a wife, the effects of this "divorce" must have been devastating to all those who chose to leave.

After all this and more, Nephi could still write, "We lived after the manner of happiness." (2 Nephi 5:27.) Isn't that incredible! They were happy because the Father and the Son were the center of their lives. How did they accomplish this seemingly impossible feat? They kept the commandments. (See 2 Nephi 5:10.) They relied on the scriptures and followed the direction of the Liahona. (See 2 Nephi 5:12.) They knew how to work. (See 2 Nephi 5:15, 17.) And they went to the temple, the House of God, and made and kept sacred covenants. (See 2 Nephi 5:16.) As a result, they maintained happiness amid affliction; they built upon the firm foundation of Christ.

As this chapter comes to a close, let us consider two more significant lessons about happiness amid affliction. Both are found in 3 Nephi 11, the account of the Savior's visit to America after his resurrection in Palestine.

The first thing the Savior said after he descended from heaven into the land Bountiful was, "Behold, I am Jesus Christ, whom the prophets testified shall come into the world." (3 Nephi 11:10.) After stating his authority, his holy name, he recognized his messengers, the prophets. Isn't that spectacular! Of all the things he could have said or done, he ratified the teachings of his servants. One of the greatest ways of finding happiness amid affliction is to stay focused on and keep our lives in harmony with the current position of the First Presidency and the Quorum of the Twelve Apostles on all issues.

The whole multitude had fallen to the ground. The Lord spoke to them, asking them to arise and come forth, one by one, to thrust their hands into his side and to feel the prints of the nails in his hands and his feet so they would know that he was truly "the God of Israel, and the God of the whole earth, and that he had been slain for the sins of the world." (See 3 Nephi 11:12–15.) Why would he do that? I'm certain there are many reasons, but I would like to briefly discuss three, one of which has much to do with being happy amid affliction.

What does section 129 of the Doctrine and Covenants say we should do if a being from the unseen world appears to us? We are to offer him our hand and request him to shake hands with us. By doing so, we will know whether this administration is from God. (See D&C 129:1–9.) The Savior is not an impostor. He waits for no one to test him. He asks those who are in his presence to come to him, to see with their eyes, feel with their hands, and know of a surety that it truly is he. (See 3 Nephi 11:15.)

Next, I believe that the Savior wants each individual to know that although he is a God, he is completely and totally approachable. His constant plea is, "Return unto me, that I may heal you." (3 Nephi 9:13.)

And finally, in the words of Elder Jeffrey R. Holland of the Quorum of the Twelve Apostles, "To those who stagger or stumble, he is there to steady and strengthen us. In the end he is there to save us, and for all this he gave his life. However dim our days may seem they have been darker for the Savior of the world.

"In fact, in a resurrected, otherwise perfected body, our Lord of this sacrament table has chosen to retain for the benefit of his disciples the wounds in his hands and his feet and his side—signs, if you will, that painful things happen even to the pure and perfect. Signs, if you will, that pain in this world is *not* evidence that God doesn't love you. It is the *wounded* Christ who is the captain of our soul—he who yet bears the scars of sacrifice, the lesions of love and humility and forgiveness.

"Those wounds are what he invites young and old, then and now, to step forward and see and feel (see 3 Ne.11:15; 18:25)." (*Ensign*, Nov. 1995, p. 69.)

Because we suffer in this life does not mean that God doesn't love us or that we have necessarily done something wrong. It is part of the "reality of mortality." We live in a fallen world where unfortunate, painful things happen to good, innocent people. The Savior suffered indescribably, and he deserved none of it.

We end this chapter as we began it, with a lesson from the line "Daddy, don't leave me here." We cannot leave these magnificent teachings and principles buried in the pages of the book. We must search them diligently each day and pray with "a sincere heart, with real intent, having faith in Christ," and by the power of the Holy Ghost we can not only know the truth of all things, but we can also take these doctrines and principles out of the pages of this glorious Book of Mormon and let them be written "in fleshy tables of the heart." (2 Corinthians 3:3; Moroni 10:4–5.)

When the words of the Book of Mormon are written in our hearts, we will be able to see and feel what our beloved President Gordon B. Hinckley sees and feels. He said, "It isn't as bad as you sometimes think it is. It all works out. Don't worry. I say that to myself every morning. It will all work out! If you do your best, it will all work out. Put your trust in God, and move forward with faith and confidence in the future. The Lord will not forsake us." (*Ensign*, Oct. 2000, p. 73.)

CHAPTER 5

Cat's in the Cradle: The Legacy of a Parent's Influence

K. DOUGLAS BASSETT

On a beautiful spring morning in 1974, my bride of only a few months announced to me that she was pregnant with our first child. Stunned and yet pleased with the news, I slid into our car and headed for my job. The drive to work each day took me through the breathtaking mountains of northern California near Shasta Lake. On this morning, heady images of fatherhood drowned out the scenery surrounding me. However, my thoughts were penetrated by a song coming from the radio. The poignant lyrics spoke directly to the emotions I was engulfed in at the moment. It was the first time I had ever heard the well-known song, "Cat's in the Cradle." The story is about a man who didn't spend time with his young son because he was too busy. The son wanted to be just like his dad when he grew up, and by the end of the song it is clear that he had indeed done so, for when the boy got older he was too busy to spend time with his father (lyrics reprinted with permission):

> My child arrived just the other day,
> He came to the world in the usual way.
> But there were planes to catch, and bills to pay.
> He learned to walk while I was away.
> And he was talking 'fore I knew it, and as he grew,

He'd say, "I'm gonna be like you, Dad.
You know I'm gonna' be like you."

And the cat's in the cradle and the silver spoon,
Little boy blue and the man on the moon.
"When you coming home, Dad?" "I don't know when,
But we'll get together then.
You know we'll have a good time then."

My son turned ten just the other day.
He said, "Thanks for the ball, Dad, come on let's play.
Can you teach me to throw?" I said, "Not today,
I got a lot to do." He said, "That's OK."
And he walked away, but his smile never dimmed,
Said, "I'm gonna' be like him, yeah,
You know I'm gonna' be like him."

And the cat's in the cradle and the silver spoon,
Little boy blue and the man on the moon.
"When you coming home, Dad?" "I don't know when.
But we'll get together then.
You know we'll have a good time then."

Well, he came from college just the other day,
So much like a man, I just had to say,
"Son, I'm proud of you. Can we sit for a while?"
He shook his head and he said with a smile,
"What I'd really like, Dad, is to borrow the car keys—
See you later. Can I have them please?"

And the cat's in the cradle and the silver spoon,
Little boy blue and the man on the moon.
"When you coming home, Son?" "I don't know when.
But we'll get together then, Dad.
You know we'll have a good time then."

I've long since retired and my son's moved away.
I called him up just the other day.
I said, "I'd like to see you if you don't mind."
He said, "I'd love to, Dad, if I could find the time.
You see my new job's a hassle, and the kid's got the flu,
But it's sure nice talking to you, Dad.
It's sure been nice talking to you."
And as I hung up the phone, it occurred to me,
He'd grown up just like me.
My boy was just like me.

And the cat's in the cradle and the silver spoon,
Little boy blue and the man on the moon.
"When you coming home, Son?" "I don't know when.
But we'll get together then, Dad.
You know we'll have a good time then."

This song by Harry Chapin hit me with such impact that I pulled over to the side of the road. Over and over I pondered the message behind the lyrics. I began to realize that in the next few decades of my life I could become like the father in the song. I prayed to my Heavenly Father that my children would grow up with a father who cared about them and who expressed his love verbally as well as by spending time with them.

A Pakistani folktale with a similar message was retold by President Thomas S. Monson in a general conference address:

"An ancient grandmother lived with her daughter and grandson. As she grew frail and feeble, instead of being a help around the house, she became a constant trial. She broke plates and cups, lost knives, spilled water. One day, exasperated because the old woman had broken another precious plate, the daughter sent the grandson to buy his grandmother a wooden plate. The boy hesitated because he knew a wooden plate would humiliate his grandmother. But his mother insisted, so off he went. He returned bringing not one, but two wooden plates.

"'I only asked you to buy one,' his mother said. 'Didn't you hear me?'

"'Yes,' said the boy. 'But I bought the second one so there would be one for you when you get old.'" (*Ensign*, May 1993, p. 62.)

How adults react in times of stress often reveals the experiences of their youth in connection with their own parents. This is illustrated by a story that took place many years ago. A young boy was given a summer job of sitting on the back of the harvester. His father had given him the responsibility of relaying to his older brothers, who sat at the front of the harvester, when the machine had broken down. Even though he was young he realized that the value of the job had nothing to do with the job description. It was just a way to keep him occupied and out of mischief during the harvest time. This task of sitting on the back of the harvester lasted for only a few summers, but an impression was branded on his mind that would remain with him forever.

Of course, it was not uncommon for the machine to break down a few times during each harvest season. Obviously his brothers didn't need his help in telling them what had happened. But that was not the part that bothered him the most. Each time the harvester broke down, within minutes his father would be racing in his pickup truck from the house or the barn through the field where his sons were working. In a rush he would jump out of the truck and stand in front of his youngest son. With his eyes penetrating displeasure, he would grab his big western belt buckle with both hands; then his hands would travel to the brim of his own hat. Bending it down in the direction of the boy standing in front of him, he would blurt out, "What's the problem?" His words were delivered more like an accusation than a question.

Each time this happened, his young son felt rebuked for something that was clearly no one's fault. The harvester had simply experienced a mechanical breakdown. It was not necessary to place blame, or put anyone in a position to feel cast down. Even though this happened just a few times over those two summers, the young boy made a commitment that when he became a man he would never do what his father had done to him.

Years later, this young boy was set apart as an elder and had the wonderful opportunity of serving a full-time mission for the Lord. He put his heart into the work, and as the months passed he was called to a leadership position. On one occasion, he and his companion were scheduled to work with another team of missionaries. He arrived at the other elders' apartment door at 7 A.M., and although the missionaries should have been awake and out of bed for thirty minutes, such was not the case. To make matters worse, the temperature outside was below freezing. In the hope of waking up the missionaries without disturbing the landlady, this young elder tried gently knocking on the front door. When this failed to awaken the sleeping missionaries, he and his companion migrated to the side of the house and began tossing pebbles against the upstairs window shielding the two sleepyheads. The fruits of their labor yielded only frozen fingers because they had to remove their warm gloves to pick up and throw the pebbles. Exasperated, this former farm boy stomped to the front door and began pounding on it with his fist. His reward was a very irritated landlady standing in the doorway. Without uttering a word, she pointed upstairs to where the missionaries remained fast asleep.

The young man's long strides quickly carried him to the top of the stairs; without knocking, he grasped the doorknob and flung the door open with a determined flip of his wrist. As the door quickly swung around it met the wall with an abrupt thud. The two sleepy elders sat up in bed like they had been instantly resurrected from the dead, and through glazed eyes they gazed at their leader. He stood before them, his eyes full of anger. Instinctively, he grabbed his belt buckle with both hands. His hands then clasped the brim of his hat, which he had neglected to remove when he entered the building. Pulling the brim down in the direction of the two guilty elders, he blurted out, "What's the problem?"

In an instant, he was no longer a missionary but a young boy standing before his father, silently making a commitment to himself: *I will never do that when I become a man!* His hands fell limp to his sides as he slowly stepped back and leaned against the wall. He had done the thing he said he would never do. It did not matter whether or not the elders had deserved his rebuke. He had told himself that he would never do it, and he had. Taking a deep breath, and silently promising himself that it would not happen again, he changed the tone of his voice and proceeded with the day's labors.

Sometimes it takes a conscious effort on the part of children to change patterns of behavior or thinking instilled in them by parents who did not model Christlike behavior. Likewise, overcoming this "Cat's in the Cradle" syndrome (where children turn out just like their parents) can be difficult for children who come from positive homes as well as negative. To the Saints of England, President Spencer W. Kimball said in an area conference: "Most people are largely the result of their home environment, good or bad. As Lehi said, on the brink of the grave, to his children, 'I know that if ye are brought up in the way ye should go, ye will not depart from it.' (2 Nephi 4:5.) Our conclusions must therefore be taking life at its best and life at its worst; the difference seems to be the catalyst of love and family solidarity." (British Area Conference Report, Aug. 1971, p. 82.)

Many years ago I read a poem about a son who could not understand why his father would not accompany him to church. I wrote a spin-off to the poem, instead making application to scripture study:

> *Daddy says it's great to read the scriptures,*
> > *And learn them all by heart.*
> *But when it's time for family study,*
> > *We never really start.*
> *Each evening I go to my room to study on my own,*

> *While Daddy stays at the office,*
> *And elects to work alone.*
> *Sometimes I wonder, yes time and time again,*
> *Why scripture study is so good for boys,*
> *And not so good for men.*

As parents we sometimes hope that our children will rise above our failings. The evidence, as well as the counsel of our leaders, indicates that all too often this is not something we can count on.

CAT'S IN THE CRADLE AND THE BOOK OF MORMON

As my life has given way to time and study, I have come to understand that the "Cat's in the Cradle" syndrome was not introduced by Harry Chapin and his thought-provoking song. Throughout all 531 pages of the Book of Mormon is recognition of a connecting, behavioral link between parent and child down through the generations of the book's history. Many sons and many daughters have turned out to be just like their parents.

Nephi's first recorded experience with the Lord is tied directly to his father's influence: "I, Nephi, . . . having great desires to know of the mysteries of God, wherefore, I did cry unto the Lord; and behold he did visit me, and did soften my heart that I did believe all the words which had been spoken by my father." (1 Nephi 2:16.) Among the "mysteries" that Nephi sought was to know the truth of the things his father had seen in the vision recorded in 1 Nephi 1:6–14. The Spirit could not have borne witness to Lehi's teachings if Lehi had not taught the truth. Parents in Zion are admonished to teach in such a fashion that the Spirit can do the same for their children. (See 1 Nephi 1:1; Mosiah 1:2.)

Following Lehi's account of the tree of life dream to his family, Nephi sought to obtain the same manifestation. In a "face to face" visit with the Spirit of the Lord, Nephi declared, "I desire to behold the things which my father saw." (1 Nephi 11:3.) If our children prayed to behold the things we have experienced spiritually, and if our spiritual experiences were duplicated for them, would they be brought to Christ and receive a stronger testimony? The Spirit of the Lord asked Nephi, "Believest thou that thy father saw the tree . . . ?" (1 Nephi 11:4.) To which Nephi replied, "Yea, thou knowest that I believe all the words of my father." (1 Nephi 11:5.) Could a son give a greater tribute to his father? The Spirit of the Lord celebrated "with a loud voice, saying: Hosanna to the Lord." (1 Nephi 11:6.) He was overjoyed that a father taught in such a way that a son could believe and the Spirit could bear witness.

Each of us must obtain a testimony based on sincere, personal striving for the truth, but as students of the Book of Mormon we must also recognize that Nephi's journey for truth was connected to a father who accepted his role. Truly the "Cat's in the Cradle" syndrome can have a positive tune, as shown in the relationship between Lehi and Nephi.

Consider the words of Enos concerning his father: "I, Enos, knowing my father that he was a just man—for he taught me . . . in the nurture and admonition of the Lord." (Enos 1:1.) Enos went on to relate his "wrestle" in obtaining "a remission of . . . sins." (Enos 1:2.) The experience of praying all day and into the night before receiving this remission was preceded by a session of very deep pondering. Enos recorded: "The words which I had often heard my father speak . . . sunk deep into my heart." (Enos 1:3.) Obviously, it was the Savior who removed the stain of sin, but consider the role of Enos' father, Jacob, in this process. Jacob could not give his son a "sacred grove" experience, but *it was his responsibility to show him the pathway there*. It would have been very difficult for Jacob to show his son the path had he not been there himself.

This is not unlike Alma the Younger, who for three long days was "racked with torment, . . . [and] harrowed up by the memory of [his] many sins." (Alma 36:17.) During this time of suffering, Alma's mind turned to the words of his father: "I remembered also to have heard my father prophesy . . . concerning . . . Jesus Christ." (Alma 36:17.) Upon crying out to the Savior, he stated, "I could remember my pains no more; yea, I was harrowed up by the memory of my sins no more." (Alma 36:19.) Again, notice the role of the father in the process of spiritual growth. The Savior removed Alma's pain and stain of sin, but *the words of the elder Alma lead his son to the fruits of Gethsemane.* The quality of spiritual example and instruction by parents illuminated the strait and narrow path for many of those who have become our heroes in the Book of Mormon. (See Helaman 5:5–6.)

The promises of the Lord carry over from generation to generation as exemplified by the Lamanite converts of the sons of Mosiah who took on the name of Anti-Nephi-Lehies. Some 2,000 of their sons became the "stripling warriors" when they enlisted in the Nephite army. These youthful patriots were untested in battle yet they illustrated no fear at the prospect of death. The reason for this being that "they had been taught by their mothers, that if they did not doubt, God would deliver them." (Alma 56:47.) Notice if they did not doubt *something* then God would deliver them. What was it that they were not to doubt? That their mothers were telling the truth? That the gospel was true? Not to doubt Helaman their military leader, and obey with exactness? (See Alma 57:21.) Not to doubt the oath they had taken to defend the freedom of their fathers and the Nephites? (See Alma 53:17; 56:47.) Not to doubt that God would deliver them? Yes, perhaps the answer encompasses all of these—but there is more.

Remember, that at an earlier time their parents were a part of the Anti-Nephi-Lehies, many whom were slaughtered by their brethren, the Lamanites, because they would not take up arms to defend themselves. (See Alma 24:13–23.) Those who lived through the slaughter eventually went to Ammon and asked him to "inquire of the Lord" as to what to do. (See Alma 27:10.) The Lord responded to his inquiry by giving a blessing of protection to the parents of these stripling warriors: "Blessed are this people . . . I will *preserve* them." (Alma 27:12;

italics added.) In this context *preserve* meant to deliver or to protect. And that was just what he did. The text records no more slaughter among these newly converted Lamanites. This became the same promise given to the stripling warriors by their mothers that "God would deliver them." (Alma 56:47.) This promise was not new to the stripling warriors when they went to battle for the first time; they grew up with it because it was the promise given to their parents by the Lord. It was not hard for them to believe in "deliverance" in battle because *this promise of "preservation" had been true in their families long before they became warriors.* This example of spiritual success with the "Cat's in the Cradle" syndrome does not end here. Ammon, the missionary who had received the revelation giving the Anti-Nephi-Lehi's their blessing of "preservation" (see Alma 27:12), received the same blessing from the Lord many years earlier when he and the other sons of Mosiah inquired of their father if they could preach the gospel to the Lamanites. The Lord spoke these words to Mosiah: "I will deliver thy sons out of the hands of the Lamanites." (Mosiah 28:7.) The sons of Mosiah received the same blessing given later to their converts the Anti-Nephi-Lehies, which naturally carried over to their sons, the stripling warriors. The faith of these youthful sons mirrors the faith of their parents and the missionaries who taught them. The promises of the Lord continue from generation to generation when his children are faithful. (See Abraham 2:9–11.)

GOSPEL PARENTING CANNOT BE DELEGATED

Latter-day prophets and ancient scriptural text adequately detail parents' responsibilities to help their children find the path that leads to spiritual victory. As parents we cannot delegate our responsibilities to teach our children. Certainly our children have other teachers in the Church, but the responsibility of ensuring that our children understand the gospel rests on our shoulders. Parents can't delegate that responsibility to the Church. Consider the words of the prophet

Harold B. Lee: "Sometimes as I go throughout the Church, I think I am seeing a man who is using his church work as a kind of escape from family responsibility. And sometimes when we've talked about whether or not he's giving attention to his family, his children and his wife, he says something like this: 'Well, I'm so busy taking care of the Lord's work that I really don't have time.' And I say to him, 'My dear brother, the greatest of the Lord's work that you and I will ever do is the work that we do within the walls of our own home.' Now don't you get any misconception about where the Lord's work starts. That's the most important of all the Lord's work. And you wives may have to remind your husbands of that occasionally." (Address to seminary and institute personnel at Brigham Young University, July 8, 1966.)

In the final blessing given to the children of Laman by their grandfather, Lehi said: "I leave my blessing upon you, that the cursing may be taken from you and be answered upon the heads of your parents." (2 Nephi 4:6.) The Lord has given to parents the responsibility of teaching their young children the gospel. If this responsibility is not accepted, then "the sin be upon the heads of the parents." (D&C 68:25.) President Spencer W. Kimball stated to the Saints in Japan: "But we the parents cannot escape the responsibility that is ours of training our children." (Tokyo Area Conference Report, Aug. 1975, pp. 38–39.) This responsibility of teaching our young children is reaffirmed in the words of the prophet David O. McKay: "There are parents who say: We will let our children grow to manhood and womanhood and choose for themselves. In taking this attitude, parents fail the discharging of a parental responsibility. Parents and teachers are God's fellow workers. The Father of all mankind expects parents, as his representatives, to assist him in shaping and guiding human lives." (Conference Report, April 1955, p. 27.)

The Savior quoted Malachi to the Nephites: "Behold, I will send you Elijah the prophet before the coming of the great and dreadful day of the Lord: And he shall turn the heart of the fathers to the children, and the heart of the children to their fathers, lest I come and smite the earth with a curse." (Malachi 4:5–6; 3 Nephi 25:5–6.) Many Saints have an understanding that this refers only to our connection with our departed relatives. The prophet Harold B. Lee stated that this refers to a parental responsibility on this side of the veil as well. He said:

> When the full measure of Elijah's mission is understood, . . . the hearts of the children will be turned to the fathers, and the fathers to the children. It applies just as much on this side of the veil as it does on the other side of the veil. If we neglect our families here in having family home night and we fail in our responsibility here, how would heaven look if we lost some of those through our own neglect? Heaven would not be heaven. . . . So, the hearts of you fathers and mothers must be turned to your children right now, if you have the true spirit of Elijah, and not think it applies merely to those who are beyond the veil. Let your hearts be turned to your children, and teach your children; but you must do it when they are young enough to be properly schooled. And if you are neglecting your family home evening, you are neglecting the beginning of the mission of Elijah just as certainly as if you were neglecting your research work of genealogy." (*Teachings of Harold B. Lee*, 281.)

TEACHING CHILDREN WHEN THEY ARE YOUNG

Sometimes parents neglect the teaching of the gospel to their young children because they feel the children are too young to understand or that their children just don't need it until they are older. Spiritually speaking, this philosophy can be fatal to a child. Prior to the age of accountability, "power is not given unto Satan to tempt little children." (D&C 29:47.) Therefore, it is imperative that gospel instruction begins at an early age before the adversary can influence our children. In a general conference address, Elder Merlin R. Lybbert of the

Seventy explained why the teaching of the gospel must begin when our children are young:

> This teaching is to be done before a child reaches the age of accountability, and while innocent and sin-free. This is pro- tected time for parents to teach the principles and ordinances of salvation to their children without interference from Satan. It is a time to dress them in armor in preparation for the battle against sin. When this preparation time is neglected, they are left vulnerable to the enemy. To permit a child to enter into that period of his life when he will be buffeted and tempted by the evil one, without faith in the Lord Jesus Christ and an understanding of the basic principles of the gospel, is to set him adrift in a world of wickedness. During these formative, innocent years, a child may learn wrong behavior; but such is not the result of Satan's temptations, but comes from the wrong teachings and the bad example of others. In this con- text, the Savior's harsh judgment of adults who offend children is better understood, wherein he said, "It were better for him that a millstone were hanged about his neck, and he cast into the sea, than that he should offend one of these little ones." (Luke 17:2.)
>
> We offend a child by any teaching or example which leads a little one to violate a moral law; causes him to stumble, or go astray; excites him to anger; creates resentment; or perhaps even leads him to become displeasing and disagreeable. (*Ensign*, May 1994, pp. 31–32.)

President J. Reuben Clark Jr., a former member of the First Presidency, reminded the teachers of youth in the Church that our children have a much greater capacity for spiritual instruction than they are oftentimes given credit: "Our youth are not children spiritu- ally; they are well on towards the normal spiritual maturity. . . . You do not need to disguise religious truths with a cloak of worldly things; you can bring these truths to [them] openly, in their natural guise. . . . There is no need for gradual approaches, . . . for coddling, for patronizing, or for any of the other childish devices used in efforts to reach those spiritually inexperienced." (Cited in Boyd K. Packer, *Teach Ye Diligently*, p. 317.)

President Gordon B. Hinckley reaffirmed the consequences of not teaching our children when they are young:

Not long after we were married, we built our first home. . . . The first of many trees that I planted was a thornless honey locust. . . . It was so supple that I could bend it with ease in any direction. I paid little attention to it as the years passed.

Then one winter day, . . . I chanced to look out the window at it. I noticed that it was leaning to the west, misshapen and out of balance. . . . I went out and braced myself against it as if to push it upright. But the trunk was now nearly a foot in diameter. . . . It seemed to say, "You can't straighten me. It's too late. I've grown this way because of your neglect, and I will not bend."

Finally in desperation I took my saw and cut off the great heavy branch on the west side. The saw left an ugly scar, more than eight inches across. . . . I had cut off the major part of the tree, leaving only one branch growing skyward.

More than half a century has passed since I planted that tree. . . . The other day I looked again at the tree. It is large. Its shape is better. . . . But how serious was the trauma of its youth and how brutal the treatment I used to straighten it.

When it was first planted, a piece of string would have held it in place against the forces of the wind. . . .

I have seen a similar thing, many times, in children whose lives I have observed. The parents who brought them into the world seem almost to have abdicated their responsibility. The results have been tragic. A few simple anchors would have given them the strength to withstand the forces that have shaped their lives. Now it appears it is too late. (*Teachings of Gordon B. Hinckley*, pp. 419–20.)

CHILDREN WHO GO ASTRAY

What of parents who have been obedient to the commandments and who have taught their children to do the same, they who have done everything in their power, and after all their efforts, the lives of their children have not reflected the gospel? To those parents it may seem that "Cat's in the Cradle" has not been the theme song playing throughout their relationship with their children. These children have gone astray even though the parents met their responsibilities. It is to these parents that Elder Boyd K. Packer has spoken:

> The measure of our success as parents, however, will not rest solely on how our children turn out. That judgment would be just only if we could raise our families in a perfectly moral environment, and that now is not possible.
>
> It is not uncommon for responsible parents to lose one of their children, for a time, to influences over which they have no control. They agonize over rebellious sons or daughters. They are puzzled over why they are so helpless when they have tried so hard to do what they should.
>
> It is my conviction that those wicked influences one day will be overruled.
>
> "The Prophet Joseph Smith declared—and he never taught a more comforting doctrine—that the eternal sealings of faithful parents and the divine promises made to them for valiant service in the Cause of Truth, would save not only themselves, but likewise their posterity. Though some of the sheep may wander, the eye of the Shepherd is upon them, and

sooner or later they will feel the tentacles of Divine Providence reaching out after them and drawing them back to the fold. Either in this life or the life to come, they will return. They will have to pay their debt to justice; they will suffer for their sins; and may tread a thorny path; but if it leads them at last, like the penitent Prodigal, to a loving and forgiving father's heart and home, the painful experience will not have been in vain. Pray for your careless and disobedient children; hold on to them with your faith. Hope on, trust on, till you see the salvation of God." (Orson F. Whitney, in Conference Report, Apr. 1929, p. 110.)

We cannot overemphasize the value of temple marriage, the binding ties of the sealing ordinance, and the standards of worthiness required of them When parents keep the covenants they have made at the altar of the temple, their children will be forever bound to them. (*The Shield of Faith*, pp. 125–26.)

Elder Vaughn J. Featherstone of the Seventy referred to this concept when he encouraged married couples to serve full-time missions: "There is a need, *not* to leave homes forever, but for a time—then return and reap the rich harvest of the faithful labor. Your children and grandchildren will be blessed. . . . President Harold B. Lee taught the principle that only as we make ourselves totally available are we worthy disciples of Christ and obtain another promise that reaches beyond us. We worry and ache and pain over family members who have erred. The 31st section of the Doctrine and Covenants provides a great key in verse five: 'Therefore, thrust in your sickle with all your soul, and your sins are forgiven you, and you shall be laden with sheaves upon your back, for the laborer is worthy of his hire. Wherefore, your family shall live.' . . . The promise is sure, 'Wherefore, your family shall live.' *Blessings will come to our wayward or wandering children,* even those who are married and have children of their own. . . . What better way have we to prepare to meet our God than to serve a mission when the

d winter of life is upon us?" (*Ensign*, May 1992, pp. 42–44;
d.)

are powerful promises, and notice that Elder Packer and
Elder Featherstone quote other prophets in their appeal to parents to
stay focused on the blessings of the Lord to the wayward children of
those parents who are "worthy disciples of Christ."

It may be difficult, if not impossible, to see the connection between
our own child's ill behavior and ourselves. Oftentimes the effort at this
approach becomes futile in the sense that we may become connected
more to the problem than to the solution. The answer to breaking the
connection is sometimes as simple as strengthening the bond of love
between parent and child. An example from the life of Arun Ghandi,
the grandson of the great leader Mahatma Ghandi, illustrates the point:

> One Saturday my father had to go to town to attend a con-
> ference, and he didn't feel like driving, so he asked me if I
> would drive him into town and bring him back in the evening.
> . . . Since I was going into town, my mom gave me a list of gro-
> ceries she needed, and on the way into town, my dad told me
> that there were many small chores that had been pending for a
> long time, like getting the car serviced and the oil changed.
>
> When I left my father at the conference venue, he said,
> "At 5 o'clock in the evening, I will wait for you outside this
> auditorium. Come here and pick me up, and we'll go home
> together."
>
> I said, "Fine." I rushed off and I did all my chores as quickly
> as possible—I bought the groceries, I left the car in the garage
> with instructions to do whatever was necessary—and I went
> straight to the nearest movie theatre. In those days, being a 16-
> year-old, I was extremely interested in cowboy movies. . . . I
> got so engrossed in a John Wayne double feature that I didn't
> realize the passage of time. The movie ended at 5:30, and I
> came out and ran to the garage and rushed to where Dad was

waiting for me. It was almost 6 o'clock when I reached there, and he was anxious and pacing up and down wondering what had happened to me. The first question he asked me was, "Why are you late?"

Instead of telling him the truth, I lied to him, and I said, "The car wasn't ready; I had to wait for the car," not realizing that he had already called the garage.

When he caught me in the lie, he said, "There's something wrong in the way I brought you up that didn't give you the confidence to tell me the truth, that made you feel you had to lie to me. I've got to find out where I went wrong with you, and to do that," he said, "I'm going to walk home—18 miles. I'm not coming with you in the car." There was absolutely nothing I could do to make him change his mind.

It was after 6 o'clock in the evening when he started walking. Much of those 18 miles were through sugarcane plantations—dirt roads, no lights, it was late in the night—and I couldn't leave him and go away. For five and a half hours I crawled along in the car behind Father, watching him go through all this pain and agony for a stupid lie. I decided there and then that I was never going to lie again.

I think of that episode often. It's almost 50 years since the event, and every time I talk or think about it I still get goose bumps. . . . Anything that is brought by fear doesn't last. But anything that is done by love lasts forever." (*Brigham Young Magazine*, Spring 2000, pp. 37–43.)

Love alone may not be the only answer, but it is certain that any effort to reach a wayward child without love will surely fail.

PARENTS WHO GO ASTRAY

There may be someone reading this who has been raised in a negative or even an abusive environment, who may be fearful that they are bound to repeat the cycle of behavior they witnessed in their own youth. Even though the "Cat's in the Cradle" syndrome is powerful in a negative environment, I will remind the reader of the words of Elder Neal A. Maxwell to the students of Brigham Young University: "No one was foreordained to fail or to be wicked. . . . Let us remember that we were measured before and were found equal to our tasks. . . . When we feel overwhelmed, let us recall the assurance that God will not over-program us; he will not press upon us more than we can bear." (*1978 Devotional Speeches of the Year*, p. 156.)

The words of Elder Boyd K. Packer also give comfort to those who fear that they may repeat the negative behavior of their parents. "To you adults who repeat the pattern of neglect and abuse you endured as little children, believing that you are entrapped in a cycle of behavior from which there is no escape, I say: It is contrary to the order of heaven for any soul to be locked into compulsive, immoral behavior with no way out! It is consistent with the workings of the adversary to deceive you into believing that you are." (*Ensign*, Nov. 1986, p. 18.)

President Spencer W. Kimball gave similar counsel to the members of the Church: "There are those today who say that man is the result of his environment and cannot rise above it. . . . Surely the environmental conditions found in childhood and youth are an influence of power. But the fact remains that every normal soul has its free agency and the power to row against the current and to lift itself to new planes of activity and thought and development. . . . . It is within his power to lift himself by his very bootstraps from the plane on which he finds himself to the plane on which he should be. . . . In other words, environment need not be our limit. Circumstance may not need to be our ruler." (*Ensign*, July 1978, pp. 3–7.)

CONCLUSION

Another story is told of the great Mahatma Gandhi, who was approached by a woman who had been told by her doctor that her son should not eat sugar. "I am deeply concerned about his health," she said. "He looks up to you. If you would suggest to him to stop eating sugar, I'm confident that he would follow your advice." After pondering her request, Gandhi determined that he would attempt to help her son. He asked her to bring her son to him no sooner than in two weeks. A few weeks later the mother returned with her child, and Gandhi visited privately with the son. The boy agreed to follow the words of his leader. The mother, overwhelmed by her son's decision, inquired of Gandhi why he had insisted on the two-week delay. He replied, "I needed to go two weeks without eating sugar myself." (Cited in Al Gore, *Earth in the Balance*, p. 14.)

The message is profound but extremely exacting in its results: We must set the example in whatever behavior we would want those in our care to display. Good parental instruction and bad parental examples are not compatible when the goal is to raise righteous children. The "Cat's in the Cradle" concept is captured by these words of unknown origin:

> *A careful man I want to be;*
> *A little fellow follows me.*
> *I do not dare to fall astray,*
> *For fear he'll go the self same way.*

Elder Matthew Cowley bore a powerful witness to the mothers in Zion regarding the power of a parent's influence:

> I was talking the other day to one of my friends, . . . who was drunk for twenty-seven years, and then finally turned his life back to God. He is now active in the Church and has not had a drink for fifteen years. I asked him how he was able to overcome that habit. . . . He said to me: "Matt, if I had not had the fortification which came to me in my childhood from a righteous mother, I never would have been able to overcome this terrible habit. The influence of that mother in my home

is what has given me the courage and the strength and the fortitude to overcome this drinking habit.'

. . . You may not live to see the fruits of your teaching in the lives of your children. . . . You may not see them turn their lives back to God, but the day will come, if you give them the fortification in their childhood, . . . the day will come . . . , because of you, . . . [when they will] turn their lives and their characters back to God and be influenced by him. (*Matthew Cowley Speaks*, pp. 108–9.)

The gospel invitation to parents is to live the gospel, honestly and completely, and to teach their children to do the same. If we are parents, we are teachers, no matter what other talents we possess—we are teachers to our own children and that cannot be delegated away. Our children are also children of God, and his "work and . . . glory [is] to bring to pass the immortality and eternal life" of all his children. (Moses 1:39.) Neal A. Maxwell of the Quorum of the Twelve stated, "Our Heavenly Father has no distracting hobbies—we are His work." (Missionary Training Center fireside, May 26, 1987.) As parents, our responsibility is to go forth with "no distracting hobbies" until our family is secure as a unit in the celestial kingdom.

I have had many occasions over the past twenty-seven years to hear Harry Chapin's "Cat's in the Cradle." During that time, my wife and I have had eight children. Through it all, I still feel the weight of the haunting lyrics toward the end of the song: "As I hung up the phone it occurred to me, he'd grown up just like me, my boy was just like me."

CHAPTER 6

Satan's Careful Chains

K. DOUGLAS BASSETT

The story is told of a time in old Alaska when wolves wreaked havoc among the settlers in the frozen countryside. In an effort to avoid starvation, the wolves would come down from the hills into the rural communities and destroy chickens and other farm animals. The citizens laid their traps out on the frozen ground and baited them with meat, which they were confident would attract the attention of the hungry wolves when they came down at night.

This plan had an unexpected consequence because of the severe winter conditions. The hinges in the traps became so frozen that when the wolves attempted to take the bait (thus springing the trap), the steel jaws of these terrible weapons would not completely snap shut. The wolf, who was severely wounded by these cruel iron teeth, would eventually wiggle free from these powerful jaws only to strike the chickens again. This time the wolf's attack was far more destructive, because often it became so diseased that in its crazed condition, anything it attacked, animal or human, would become very ill and would sometimes die just from a single bite.

The men made an attempt to control the wolves with the use of their rifles, but this took precious time away from sleep, chores, and other things that needed to be done. Finally it was decided to use the basic nature of the wolf in winter against itself—this being the need to satisfy its intense hunger for food. The blades of large knives were covered with the grease left over from frying meat such as bacon. Shallow holes were then dug in the ice, just deep enough to completely bury the knife except for the edge of the blade. The ice was then packed down all around, with the blade of the knife barely visible. There it would lie, with the smell of bacon grease inviting the wolves with the promise of what lay just beneath the snow. Sure enough, eventually the hungry wolves would come down in the middle of the night, drawn to the smell of bacon by their keen senses.

In an attempt to unearth the buried treasure and at the same time partake of the wonderful taste of meat, they would lick and lick. In the frozen conditions of the night, the sensation of cold and pain are often indistinguishable. The wolves' pain was masked by the cold just long enough for the knife to complete its task. Their tremendous drive to satisfy their hunger drove the wolves to lick repeatedly. Then they were overcome with the pain of what they had done to themselves. The momentary pleasure of the taste of bacon was soon replaced by the unexpected and abrupt end to their lives. In the morning their bodies were usually discovered within fifty yards of the knife, which still lay there, waiting like an invitation for the next evening.

Harsh conditions led these citizens of the cold north to make a choice between their own survival and that of the wolves. In our day these measures may seem cruel and unnecessary. Perhaps if we were a part of their time, conditions, and challenges, we might see it differently.

However, is there not a lesson in their experience from which we may profit? Consider the strategy used by these pioneers of old. They understood that the wolf was so driven by its hunger that it would stop at nothing to satisfy this natural instinct. The bacon grease was used as an enticement to invite the wolf to unwittingly destroy itself. Is not this the same strategy Satan has been using since the beginning of his reign here on earth? He finds those children of God who are completely driven by the needs of the natural man. (See Mosiah 3:19.) Then he places snares in their path, with an invitation to satisfy the moment. Then, over a period of time, the participants discover that they have traded their eternal lives for the momentary pleasures of what may amount to little more than "bacon grease."

Let us consider another analogy with a similar message. One of the natural instincts for all children, even after they have obtained a full set of teeth, is to quickly swallow things that taste good. Their immediate desire when something stimulates their taste buds is to chew it no longer than it takes to be able to ingest it. For example, it is difficult for a young child to chew gum without swallowing it or even suck on a lifesaver for any length of time without doing the same. Thus, parents constantly remind their children to chew their food when they eat.

For many years, prior to the invention of the childproof cap on medicine containers, one of the most tragic causes of death among small children was candy-coated pills. Children would sometimes place candy-coated pills into their mouths and, rather than chewing long enough to discover the bitter taste of the medicine, they did what only comes naturally—swallowed as fast as possible. Sometimes this process was repeated with many pills, placing children without immediate assistance in grave danger. Their natural curiosity, coupled with their basic instinct to swallow, drove them to do that which was not in their own best interest. Injury and even death were too often the result of this immature desire for immediate gratification.

We can easily see Satan's strategy with God's children of all ages in the example of candy-coated pills. Satan deals with immediate physical gratification at the expense of a lifetime of joy and growth. He entices his victims, young and old, into trading their tomorrows, filled with so much joy and hope, for momentary pleasures that lead to addictive slavery and eventual death. By the time many people are aware of the momentary nature of the candy coating offered by the adversary, they have already swallowed the poison. Satan deals in this type of short-term physical pleasure connected with long-term spiritual regrets. Isaiah seems to be referring to Satan's ability to fool us with candy-coated lies when he warns, "Woe unto them that call evil good, and good evil; . . . that put bitter for sweet, and sweet for bitter!" (Isaiah 5:20.)

Let us look to the Book of Mormon for an example of this phenomenon. Laman and Lemuel were engulfed in what seemed to their father to be a short-term perspective that blinded them to the consequences of their own behavior. In his final blessing to his sons, Lehi made an attempt to extend their vision beyond their momentary needs: "O that ye would awake; awake from a deep sleep, yea, even from the sleep of hell, and shake off the awful *chains* by which ye are bound, which are the *chains* which bind the children of men, that they are carried away captive down to the eternal gulf of misery and woe." (2 Nephi 1:13; italics added.) A few verses later he continued, "Awake, my sons; put on the armor of righteousness. Shake off the *chains* with which ye are bound." (2 Nephi 1:23; italics added.)

The first time I read this verse many years ago, I was fascinated by Lehi's use of the word *chains*. I wondered what the word must have meant from Lehi's perspective. Over the years, I have studied the ancient society of the Assyrians as well as the Babylonians and the way they bound and transported the masses they had conquered. With this background, it became obvious what Lehi was trying to communicate to his sons. The torturous ways of these societies were always connected with the concept of cruelly binding with ropes or chains the people they had conquered. It would have been nearly impossible for Laman and Lemuel not to understand the imagery their father was trying to use to get them to wake up spiritually. By using the terrifying mental picture of the chains used by conquering nations, Lehi wanted to impress upon his sons the power of Satan to dominate and control the people he captures.

Elder Carlos E. Asay helps us apply this idea to our day: "'*Shake off the awful chains by which ye are bound*' indicates the need to overcome bad habits, even the seemingly little habits that grow into strong 'chains of hell.'" (*Ensign*, May 1992, p. 41.)

Later in the Book of Mormon, Alma connects the word *chains* with those who "will harden their hearts." He continues, "They are taken captive by the devil, and led by his will down to destruction. Now this is what is meant by the chains of hell." (Alma 12:11.)

Gospel scholar Robert J. Matthews referred to these hardhearted people when he said, "Such unbelievers are actually in a spiritual deep-freeze and are in danger of freezing to death, but don't even know that they are cold. Unless they are awakened and aroused and made to exercise, they will die spiritually. The devil slips his chains around them so subtly and carefully that he snares and binds them almost before they realize it." (In *Alma, the Testimony of the Word*, p. 53.)

Nephi saw our day and even spoke to us about the chains we may be wearing. He spoke to those whose hearts are in tune with the devil and encouraged them to "be stirred up unto repentance, or the devil will grasp them with his everlasting *chains*, and they be stirred up to anger." (2 Nephi 28:19; italics added.)

In this verse, notice the connection between Satan's chains and those who are "stirred up to anger." What a contrast between those who please Satan through anger and those who submit to the Lord by becoming "child[like], . . . meek, humble, patient, [and] full of love." (Mosiah 3:19.)

Nephi continued this line of reasoning by speaking to the audience that also includes the youth of our time: "At that day shall he rage in the hearts of the children of men, and stir them up to anger against that which is good." (2 Nephi 28:20.) In the previous verse, he spoke of those of the latter-days who wear the chains of anger, but in this verse he includes "the children of men" who "anger against that which is good." Isn't it possible that some of that anger is reflected in the fashion of some of our youth in their body piercing, tattoos, radical hairstyles, and general conduct?

Nephi included this group with many of the older generation when he said, "Others he flattereth away, and telleth them there is no hell; and he saith unto them: I am no devil, . . . and thus he whispereth in their ears." (2 Nephi 28:22.) This "whispering" is one of the ways Satan has of reaching the ears of some of our troubled youth through music and other forms of media. Nephi then spoke to us about the power of this negative media: ". . . until he grasps them with his awful *chains*, from whence there is no deliverance." (2 Nephi 28:22; italics added.) Elder Boyd K. Packer echoed Nephi's testimony: "The world grows increasingly noisy. . . . Raucous music, with obscene lyrics [is] blasted through amplifiers. . . . The first order issued by a commander mounting a military invasion is the jamming of the channels of communication of those he intends to conquer. Irreverence suits the purposes of the adversary by obstructing the delicate channels of revelation." (Conference Report, Oct. 1991, pp. 27–28.)

In these words we can almost see the same vision as the prophet Enoch when he "beheld Satan; . . . [who] had a great *chain* in his hand, . . . and he . . . laughed, and his angels rejoiced." (Moses 7:26; italics added.) Can we not see his hand in the challenges that try the souls of many of our youth?

There may be some who see themselves as active in the Church but because they are blessed economically, have settled into a comfortable form of spiritual laziness. They may be fooled into fostering the false assumption that they are active simply because they attend meetings regularly in a chapel that requires little more sacrifice than to walk or drive a short distance from their homes. In a sense they are enjoying the taste of an adult kind of pacifier as they wean themselves from true spirituality to something that resembles a spiritual coma.

It is to us that Nephi wrote these words: "Others will he pacify, and lull them away into carnal security, that they will say: All is well in

Zion; yea, Zion prospereth, all is well." (2 Nephi 28:21.) Nephi warned the Saints who have pacified themselves with this kind of thinking: "Wo be unto him that is at ease in Zion! Wo be unto him that crieth: All is well." (2 Nephi 28:24–25.)

Speaking to our day, Nephi tried to wake us up in the same manner in which Lehi tried to wake up his slumbering sons: "Thus the devil cheateth their souls, and *leadeth them away carefully down to hell."* (2 Nephi 28:21; italics added.)

President Ezra Taft Benson referred to this verse when he said, "I like that word 'carefully.' In other words, don't shake them, you might awake them." (Conference Report, Apr. 1965, p. 124.) President Gordon B. Hinckley applied this verse to our time when he said, "There is so much of the good and the beautiful and the uplifting in literature and art and life itself that there should be no time for any man who holds the priesthood of God to patronize, to watch, to buy that which only *'carefully leads him down to hell.'"* (Conference Report, Oct. 1983, pp. 67–68; italics added.) It is to us, not the Nephites, that Nephi and these two great latter-day prophets are referring.

FLAXEN CORDS

How is it possible for those who have willingly made covenants before this life, as well as in mortality, to trade their tomorrows for that which has no more lasting value than candy-coated poison or knives smothered in bacon grease? Once again, Nephi gives us a clue by explaining the nature of Satan's chains. "He leadeth them by the neck with a *flaxen cord,* until he bindeth them with his strong cords forever." (2 Nephi 26:22; italics added.)

Clyde J. Williams of the Ancient Scripture Department at BYU wrote, "A flaxen cord would be made of the fine, light-colored fiber manufactured from flax. It would be soft and thin and easily broken. Nevertheless, if we continue to rationalize our involvement with flaxen cords, or 'little sins,' eventually we will become bound with the 'strong cords' and find ourselves subject to Satan." (In *Doctrines of the Book of Mormon*, p. 249.) Too often we like those flaxen cords because they please our physical senses. It is only after we have entangled ourselves in them that we realize they have become as strong as chains in the hands of the adversary.

A number of years ago, my calling in the Church was to be a religious counselor to the inmates at the Utah State Prison. I drew close to many of the citizens of that institution. I became particular friends with one of the inmates whom I will call Bill. Even though he had served a full-time mission for the Church and had married in the temple, he had later committed crimes that had violated the virtue of his own daughters. He despised himself for it and would not forgive himself for the vile deeds of his life. He spent a number of hours each day in the weight room, trying desperately to escape the tension of his life. As he expressed it, "I can't stand to be alone in my cell with the memory of my crimes."

Like almost all the inmates, he hated being incarcerated. But unlike his peers behind bars, he had no desire to leave prison for fear that he might commit the same crime again. Prison was the place he felt he deserved to be, and a place he felt he should remain for the protection of others.

But what of the road that had led him to prison? As a young man he'd had all the hopes and dreams of any boy growing up in the Church. He'd had no desire to wind up in jail or, worse yet, to travel the road of sin that led him to this place. He was living proof that we do not have to die to go to hell. The weeping and wailing of the damned does not begin when they die any more than celestial people must wait to have charity until they reach the gates of heaven. Heaven and hell are attitudes and actions in the lives of people long before those same people become eternal residents of the actual places.

One particular Sunday I happened to be assigned to give a gospel doctrine lesson to a group of inmates (including Bill) who had committed the same type of crimes he had been guilty of. Following a scriptural journey through the concept of the addictive nature of Satan's chains, I tried something a bit risky in an effort to help them make the connection with themselves and flaxen cords. I had brought with me an expensive spool of thread that was light and silky. It was so fine that an individual strand of this thread was barely detectable to the eye.

I invited Bill to come forward and help me make a point in my lesson. My experience had taught me that the road to prison almost always intersects somewhere along the way with pornography. This was one of the flaxen cords leading to the chains of Satan that kept these men bound.

I asked Bill to make a fist with both of his hands and then bring them together in front of his body. I then asked him to extend the forefinger of each hand so he was pointing forward with both index fingers side by side. Following this, I wrapped one strand of thread around his fingers as close to his knuckles as possible so it would be up against the tender upper portion of the sides of his fingers. I said that this represented the first time he had looked at pornography. I asked if he could remember the first time he had done it. He said that he could not forget it.*

I then asked him to pull his fingers apart and break the thread. With a little bit of effort he did so. Quickly I grabbed one of his hands and held up one of his forefingers so the other inmates could see the line on the inside of the finger where he had broken free.

I asked the other inmates what they were witnessing as they looked at his finger. They indicated in one voice that the line was disappearing.

---

*How ironic it is that when we commit sin without repentance, our lives become so wrapped up in flaxen cords that we begin to actually lose spiritual memory. Bill could easily remember the first time he looked at pornography, but he found it difficult to remember the sacred covenants he had made. His connection to sin created a kind of spiritual amnesia about his covenants and sacred experiences. Similarly, Nephi said that his rebellious brothers had forgotten the spiritual power that had delivered them because of their sins. (See 1 Nephi 18:9.) Remembering two masters becomes very difficult when they oppose each other. (See 3 Nephi 13:19–24.)

I said to them that this is what happens when we repent. The scar is removed and the pain of breaking free is eventually replaced with a new beginning.

I asked Bill if the tender portion of the inside of his index fingers had hurt when he had broken free of the thread. He said that it had. I reminded him, as well as the rest of the group, that there is discomfort and even pain that must be experienced in order to obtain forgiveness—it is not simply a free ride on our part. I told Bill that, symbolically speaking, this is what could have happened had he gone to his bishop and sought the help needed to free himself of his attraction to pornography. When I asked him if he had done this, he said that he had not.

Next, I told him I was going to wrap the thread around his fingers over and over again. Each time around was to represent an occasion when he had looked at pornography. I asked him to stop me when I had reached the correct number. As he looked at me in disbelief, I began wrapping the flaxen cord around and around his fingers without saying a word. Even though the silence did not extend beyond thirty seconds, I'm sure it seemed a lot longer to Bill than anyone else in the room. It did not take long for the thin flaxen thread to weave into a strong cord, like one link in a chain.

I interrupted the silence by saying that this was the point Bill had reached in his life right then. I challenged him to break free of the flaxen cord as he had done before. He strained and strained until the tenderness on the soft skin of his forefingers had turned to real pain. He stood there, defeated in his own attempt to break free.

I placed the spool, which was still connected to the thread wrapped around his fingers, on the edge of my shoulder. I put the little finger of my right hand on top of the spool, holding it down on my shoulder. I then took two steps to the side. His fingers were so tender that he did not resist the direction I was taking him. I looked at my defeated friend and said, "That's where you are right now. All Satan has to do is to place a little pornography in front of you, and you will follow him the way you just followed me when I directed you ever so slightly. You have abused your agency to the point that it is almost lost."

He looked at me with a pained, almost embarrassed expression. I'm sure that only his knowledge of my love for him kept him from being very upset with me. I had taken liberties in order to teach a principle, and he had been kind enough to allow it to happen.

We rehearsed how life could seem so normal for Bill until he encountered the lethal combination of stress and pornography. The path that had led him to this place was well traveled by all the inmates in that room. I reminded Bill that with all the strength he had acquired by spending time in the weight room at the prison, he still wasn't strong enough to lift himself. We agreed that no one but a Savior could lift him from what he had become. I encouraged him as well as the other inmates to recognize the Savior's role in freeing himself from the chains of Satan.

I was constantly amazed that the Spirit was so strong in that church setting with those inmates who had committed such vile crimes. I think it was because many of them had a total dependency on the idea that no one but a Savior could relieve them of their burdens. I fear that sometimes in our own wards, the lack of Spirit in some meetings comes from the fact that we think we have our salvation under control. Unconsciously, we carry this to the point that our need for the Savior from moment to moment is not as great as with those inmates in prison. We recognize that we will depend on the Lord at the end of our lives and at various points in between, but not today when the sun is shining and life is good. That mind-set, in and of itself, may be a flaxen cord.

As I worked with Bill and the other inmates to get them to accept responsibility for their flaxen cords and then work to get free of these traps of the adversary, I found the words of President Ezra Taft Benson very applicable: "We are free to choose, but we are not free to alter the consequences of those choices." (*Come unto Christ*, p. 40.) These men had been free to entangle themselves with flaxen cords but not to release themselves from the chains that the flaxen cords had eventually become. Few people would intentionally place a chain around their necks, but a flaxen cord is a different story. But when we place one around our necks, we have unknowingly embraced the other. The chain becomes part of the consequences of our choice to wear a flaxen cord. In a sense, the flaxen cord is the candy-coating and the chain is the poison. Through the passing of time, the freedom of these inmates had slowly disappeared until they recognized that the chains of Satan they now wore began as deceptively harmless packages that were carefully wrapped with an appealing flaxen ribbon.

WATCH AND PRAY ALWAYS

During the Savior's visit to the Nephites, he warned them, "Watch and pray always, lest ye be tempted by the devil, and ye be led away captive by him." (3 Nephi 18:15.) A few verses later he bore a second witness to the danger of the adversary: "Ye must watch and pray always lest ye enter into temptation; for Satan desireth to have you." (3 Nephi 18:18.)

The town that my family and I have lived in the past few years lies in a valley up against a section of one of the most beautiful peaks along the Wasatch Mountain Range. Within a few miles of my house are a number of old mining caves. When I first moved to this town, I was talking to a few of my neighbors as to the whereabouts of these wonderful places of adventure. They filled my head with stories that excited the little boy within me. Following our conversation, one of the fellows said, "Remember not to go cavin' up there in August." When I inquired as to his reasoning, he simply said, "Snakes—rattlesnakes."

His words immediately sent a chill down my spine, and I was reminded of my fear of these belly-crawling creatures. But with the passing of time, the weather began to warm up, and naturally I began to explore the territory around the nearby hills. The area just echoed adventure as my family and I used much of our free time to explore the mountains near our home. Summer continued until we found ourselves in the dry month of August. By this time I had forgotten the counsel of my neighbor. My son Blaine and I were riding motorcycles along the foothills on a hot August afternoon when my eyes caught sight of a mining cave that I had not yet shared with my son. The child within me burst forth as I exclaimed, "Let's go cavin'!" He joyfully followed my lead.

We drove our motorcycles as close to the cave as possible, parking them about a quarter mile from the cave's opening. As we hiked up the trail, we were surrounded by the sound of katydids and grasshoppers. It was a beautiful day, and we were two boys in a world of adventure. After an hour or so in the cool confines of the cave, we made our way back down to the motorcycles. My heart was full, and my eyes moved back and forth and all around in an effort to drink up all the scenery that surrounded us. When we reached a place in the trail that seemed to have the best vantage point to partake of all the natural beauty, I asked my son to stop and enjoy the sight. In my moment of wonder I proclaimed, "It doesn't get any better than this!"

My thoughts were interrupted by a sound I couldn't identify because it was so muffled by the clatter of the grasshoppers and katydids. I stepped toward a bush only a few feet away to get a better view. As I leaned over the bush, my eyes caught hold of its occupant. Staring back at me was a rattlesnake coiled and ready to strike, and there was no question as to its target.

In the newspaper a few years ago I read a movie title called *White Men Can't Jump*. In an instant I proved that movie's title false. I even proved that old white men can jump as I instantly became vertical as well as horizontal in the air, like one of those cartoon characters I had grown up seeing on TV. It was a shame the Guinness Book of World

Records could not have been there to record my leap. At the very least it would have been a record for my age group.

It's amazing how quickly life can change from moment to moment. One moment I was strolling down a mountain trail with my son, soaking up the world around me, and in the next instant my heart was filled with terror. Quickly I grabbed my son's arm, and we ran down the trail to our motorcycles. As we sat there on our bikes catching our breath, those words of advice came back to me: "Remember not to go cavin' up there in August."

I had forgotten the counsel because I had been caught up in the moment. I placed myself as well as my son in a position to alter our tomorrows because of my preoccupation with the moment. We were fortunate not to have paid for my lack of obedience to the counsel of those who had been down that trail before us.

We can learn from the experiences of others, or we can make life's mistakes on our own. If I had just waited for another season, our adventure would not have been so perilous. I thought of Alma's words to the Nephites: "Watch and pray continually, that ye may not be tempted above that which ye can bear." (Alma 13:28.) I had let down my guard by not watching continually, and I was fortunate to have had no more than just a story to tell.

CONCLUSION

In a term paper a university student once described his experience as a deep-sea diver: "En route to the floor of the ocean the diver first passes through the 'belt of the fishes.' This is a wide band of light reflected from the surface of the sea. From this area he moves to a depth of water that cannot be penetrated by light above the surface. It is *dark, foreboding, and eerie*. The diver's immediate reaction is apt to be one of *fear* and sometimes a sudden spasm of *panic* that soon passes. As he drops deeper and deeper into the abyss, slowly his eyes begin to pick up the *luminous quality of the darkness; what was fear is relaxed and*

he moves into the lower region with confidence and peculiar vision."
(Howard Thurman, *The Luminous Darkness*, pp. vii–viii; italics added.)

While there is nothing wrong in the adventure shared by this student, it is similar to how the path of Satan is traveled by those he wishes to ensnare in his "careful chains." The attraction to swim in safe water is one thing, but to be drawn to the depths of that which is "dark, foreboding, and eerie" is another. As the person continues on his journey downward, his initial "fear" and even "panic" of darkness is replaced with a vision of the "luminous quality of the darkness." This false sense of light invites the swimmer to extend his stay in the darkness until he risks the danger of becoming lost or even drowned. Satan can't draw us into the depths of dangerous waters unless we are tricked into thinking that it is safe to swim in areas that are "dark, foreboding, and eerie." It is at that moment when that which "was [once] fear[ed] is relaxed and [we move] into the lower region with confidence and peculiar vision." It is to those who are "confident" in swimming in forbidden waters that Satan, like a shark, is drawn. Let us never be fooled into thinking that any of the light of Christ is to be found in the "luminous quality of darkness."

It is a sad truth that those who have been fooled into accepting darkness for light are those who will be able to bear personal witness of the careful chains of Satan. If we had the ability to listen carefully through the veil and hear the voices of those in spirit prison, perhaps we could hear Laman and Lemuel bearing testimony of their father Lehi's warning about the careful chains of Satan.

CHAPTER 7

FACES OF PRIDE IN THE BOOK OF MORMON

K. DOUGLAS BASSETT

In introducing himself to the latter-day audience who would read his record, Moroni wrote, "Jesus Christ hath shown you unto me, and I know your doing. And I know that ye do walk in the pride of your hearts." (Mormon 8:35–36.) Many in the world today think of pride as a positive thing, a driving force for success in our society, but despite that prevailing attitude, President Ezra Taft Benson reminded us, "In the scriptures there is no such thing as righteous pride—it is always considered a sin. Therefore, no matter how the world uses the term, we must understand how God uses the term." (Conference Report, April 1989, p. 3.) (The major writers of the Book of Mormon saw our day and shaped their message for us.)

President Benson also said: "Mormon . . . [chose] the stories, speeches, and events that would be most helpful to us. Each of the major writers of the Book of Mormon . . . wrote for future generations. . . . They saw our day and chose those things which would be of greatest worth to us." (Conference Report, Oct. 1986, p. 5.)

Moroni introduced himself to the readers of the Book of Mormon by declaring that the Lord had granted him a vision of our day: "The Lord hath shown unto me great and marvelous things concerning . . . that day when these things shall come forth among you." (Mormon

8:34.) He continued: "I speak unto you as if ye were present, and yet ye are not. But behold, Jesus Christ hath shown you unto me, and I know your doing." (Mormon 8:35.) It is ironic that he saw us in mortal bodies, hundreds of years before we were born, and we are now getting acquainted with his mortal ministry hundreds of years after he has left his mortal body behind.

Nephi also saw our day and recorded the things he witnessed: "I prophesy . . . concerning the last days; concerning the days when the Lord God shall bring these things forth unto the children of men." (2 Nephi 26:14.)

It is the idea that the Lord granted the major prophets of the Book of Mormon an opportunity to see us before they made their record that makes the following words of Elder Jeffrey R. Holland true: "No other book has ever been written with such a full view of the future dispensation to which that record would eventually come." (*Christ and the New Covenant,* p. 9.)

Is it any wonder that the first major war in this country following the arrival of the Book of Mormon was the bloody conflict known as the Civil War which saw brothers fighting brothers? This idea of brothers fighting brothers in the promised land is one of the major themes running throughout the text of the Book of Mormon. Based on the words of President Benson and Elder Holland, this would have to be prophetic rather than coincidental.

Other Book of Mormon themes such as family conflicts, secret combinations, educational pride, wealth, the coming of Christ, and many others, have direct application to our day because the writers seemed to be recording those things from their society which mirrored our society. They were doing more than just speaking to us; they were using those examples from their history and times which reflected that which they saw in our day. In a prophetic sense, the Book of Mormon reads like today's newspaper because so much of what we read in that book can be found in today's newspaper. This may explain the ease many readers find in likening it to themselves.

The Book of Mormon helps us do that. Toward the end of the Nephite text, Moroni included a letter written by his father, Mormon, concerning the people of their society: "Behold, the pride of this nation, or the people of the Nephites, hath proven their destruction except they should repent." (Moroni 8:27.) Hundreds of years before Mormon's epistle, Nephi, the man for whom the Nephite nation was named, prophesied concerning his seed: "For the reward of their pride and their foolishness they shall reap destruction." (2 Nephi 26:10.) Nephi and Mormon were speaking almost a thousand years apart, yet both were referring to the same event. Nephi prophesied and Mormon confirmed that pride was the cause of the destruction of the Nephite nation.

If pride proved the downfall of the covenant people who dwelt on this promised land anciently, then of what import is pride to the covenant people who inhabit this promised land today? In the Doctrine and Covenants, the Savior repeats the ancient warning against pride: "Beware of pride, lest ye become as the Nephites of old." (38:39.)

President Benson brought the same message to our doorstep with a warning: "Pride is the great stumbling block to Zion. I repeat: Pride is the great stumbling block to Zion." (Conference Report, Apr. 1989, p. 7.) He also explained the meaning of pride: "The central feature of pride is enmity—enmity toward God and enmity toward our fellowmen. *Enmity* means 'hatred toward, hostility to, or a state of opposition.' It is the power by which Satan wishes to reign over us. . . . Our enmity toward God takes on many labels, such as rebellion, hardheartedness, stiff-neckedness, unrepentant, puffed up, easily offended, and sign seekers. The proud wish God would agree with them. They aren't interested in changing their opinions to agree with God's." (Ibid., pp. 3–4.)

GREAT AND SPACIOUS DESIRES

It may be helpful for us to identify the desires or ambitions of those whose hearts were filled with pride in the Book of Mormon. The pride of the great and spacious building associated with the tree of life dream (see 1 Nephi 11:36; 12:18) is embodied in the great and abominable church spoken of by Nephi in 1 Nephi 13:5–9. Later, Nephi tells us that the people within the churches of the devil in the last days have the prideful objectives of *gain, power, popularity,* and *lusts of the flesh.* (See 1 Nephi 22:22–23.) Recognizing these four ambitions allows us to break down pride into its component parts. It also helps us to recognize when we might be mirroring the type of pride spoken of in the Book of Mormon. As we look carefully at these four ambitions, it becomes clear that all sins fall into at least one of these categories. The people of our day whose hearts belong to any of these four areas spoken of by Nephi are engulfed to one degree or another in the kind of pride spoken of in the Book of Mormon.

Notice how these four desires are Satan's counterfeits of four wonderful virtues given to us by our Heavenly Father. (1) *Gain* is Satan's attempt at corrupting individual financial responsibility. (2) *Power* takes the virtue of self-control and corrupts it with the unrighteous desire to control or dominate others. (3) *Popularity* takes the virtue of needing to be valued and appreciated by others and turns it into a vice—the need to define oneself through the eyes and opinions of others. (4) *Lust of the flesh* is Satan's attempt at corrupting the commandment given to Adam and Eve to "multiply, and replenish the earth." (Moses 2:28.) It removes covenants from procreation and connects it to individual self-gratification. Indeed, all virtues quickly turn to prideful vice with the addition of selfishness.

It would be incorrect for us to assume that membership in The Church of Jesus Christ of Latter-day Saints somehow gives us immunity from the great and spacious agendas of gain, power, popularity, or lusts of the flesh. Stephen E. Robinson of the Department of Ancient

Scripture at Brigham Young University wrote, "Individual orientation to the Church of the Lamb or to the great and abominable church is not by membership but by loyalty. Just as there are Latter-day Saints who belong to the great and abominable church because of their loyalty to Satan and his life-style [2 Nephi 10:16], so there are members of other churches who belong to the Lamb because of their loyalty to him and his life-style. *Membership is based more on who has your heart than on who has your records.*" (*Ensign*, Jan. 1988, p. 37.)

Regarding these four ambitions of the great and abominable church, perhaps the only one needing further explanation is *gain*. To say that *money* is a synonym for *gain* is incorrect, because temples, churches, missionaries, seminaries, and most things associated with building the kingdom of the Lord are connected to money in one way or another. Gain could be correctly defined as what the scriptures call "lucre." (See Mosiah 29:40; Alma 11:24.) Lucre is money used to promote greedy or unrighteous agendas. Gain involves not just money but all the things money can buy for all the wrong reasons. *Gain* brings to mind a race, where one runner is *gaining* on another. In this context, gain is only concerned with one person in comparison with another. Gain, then, becomes a financial footrace, where the priority is to have more than the next person. The concern is based more on a person's *wants* than a person's *needs*. And what does the person with gain want? Simply to have more than the next person trailing him in the race for mammon, while at the same time *gaining* financially on the fellow ahead of him.

A review of the Book of Mormon shows that success in any of the four prideful desires is often short-lived; in reality, it becomes little more than postponed failure. It appears that from the beginning of time, the appealing voices of the world have cried out that in order to have winners we must create losers. But the gospel of Christ has consistently proclaimed that success in this world without consideration of what God expects of us, and without a sensitivity for the divine nature of others, is a feast devoid of flavor. Pride introduces itself early in the Book of Mormon and wears various faces throughout the text. I will identify three of these faces of pride that have immediate practical application in our day.

COSTLY APPAREL, OR CONSPICUOUS CONSUMPTION

Nephi identified the great and spacious building that his father saw in a dream as the "vain imaginations and the pride of the children of men." (1 Nephi 12:18.) He said that pride and vanity are inseparably connected with this great building with no foundation. Nephi's younger brother Jacob chastised the vanity of the Nephites by saying, "Ye are lifted up in the pride of your hearts, and wear stiff necks and high heads because of the costliness of your apparel." (Jacob 2:13.) Jacob added that this pride based on clothing caused the Nephites to persecute their brethren, noting, "Ye suppose that ye are better than they." (Jacob 2:13.) It is not difficult to see how the great and spacious desires of power, popularity, gain, and lust of the flesh are connected to costly apparel.

In the first year of the reign of the judges, a wicked man named Nehor became known among the Nephites. Mormon described Nehor's priestcraft: "He began to be lifted up in the pride of his heart, and to wear very costly apparel, yea, and even began to establish a church after the manner of his preaching." (Alma 1:6.) Nehor's church was founded on the concept of pride. It seems that this philosophy still had an effect on the members of the true church some eight years after Nehor had left the scene: "The people of the church began to wax proud, because of their exceeding riches, . . . for they began to wear very costly apparel." (Alma 4:6.) Alma gave up his political position as chief judge to preach the gospel to the Nephites, who were ripening for destruction. To those Nephites Alma boldly proclaimed, "Can ye be puffed up in the pride of your hearts; yea, will ye still persist in the wearing of costly apparel?" (Alma 5:53.)

Hierarchy based on what a person wore was not unique to this period in the Book of Mormon. Nearly twenty years later Alma preached to an apostate group of Nephites called Zoramites—a people whose spiritual values included the idea that some individuals were excluded from attending church. Speaking of those who were not allowed to enter, Mormon wrote, "They were cast out of the synagogues because of the coarseness of their apparel." (Alma 32:2.) Of what value would it be for us to learn of an ancient people who placed an inappropriate priority on the way they dressed?

This question brings to mind an experience I witnessed many years ago with one of my seminary students. My six-year-old son Boyd, who was in the final months of a battle with cystic fibrosis, became very close to one of my students whom I will call Tom. When I would bring Boyd to seminary, he and Tom were inseparable. I'm sure Tom's major motivation for coming to class was connected with his desire to be with my son. The school where I taught was one of the wealthiest in the area, and wearing the "right" clothing was very important to the majority of the students. However, Tom's parents did not have a great deal of money, which was reflected in the clothes he wore to school. Perhaps this is one of the reasons he connected so well with my son. Tom's unfashionable apparel, as well as his social isolation in school, gave him an instant identification with this little boy whose body was not so fashionable either.

My son's condition continually grew worse, and near the end of the school year he passed away. His funeral was held at the church where I taught seminary, next to the high school. Like so many of my students, Tom came directly from his classes to attend the funeral. As he entered the chapel, he was stopped by one of the employees of the mortuary, who inquired, "Do you think you're dressed appropriately to show the necessary respect to this little boy and his family?"

Tom was devastated. He immediately left the building like a Zoramite cast out of the synagogue because of the *coarseness of his apparel*. To my knowledge he never attended seminary or church again. In his mind, this was the last straw for his already wavering testimony. As hard as I tried, I could not get him to come back. Is it possible that some of us in the Church could unwittingly be sending the same message that was given to Tom as well as to the unfashionable among the Zoramites?

President Gordon B. Hinckley has given us counsel against the improper use of body piercing and tattoos. (See *Ensign*, Nov. 2000, p. 99.) His counsel was directed to members of the Church, who are to refrain from such practices as a token of respect for our bodies, which the Savior identified as temples. (See John 2:19–21.) It is important to note that President Hinckley's words were meant for us personally; they were not given as a license to judge anyone else who chooses to participate in body piercing or tattoos. Someone with a nose ring or a tattoo might not feel welcome at church if we take President Hinckley's counsel incorrectly by casting judgmental glances or verbal innuendo about his or her appearance. If so, then it is we, the members of the Church, who take on the role of the prideful Zoramites in the Book of Mormon.

The challenge to us as members of the Church is to not judge others by their appearance while at the same time recognizing that the world will judge the Church by the appearance of its members. That is why students of church-owned schools as well as missionaries are required to dress and groom in a conservative fashion. At the conclusion of their missions, missionaries are counseled by their mission presidents to maintain their missionary grooming and conservative dress standards, not only for themselves but as a light for those who would follow in their footsteps by also serving missions.

While serving my full-time mission to England, I had the privilege of meeting several General Authorities. One who made a lasting impression on me was President Gordon B. Hinckley. Oddly enough, the greatest impact he had on my life came after I returned from the British Isles to my home in Redding, California.

About a year after arriving home, I acquired a job as a waiter at a posh restaurant. The waiters were required to dress in suits with white shirts and bow ties. We were also asked to grow our hair long and wear mustaches. It does not take a lot of imagination to realize that I looked very different than I did while serving as a full-time missionary. A few months after I started the job, my father was called to be a bishop. President Hinckley was sent out from Salt Lake City to set him apart in his new calling.

My wife and I, as well as my extended family, sat in the high council room of the stake center, anxiously awaiting the arrival of Elder Hinckley. As he entered the room, the atmosphere was full of his gentle enthusiasm. Instantly, my mind was brimming with a flood of memories of England, and my heart was full. Seeing him again made me yearn for the time in England that could never be revisited.

Each person in the room felt of his special spirit as he shook their hands one by one. As he came toward me, I reached out and gave him an enthusiastic missionary handshake, which seemed to catch him off guard a little bit. My energetic greeting caused him to step back.

Smiling at me he said, "You'll have to excuse me; your greeting makes me feel like we're old friends." He inquired, "Have we met before?"

"Yes," I said. "I'm Doug Bassett; I met you in London while serving my mission."

He hesitated for a moment, perhaps to assess how teachable I was. Placing his hand on my shoulder, he drew me closer to him. Drawing his mouth near my ear, he spoke in a manner that ensured that I would hear his message. His voice came forth in a soft tone of regret: "You'll have to forgive me for not recognizing you, Elder Bassett; you no longer have the look of a missionary."

He then stepped back and studied me just long enough to make sure I understood the message he had delivered. Following a gentle squeeze on my shoulder, he moved on.

I was not upset at him; I loved and respected him too much for that. But make no mistake about it, his message had found its mark—like an arrow to my heart. He wanted me to know that while he was not judging me personally, younger men than myself would judge a mission and its ability to change the life of a missionary simply by my appearance. Just because I was not to judge others did not mean these young men would not judge me or the Church by my appearance.

Moroni spoke directly to us—his latter-day audience—about our preoccupation with costly apparel and our priorities: "I know that ye do walk in the pride of your hearts; and there are none save a few only who do not lift themselves up in the pride of their hearts, unto the wearing of very fine apparel. . . . For behold, ye do love money, and your substance, and your fine apparel, and the adorning of your churches, more than ye love the poor and the needy, the sick and the afflicted." (Mormon 8:36–37.) Notice that Moroni did not speak out against the "adorning of your churches"; rather, he identified those who "love . . . the adorning of . . . churches more than [they] love the poor and the needy, the sick and the afflicted." His point is one of priority; the sin is in loving things—even consecrated buildings—more than people. In speaking to us, Moroni is connecting our churches and perhaps even our temples to costly apparel for those of us whose hearts are filled with the pride of the Zoramites.

Hundreds of years earlier Nephi also prophesied concerning the practices of some churches in the latter days when the Book of Mormon would come forth: "Their churches are lifted up; because of pride they are puffed up. . . . They rob the poor because of their fine clothing." (2 Nephi 28:12–13.) These two Book of Mormon prophets serve as powerful witnesses regarding the evils of pride in our time. Their words echo the oft-repeated play on words of our own day: "Love people and use things; don't love things and use people." Those things we love more than people become our costly apparel. According to the

Book of Mormon, such a misuse of priorities can have eternal consequences.

Even though costly apparel was and is a physical manifestation, Mae Blanch, a professor of English at BYU, rightly identified it as a spiritual problem: "When money and possessions become the chief marks of distinction in society, then the pursuit of money becomes the only action worthwhile. And if this pursuit requires the sacrifice of honesty, integrity, compassion, and all other virtues, then so be it, for the love of money is indeed the root of all evil. Thus the wearing of costly apparel involves the soul as much as the body." ("Challenge to the Reign of the Judges," in Kent Jackson, ed., *Studies in Scripture*, 7:292.)

I recall the experience of one of my students who drove to seminary in a very expensive sports car presented to her by her father on her sixteenth birthday. Along with my other students, I stood in the parking lot celebrating as well as coveting her brand new car. Later in the day she drove back to the seminary to visit with me one on one. With no other students around, she was free to share her feelings concerning this expensive gift. Surprisingly, her emotions were not based on the joy of receiving the beautiful car but of sorrow—almost mourning—regarding the distance between herself and her father. Her tears were interrupted by these words: "He gives me everything money can buy and nothing it can't."

I must admit that because of my middle-class background, I initially saw her words as those of a spoiled rich girl, until she said, "He has never told me he loves me. This car is his way of avoiding the issue. I would gladly give back all his expensive gifts just to hear him say, 'I love you.'"

Later that year her parents divorced, and from then on the geographical distance between her and her father equaled the emotional distance that had always been there. Without knowing it, she had identified his gifts as costly apparel. From this experience and so many others I have witnessed, costly apparel is used as a shield for people to hide behind so they don't have to make needed changes within themselves. When our hearts are filled with pride, we rationalize that if we surround ourselves with all the toys of success, then we will be thought of by others as being successful. This allows us not to have to deal with the real internal issues that keep us from progressing. We then begin to value personal possessions more than personal relationships. In this light, it is not hard to see the importance of ridding ourselves of costly apparel.

Our society may well be as guilty as the wealthy Zoramites of using fashion as "the science of appearances, inspiring us with the desire to seem rather than to be." (Edwin Hubbel Chapin, as quoted in Stephen R. Covey, *Spiritual Roots of Human Relations*, p. 26.) In our day the costly apparel syndrome may be identified as one aspect of the modern-day term *conspicuous consumption*. The word *conspicuous* alludes to the visual side of vanity—the need to be seen or recognized. *Consumption* refers to that which we take in or consume. Conspicuous consumption may be defined as that which we take to ourselves in order to be recognized and approved of by others. The person trapped in conspicuous consumption, especially as it applies to "costly apparel," must be focused on the opinions of others, because what is "in" today may be out of fashion tomorrow. Vanity then becomes its own punishment, because there is never time to be satisfied—the eyes and opinions of others can turn so quickly to embrace someone else.

As I mentioned earlier, the disease that afflicted the Zoramites encompasses more than clothing in our day. It can include cars, houses, boats, diplomas, computers, or anything else that has as a foundation the need for the approval of man more than the need to be accepted by God. Elder Ezra Taft Benson referred to this problem in general conference many years ago: "Are not many of us status-seekers—measuring the worth of a man by the size of his bank account, his house, his automobile?" (Conference Report, Oct. 1960, p. 103.)

A Society Divided into Classes

Another result of pride within a society is the separation of people into a caste system. The Book of Mormon gives ample evidence of this face of pride. Following the Lord's visit to the Nephites, "They had all things common among them; therefore there were not rich and poor, bond and free, but they were all made free, and partakers of the heavenly gift." (4 Nephi 1:3.) The record adds, "Surely there could not be a happier people among all the people who had been created by the hand of God." (4 Nephi 1:16.) What could make a people who were filled with "the heavenly gift"—a people of exquisite happiness—degenerate into a society torn by class divisions? The Book of Mormon tells us "there began to be among them those who were *lifted up* in pride." (4 Nephi 1:24; italics added.)

I had never thought much about the words "lifted up" in this verse until a student of mine contrasted them with another scripture. Ether 4:19 alludes to each faithful individual who will "be lifted up to dwell in the kingdom prepared for him." This student pointed out that in Ether 4:19 it is the Savior who "lifts up" the humble, while in 4 Nephi 1:24 it is the people themselves who were "lifted up in pride," with this *lifting up* being in their own minds as they compared themselves to others. This self-lifting rather than the Savior's lifting becomes the inner workings of what we know as the caste or class system within a society, with the motive always to be above others—to be on higher worldly ground as external evidence that one person is better than another.

Before Jesus' visit, the Nephite society had degenerated to such an extent that the Lord swept the land clean of the wicked so his people could begin anew. Just before this cleansing, the prophet Mormon explained, "The people began to be distinguished by ranks, according to their riches and their chances for learning." (3 Nephi 6:12.) Even the Church was not immune to this class system, as Mormon's words bear witness: "And thus there became a great inequality in all the land, insomuch that the church . . . was broken up in all the land." (3 Nephi 6:14.) In the next verse, Mormon identified the cancer that caused the church to be broken up: "The cause of this iniquity of the people was this—Satan had great power, . . . to the puffing them up with pride." (3 Nephi 6:15.)

Mormon's description of this soon-to-be-fallen society merits further review. He explained that the pride that caused that society to be broken up was based upon "their riches and their chances for learning." (3 Nephi 6:12.) President Benson likened this message to our day when he said, "The two groups in the Book of Mormon that seemed to have the greatest difficulty with pride are the 'learned, and the rich.'" (A Witness and a Warning, p. 79.)

President Gordon B. Hinckley reminded the men of the Church that honorable priesthood is a great weapon against this kind of pride: "My brethren, what a wonderful thing is the priesthood of God. . . . It is classless. Every worthy man, regardless of nationality, ethnic background, or any other factor, is eligible to receive the priesthood. His obedience to the commandments of God becomes the determining factor. Its bestowal is based only on worthiness before the Lord. . . . Such is the wonder of this priesthood. Wealth is not a factor. Education is not a factor. The honors of men are not a factor. The controlling factor is acceptability unto the Lord." (Conference Report, Apr. 2000, p. 63.) Just what is it about education and wealth that proved to be such a stumbling block for the Nephites? The prophet Jacob taught, "When they are learned they think they are wise, and they hearken not unto the counsel of God, for they set it aside, supposing they know of themselves." (2 Nephi 9:28.) He then turned his attention from the educated to the wealthy: "But wo unto the rich. . . . Their hearts are upon their treasures; wherefore, their treasure is their god." (2 Nephi 9:30.)

How did education enter this negative scenario? Education brought wealth to the Nephites, and wealth was needed to obtain an education. This process created an inner circle that allowed the upper class to serve itself while at the same time separating them by a wall of pride from those who had little hope of obtaining "the good life." Mormon described that wall very well: "Some were ignorant because of their poverty, and others did receive great learning because of their riches." (3 Nephi 6:12.) Wealth was the key to education, and education was the key to wealth. The lower classes never held either of the keys. It is amazing to think that education could have proven so destructive to their society.

Some time ago I was speaking to a group of people at BYU on this subject. Following my talk, a gentleman came up and visited with me. He handed me a piece of paper that read, "I am a professor of finance at the University of Memphis. In the past ten years the quality of education available in state universities versus that at private universities is diverging steadily. In many states funding for higher education is dropping steadily while tuition and giving at the prestigious private universities are growing rapidly. The better professors are migrating from state universities to private universities. The quality of education available to the wealthy is much better than that available to the poor, and the gap is widening rapidly."

Many years ago, as a young and very insecure BYU student, I had an experience that comically illustrates this point. At the old Harold B. Lee Library there were study booths, called carrels, along the interior walls of each floor. To be able to sit in one of these carrels made the difficult task of studying much easier than sitting at the large study tables in the middle of the room, which gave no privacy because of the sheer number of students at each table. In order to get a carrel during finals week, I had to arrive at the library early each morning. On the side of each one of these carrels was a sign no larger than a 3x5 card. It read, "This carrel is reserved for a graduate student and must be vacated upon request."

I never thought much about it until in the midst of my studying I was tapped on the shoulder by a rather sober fellow who announced,

"I'm a graduate student and you're not, and you're out of here." He then stood impatiently waiting for me to gather my books and papers and exit his domain. With a condescending smile he sent me on my way.

I spent the next few minutes searching for a vacant study carrel along the wall, but to no avail. In fact, there wasn't even any room at the large tables in the center of the room. With the pressure of finals mounting and the feeling of being a poor Zoramite following my quick and unwanted exit from my study carrel, I wandered around the library looking for another spot to study. There was nothing available; even most spots on the floor were taken, except in the walkways. Frustrated and cast down, I went into one of the restrooms and found a lowly seat in one of the stalls. Sitting there pondering my plight, my eyes caught hold of some graffiti on the stall door. A former occupant had written a message in felt pen: "This stall is reserved for a graduate student and must be vacated upon request." Instantly, I burst into the kind of laughter that purged my heart and soul of the frustration of the moment. I got up with a new resolve and found another place to study.

I suppose we have all felt the pains of being a level or two lower in society than we would like. But the real point of the scriptural lesson is, Do we have the kind of pride that makes us need to be above those around us? College students need to look within their hearts and see if their goal in acquiring a degree is to provide an honest living and open doors of service or to acquire wealth and gratify prideful agendas.

Jacob qualified his condemnation of learning and riches by suggesting a solution to both concerns. Regarding the educated he taught, "To be learned is good if they hearken unto the counsels of God." (2 Nephi 9:29.) He also addressed the management of wealth: "Think of your brethren like unto yourselves, and be familiar with all and free with your substance, that they may be rich like unto you. But before ye seek for riches, seek ye for the kingdom of God." (Jacob 2:17–18.)

Jacob's counsel, however, is at variance with most worldly

philosophies. The world would have us believe that the Lord helps those who help themselves, while Jacob seems to be saying that the Lord helps those who help others. This places wealth and education in a different light. When we use wealth and education to serve our fellow beings, we are placing ourselves in a better position to gain the Lord's approval. In this way a person uses wealth and education not as weapons to separate himself from others in a vain attempt to rise above the rest, but as tools to serve and lift his fellowman.

Moroni accused his latter-day readers of a class system of exclusion based upon pride: "Your churches, yea, even every one, have become polluted because of the pride of your hearts. For behold, ye do love money, and your substance, and your fine apparel, and the adorning of your churches, more than ye love the poor and the needy, the sick and the afflicted." (Mormon 8:36–37.) The magnitude of this type of pride, which deeply divides society, has been well documented. Richard E. Johnson has written, "Social commentators almost unanimously refer to the 1980s as 'America's Age of Greed.' . . . The Census Bureau reports that the richest one-fifth of American households now receive almost 10 times the average income of the poorest one-fifth, which is the highest ratio of inequality since they began keeping records following World War II." (*BYU Today*, Sept. 1990, p. 50.)

As President Harold B. Lee said during the 1970s, "Today we are basking in the lap of luxury, the like of which we have never seen in the history of the world. It would seem that probably this is the most severe test of any we have ever had in the history of the Church." (Address to LDS Church employees, Dec. 13, 1973.)

After the Saints arrived in the Salt Lake Valley, Brigham Young hinted that such a challenge would befall the Church: "This people will stand mobbing, robbing, poverty, and all manner of persecution, and be true. But my greater fear for them is that they cannot stand wealth." (In James S. Brown, *Life of a Pioneer*, p. 123.)

I can stand at a window in my house and see horses gently grazing in our pasture. As I look beyond our property, I can see our neighbors working in their yard. Extending my perspective farther, I behold the clean, blue water of the reservoir just north of our small town. But if I apply a special type of silver paint to the glass, my view of the world around me changes considerably. Because of this special paint, my window becomes a mirror. As I try to look out my window, I no longer see the world as it is; I see only myself. This is the challenge for all of us who find excess silver in our lives. Instead of viewing the world as it is, this silver may change our perspective to the point that we may not be able to see beyond our own self-indulgent desires. If our hearts are turned inward, it doesn't take much silver to blind us to the world outside our own house. But if our souls are in tune with the needs of others, if we truly care about our fellowman, then we can use whatever silver the Lord blesses us with to bless the lives of God's children in and outside our own homes.

Once again, it is easy to see how each of the prideful ambitions of *gain, power, popularity,* and *lusts of the flesh* contributed to a caste society among the Nephites. However, the challenge is our ability to make application to ourselves and our own society.

Contention

A basketball game between two Utah County high schools provided a fascinating illustration of contention. A friend of mine who is a member of the Church happened to be officiating the game with a man of another faith as his companion referee. The contest was between two crosstown rival schools whose fans came to the gym brimming with the excessive type of school spirit that can sometimes blind people to basic Christian virtues.

The parents of a particular player were sitting on the front row directly behind one of the baskets. Their son was called for a number of fouls in the first half of the game, fouls they thought were not merited. The mother of this boy was especially vocal in her attention toward the referees. Her overzealous attack didn't cease even when the buzzer sounded concluding the first half. She hustled over to the scorers' table where the officials were huddling. Her enthusiastic verbal complaints gained an audience that included all within the sound of her voice. Finally her tirade was interrupted by the non-LDS referee, who inquired, "Lady, are you a member of the Mormon Church?"

Completely caught off guard, her voice softened as she shamefully replied, "Yes, I am." To which he retorted, "Lady, it's people like you that keep people like me from joining your church." Suddenly, the game no longer carried the same impact as she quietly returned to her seat and sat in silence for the duration of the game. His rebuke was a poignant reminder to each of us that our religiosity must extend beyond the buildings in which we worship.

President Ezra Taft Benson stated, "Pride is essentially competitive in nature. . . . In the words of C. S. Lewis: 'Pride gets no pleasure out of having something, only out of having more of it than the next man. . . . Once the element of competition is gone, pride has gone.'" President Benson's words then moved from the athletic arena to focus on our homes: "Another face of pride is contention. Arguments, fights, unrighteous dominion, generation gaps, divorces, spouse abuse, riots, and disturbances all fall into this category of pride. Contention in our families drives the Spirit of the Lord away. It also drives many of our family members away. Contention ranges from a hostile spoken word to worldwide conflicts. The scriptures tell us that 'only by pride cometh contention' (Proverbs 13:10; see also Proverbs 28:25)." (Conference Report, Apr. 1989, pp. 4–5.)

Contention was an unfortunate part of Lehi's family on account of the murmuring of his two eldest sons, Laman and Lemuel. They murmured against virtually every recorded commandment given them by their father, with the possible exception of returning to Jerusalem for the daughters of Ishmael. Lehi's final blessing to his rebellious sons challenged them to "awake" (see 2 Nephi 1:13), but their spiritual slumber apparently had lapsed into a coma. After Lehi's death, Laman and Lemuel's contentious natures were fueled to the point that, as Nephi recorded, "They did seek to take away my life." (2 Nephi 5:4.) Only after the Lord commanded him to depart with his followers could Nephi say of his people, "We lived after the manner of happiness." (2 Nephi 5:27.) But that bliss was short-lived. "Forty years had passed away, and we had already had wars and contentions with our brethren." (2 Nephi 5:34.)

Even with all the fighting between the Nephites and Lamanites, the most damaging contention was among the Nephites themselves— and more specifically among those within the Church. Mormon explained that during the reign of Alma there was a "strict law" within the Church forbidding that kind of behavior. (Alma 1:21.) He continued, "Nevertheless, there were many among them who began to be proud, and began to contend warmly with their adversaries, even unto blows. . . . It was a cause of much affliction to the church; yea, it was the cause of much trial with *the church*." (Alma 1:22–23; italics added.) Once again, it becomes easy to see how the prideful ambitions of *gain*, *power*, *popularity*, and *lust of the flesh* contribute to this face of pride.

Still later, about three decades before the Savior's visit to the Nephites, peace was interrupted, not from outside the Church but from within. Mormon said of the Nephites, "There were no contentions, save it were a few that began to preach, endeavoring to prove by the scriptures that it was no more expedient to observe the law of Moses." (3 Nephi 1:24.)

After the destruction of the Nephite people who had formed this contentious society, Jesus Christ appeared to those who had been spared because they "were more righteous." (3 Nephi 9:13.) One of the first principles recorded in his teachings to these people was, "He that hath the spirit of contention is not of me, but is of the devil, who is the father of contention. . . . This is my doctrine, that such things should be done away." (3 Nephi 11:29–30.) As was mentioned earlier, these people subsequently dwelt in peace for two centuries. Mormon described their culture in these terms: "There was no contention in the land, because of the love of God which did dwell in the hearts of the people. . . . And surely there could not be a happier people among all the people who had been created by the hand of God." (4 Nephi 1:15–16.) It was not enough for them to have an absence of contention; this contention had to be replaced with the love of God. And because that process had taken place, Mormon was prompted to describe them as the happiest of all people. Mormon saw contention as such an important element that he included it four times in the first eighteen verses of 4 Nephi. (See 4 Nephi 1:2, 13, 15, 18.)

Contention did not begin with the Book of Mormon. As Elder Russell M. Nelson declared in general conference, the "war in heaven was not a war of bloodshed. It was a war of conflicting ideas—the beginning of contention. Scriptures repeatedly warn that the father of contention opposes the plan of our Heavenly Father. Satan's method relies on the infectious canker of contention." (Conference Report, Apr. 1989, p. 86.)

And what about us? Is contention a part of our society? Can it be found even among the members of the Church? These questions were also addressed by Elder Nelson, who said: "I remember a friend who would routinely sow seeds of contention in church classes. His assaults would invariably be preceded by this predictable comment: 'Let me play the role of devil's advocate.' Recently he passed away. One day he will stand before the Lord in judgment. Then, I wonder, will my friend's predictable comment again be repeated? . . . My concern is that contention is becoming accepted as a way of life. From what we see and hear in the media, the classroom, and the workplace, all are now infected to some degree with contention." (Ibid., pp. 85, 87.)

King Benjamin admonished the Nephite parents to "not suffer your children . . . [to] fight and quarrel one with another, and serve the devil." (Mosiah 4:14.) Notice that our children are actually serving the devil when they contend with each other.

President Gordon B. Hinckley rebuked fathers within the Church who introduce this same spirit into the home: "Unfortunately a few of you [sisters] may be married to men who . . . put on a fine face before the world during the day and come home in the evening, set aside their self-discipline, and on the slightest provocation fly into outbursts of anger. . . . There are children who fear their fathers, and wives who fear their husbands. . . . As a servant of the Lord I rebuke you and call you to repentance." (*Ensign*, Nov. 1996, p. 68.)

His words were brought painfully home to me one day when I became angry with one of my teenage sons who had lost the oil cap to my car. Instead of telling me of the mistake when it happened, he had stuffed a rag into the hole, hoping he could find the cap and replace it before I discovered the error. However, the car emptied itself of oil as I was driving on the freeway a few days later, thus putting an end to the engine.

When he confessed to the deed, I was incensed, and after an angry barrage of words, I inquired, "Son, why didn't you tell me you had lost the oil cap in the first place?"

To which he replied, "Because I thought you would act the way you're acting right now." I pondered his words for a moment; then I asked for a "time out" to regroup my emotions for a more suitable presentation.

While his motive for hiding the truth did not excuse his behavior or allow him to avoid the consequences, there was a lesson in this experience for me as well. Being a parent, as well as being the owner of the car, did not justify my angry tirade. The Lord admonished the Prophet Joseph to state the truth "not in haste, neither in wrath nor with strife." (D&C 60:14.) The Savior did not excuse the Nephites from contention even when they were on the side of truth. He said, "He that hath the spirit of contention is not of me, but is of the devil."

(3 Nephi 11:29.) So when I stated the truth to my son in the spirit of contention, my words were still "of the devil." Why? Because the Holy Ghost could not be there to bear witness, to comfort, and to heal. That being the case, perhaps it is easier to understand why Nephi stated that in the last days, "the children of men . . . [would] anger against that which is good." (2 Nephi 28:20.) Children, and adults, have a tendency to respond to the *method* rather than the *message* when disciplined; such was the case on the occasion of the lost oil cap.

In speaking to the young men of the Aaronic Priesthood, President Hinckley stated, "[Anger] . . . is another serious thing to which many young men become addicted. . . . With the least provocation they explode into tantrums of uncontrolled rage. . . . But even worse, they are prone to lose all sense of reason and do things which bring later regret. . . . I plead with you to begin the work of making that correction now. Otherwise you will bring only tears and sorrow into the homes which you will someday establish." (*Ensign*, May 1998, p. 50.)

In the final chapter of the Nephite history, Mormon wrote these words to his son Moroni concerning the Nephite army: "When I speak the word of God . . . they . . . anger against me." He then identified what happened as a result of this mind-set: "They have lost their love, one towards another." (Moroni 9:4–5.) Is there any parent or child reading this who can't see the connection between angry words and a loss of love?

Even in conversations between good, well-meaning Church members, falling into a trap of contention is easy when they disagree about how a particular program should be administered. Many years ago George Q. Cannon addressed that challenge: "It is better to carry out a plan that is not so wise, if you are united on it. Speaking generally, a plan or a policy that may be inferior in some respects is more effective if men are united upon it than a better plan would be upon which they were divided." (*Gospel Truth*, p. 163.) This process hints at a celestial strategy within the Church based on the Lord's program of unity. If the ancient covenant Nephites had learned this principle, the Lamanites might not have proven the overpowering adversary they turned out to be. Are we as a covenant people free from contention? We need to look no further than our homes, neighborhoods, and wards, including our participation in Church-sponsored athletic competitions, for the answer.

CONCLUSION

Costly apparel, class distinction, and contention are only three of the many faces of pride in the Book of Mormon. However, none of these would have surfaced without the prideful desires of gain, power, popularity, and lusts of the flesh (See 1 Nephi 22:23.) These four provide the strong wind that fans the selfish flame of pride. True happiness begins only when selfishness ends. This preoccupation with self is always found at the heart of pride. The remedy to this powerful illness of pride was given us by President Ezra Taft Benson:

The antidote for pride is humility—meekness, submissiveness. . . .

God will have a humble people. Either we can choose to be humble or we can be compelled to be humble. . . .

Let us choose to be humble.

We can choose to humble ourselves by conquering enmity toward our brothers and sisters, esteeming them as ourselves, and lifting them as high or higher than we are.

We can choose to humble ourselves by receiving counsel and chastisement.

We can choose to humble ourselves by forgiving those who have offended us.

We can choose to humble ourselves by rendering selfless service.

We can choose to humble ourselves by going on missions and preaching the word that can humble others.

We can choose to humble ourselves by getting to the temple more frequently.

We can choose to humble ourselves by confessing and forsaking our sins and being born of God.

We can choose to humble ourselves by loving God, submitting our will to His, and putting Him first in our lives.

Let us choose to be humble. We can do it. I know we can. (Conference Report, Apr. 1989, p. 6.)

A review of history, secular as well as religious, shows that temporary success is often little more than postponed failure. Pride is often the key ingredient in this "success" formula. Like the Nephites of old, we can choose to bask in the temporary successes of pride, which led to their eventual failure, or we can follow the word of warning spoken by the Book of Mormon prophets as well as by latter-day prophets. The two roads lie before us with their destinations clearly defined. It is for us to choose.

CHAPTER 8

Changing Weaknesses to Strengths

K. DOUGLAS BASSETT

Many years ago my bishop called me into his office for a visit. He wanted to extend a call while at the same time making sure I had the energy to take on the challenge. There was a group of eleven-year-old boys that had been a trial to their leaders the entire time they had been in Primary. He was at his wits' end and wanted so desperately for them to have a change that might prepare them for the priesthood. Because of his negative experiences in the past with this group, I almost sensed an apologetic tone to his voice as he extended the call. Following a compassionate handshake, he thanked me for accepting the call and sent me on my way.

All week long at work, I couldn't help but wonder what I had gotten myself into. However, I believed that since I was a seminary teacher I could handle anything a small group of eleven-year-olds could throw at me. However, as the week progressed, I began to take counsel from my fears to the extent that I convinced myself this was a task of massive proportions. I even began to feel a little sorry for myself. I reasoned that since I taught seminary all week long, I should be excused from teaching these little hooligans on the day of rest.

So when Sunday finally arrived, I shuffled like a condemned man to my assigned classroom in fear and trembling. I have discovered many times in my life that reality is rarely as ominous as my imagination. Such was the case in this experience, as the first day of class proved to be wonderful. At the end of the class I announced to the students that I had thoroughly enjoyed myself and couldn't wait for the next Sunday so that we could repeat the great experience we had just had. One of the students interrupted my joy by saying, "It won't be so great next week."

Stunned a bit, I retorted, "Why not?"

He answered, "Because Phil will be here." After a short pause to make sure the others were in agreement with him, he continued, "When Phil is here the teachers don't teach."

Once again I replied, "Why not?" What came next was totally unexpected. Instead of giving an answer to my query, the class laughed—a kind of mocking laugh. It was much like the kind of celebration found on the playground when young people tease one of their peers by playing "keep away." In this case they were not playing "keep away" with a ball but with the truth. They were hiding something they were not willing to share with me at that point. I feared that I would find out the next Sunday when Phil came to class. It was hard to tell if they were mocking Phil or me.

Their laughter was interrupted when one of them said, "Yeah, when Sticky Fingers is here the teachers can't teach."

I responded by repeating this new name in the form of a question: "Sticky Fingers?" The expression on my face let them know that I had never heard the title before. This only seemed to add fuel to their youthful game of "keep-away." The moment was interrupted by the sound of the bell announcing the end of class. As they ran from the room celebrating their secret, once again that same fear of the unknown I had experienced the week before fell over me like a shadow.

As the new week progressed, the passing of each day was darkened by my once again taking counsel from my fears. What could they have meant by "Sticky Fingers"? I reasoned that the only thing that name could stand for was a thief. I determined that if Phil showed up in my class on Sunday, I would keep a close eye on my wallet.

After sacrament meeting the next Sunday, with lesson manual in hand like a sword to ward off failure, I marched once again down the hall that led from the chapel to my classroom. I was ready to do battle with this child who went by the alias of Sticky Fingers. Apparently, the prediction of his attendance had not come to pass, because he did not show up. The teacher side of me was disappointed at not being able to make a difference in the life of a child of God. But the insecure part of myself let go a sigh of relief that the battle could be postponed for another week. As I looked around the room, I recognized all the faces and felt secure in the safety of knowing that I could build on the momentum of the week before.

However, about halfway through the lesson, the door opened, and in walked the child I had grown to fear, even though we'd never met. He stood in the back of the room without saying a word, silent, staring, sizing me up to see if I could be trusted. Like a missionary knocking on his very first door, I approached to introduce myself. "Phil, I've heard so much about you!" I enthusiastically held out my hand to greet him. He had a blank expression on his face, and his hands remained in his pockets as a protest to my greeting. He wasn't about to give in that easily, but neither was I. In an instant I reached around him, grabbed his right hand from his back pocket, and brought it forward to my right hand. As I shook his hand I could feel that something was different; I just couldn't tell what it was. Without thinking I turned my right hand over so I could catch a view of the hand I was holding. In a glance I understood why the kids called him Sticky Fingers. It was a cruel joke about a defect he had been born with. Every normal finger has three divisions or phalanges, with the thumb having only two. All eight of Phil's fingers had only two phalanges, just like his thumb. His hands were uniquely his, and that difference from his peers was the motivation behind the name Sticky Fingers.

As I glanced at his hand, he attempted to pull it back. Recognizing my mistake, I quickly turned my own hand back over so I could no longer view his hand, all the while holding fast to my grip. I didn't blame him for trying to pull free of my handshake. After all, none of us enjoys having others view our flaws, especially without invitation. To say the least, I had not accomplished what I had hoped for in our first meeting. Inside I prayed for a way out of the hole I had dug for myself.

Dropping down to one knee and looking him in the eye, I said, "Would you like to meet someone else with sticky fingers?" At best my question was risky. I'm sure the look on his face was based on his surprise that I knew the name he had been given by his peers. He abruptly replied, "There ain't nobody else with sticky fingers but me."

"You're wrong," I countered, "but you'll have to sit in that chair over there to find out."

He studied me for a moment, trying to discern what I was up to. He then glanced in the direction of the empty chair. I tried to encourage him one more time. "All you have to do to meet this fellow is sit in that chair over there."

He communicated his acceptance of my invitation with a simple nod, then walked slowly to the chair in a manner that said he was not totally buying into my ploy. With all the other children watching in silence, I knelt on one knee in front of Phil, opened the Book of Mormon to Ether, chapter 12, and set the book on his lap.

Looking at Phil, I said, "There was once a man named Moroni, and he wrote a book called Ether. When he finished his book, he was not very pleased with his writing and had a visit with Jesus Christ about it." I continued, "Phil, let me have you read the first couple of lines in verse 23."

With great trepidation, and a little help from the teacher, Phil read, "And I said unto him: Lord, the Gentiles will mock at these things, because of our weakness in writing." He stopped and said, "This doesn't say he had hands like mine."

Without commenting on his statement, I encouraged him to read verse 24. Almost in protest, he looked back at the book and read, "And thou hast made us that we could write but little, because of the awkwardness of our hands." His voice slowed down as he read the words "awkwardness of our hands." His countenance changed to that of a student—he was no longer a participant under protest.

Staring at the text a little longer, he lifted his head toward me and asked, "Did he have hands like mine?"

I answered him by saying, "He may not have had hands that looked like yours, but I'm sure he had hands that felt like yours." I asked, "How do your hands feel?"

He looked at the other boys for a cold moment and then focused his attention in my direction. "Different, real different."

I then inquired, "Phil, who gave you those hands?"

Pausing long enough to ponder why I was asking such odd questions, he stated the obvious: "My mom, I guess."

I responded, "The scriptures not only tell you who really gave you those hands, but they also tell you why. In verse 27 Jesus is speaking to Moroni about his hands. 'I give unto men weakness that they may be humble; . . . for if they humble themselves before me, and have faith in me, then will I make weak things become strong unto them.'"

I reviewed with Phil that his hands were a wonderful gift that connected him with the Lord. I reminded him that the Savior would use his hands as a teaching tool if Phil would only let him. If Phil would humble himself and learn to have faith in Christ, the Lord would perform the marvelous miracle of turning his "sticky fingers" or weakness into a greater strength than he could ever imagine.

I then asked, "Phil, what do you do better than anything else?"

"I draw great rockets and cars!" he stated proudly.

I then asked, "What do you draw those rockets and cars with?"

Hesitating long enough to look down at his fingers, he responded almost apologetically, "These hands."

Everything that had happened so far in our first encounter had led up to this teaching moment. "Isn't it interesting that your weakness is also your strength. But you won't really find out how much of a strength it is until you stop using those hands to fight those who say cruel things, and begin to do as the Lord encouraged Moroni, to humble yourself and have faith in him."

Turning to the other boys I said, "You have weaknesses too; they are just not as obvious as a pair of hands. How would you like people talking about your weaknesses and then connecting cruel names to them like Sticky Fingers? How would you like it if I did some research over this next week and announced to everyone which of you boys wet your beds in the past few years, or who has been caught by their parents doing something else that would really be embarrassing if your friends found out?" I continued, "I won't do it, but how would you feel if I did?" Answering my own question, I said, "You would feel just as bad as Phil does each time he hears you call him Sticky Fingers. Notice what the Lord told Moroni about people who make fun of other people's weaknesses." I then read verse 26 of Ether 12: "Fools mock, but they shall mourn."

Each agreed that the last thing he wanted to be was a fool. I admonished them to change their behavior and not to mock Phil or anyone else, but to look for the good and comment on it as they would want other people to do with them. Unlike the week before, this class period ended with a sense of greater compassion from those boys and a commitment that they would try harder to lift each other, and to use words as a tool to unite rather than to divide. As you can imagine, the changes came slowly, but there was a noticeable improvement, at least in their behavior in class.

My season with those boys was short, lasting less than two months, and I have lost track of most of them, including Phil, as they have long since traveled into manhood.

I hope this story not only reminds us of an important principle but also pays tribute to a wonderful boy who had much in common with all of us. How great is the wisdom of the Lord, who wants us all to become perfect and places us here in mortal tabernacles filled with weakness to accomplish that very purpose. These weaknesses are designed as an aid to connect us with him. Through humility, we can develop the faith that places us on the path to perfection. I have hoped many times that Phil has been able to turn his "sticky fingers" into the strength the Lord had in mind for him. Phil, as the rest of us, can be living proof of the Lord's blessing to Moroni: "Because thou hast seen thy weakness thou shalt be made strong." (Ether 12:37.)

The Savior's words to Moroni, "I give unto men weakness" (Ether 12:27), are echoed by prophets in the latter-days. President Howard W. Hunter said, "Obviously, the personal burdens of life vary from person to person, but every one of us has them. Furthermore, *each trial in life is tailored to the individual's capacities and needs as known by a loving Father in Heaven.*" (Conference Report, Oct. 1990, p. 20; italics added.)

This divine custom-engineering of our weaknesses may be difficult for some to accept, but the truth is ever before us, as stated by Elder Bruce R. McConkie: "Everything the Lord does is for the benefit and blessing of his children. And *each of those children is subjected to the very trials and experiences that Omniscient Wisdom knows he should have.*" (*The Millennial Messiah*, p. 660; italics added.)

This doctrine explains the predisposition each of us has to be challenged in various areas of sin, while at the same time not giving us the license to give in to those desires. Nevertheless, there are those who, speaking of their own "weaknesses," say, "If these desires aren't good then why did God place them within me?" or, "What I am doing can't be a sin because I am only following the feelings put inside me by God." In truth, the disposition may be given as a test but not as an excuse to give in to it. Weaknesses are often given as a gift from God, to be developed into strengths through the atoning sacrifice of his Son and our willingness to work with the Lord in the process of perfection. Elder Hartman Rector Jr. spoke of this:

> Where do you suppose we get these weaknesses? . . . Some will say . . . weaknesses come from heredity or environment; in either instance, we are passing the responsibility to someone else, either our parents or our neighborhood. Both of these sources have great influence upon us, but they do not give us our weaknesses. Still another may blame Lucifer, the devil, for their weaknesses; surely he is always on the job, but this is not where we get our weaknesses, either. Where do they really come from?
>
> . . . We get them from the Lord; the Lord gives us weaknesses so we will be humble. This makes us teachable. Now don't misunderstand me—the Lord is not responsible for the sin; he is only responsible for the weakness. It seems that all men have weaknesses in one form or another, character traits that make one more subject to a particular temptation than another. . . .
>
> Giving us weakness, however, is one of the Lord's ways of getting our attention. He says this is the means he uses to make us humble, but he also says that if we will come unto him and have faith in him, he will make us strong wherein we were weak. (Conference Report, Apr. 1970, pp. 139–40.)

Our Savior took much more than just our sins upon himself in Gethsemane. In that sacred place Christ took upon himself our weaknesses as well, in the hope that we might one day be willing to participate in the process of changing them into strengths. The Book of Mormon states, "He will take upon him the pains and the sicknesses of his people . . . and he will take upon him their infirmities." (Alma 7:11–12.)

Gerald N. Lund wrote, "He . . . chose to suffer, not only for our sins, but for the infirmities, sicknesses, and illnesses of mankind." (In *Doctrines of the Book of Mormon*, p. 87.) Elder Neal A. Maxwell said, "Since not all human sorrow and pain is connected to sin, the full intensiveness of the Atonement involved bearing our pains, infirmities, and sicknesses, as well as our sins." (In ibid.)

This journey from weaknesses to strengths is portrayed in many ways within the scriptures. Even great prophets like Enoch and Moses found that the strengthening process of the Lord began in the gifts the Lord had given them in the form of weakness. (See Moses 6:31; Numbers 12:3.) Lehi bore similar testimony about the Prophet Joseph Smith: "Out of weakness he shall be made strong." (2 Nephi 3:13.)

These weaknesses do not always have to be in the context of a genetic weakness like Phil's hands; often they come through the daily circumstances with which we find ourselves having to deal. Mormon told us that the Lord places many weaknesses in our path in the form of trials to keep us relying on Him. It is our natural disposition to turn away from the Lord when the waters of life are calm and the sailing is smooth. When all is well in our lives, "then is the time that [we] do harden [our] hearts, and do forget the Lord . . . yea, and this because of [our] ease." (Helaman 12:2.)

In this context, the counsel of Lehi to his son Jacob is understood: "In thy childhood thou hast suffered afflictions and much sorrow." (2 Nephi 2:1.) Immediately following this he added, "Thou knowest the greatness of God; and he shall consecrate thine afflictions for thy gain." (2 Nephi 2:2.) Receiving "afflictions for thy gain" is a concept similar to changing "weaknesses to strength." It seems to be a natural order of progression in the lives of many of the faithful.

Moroni hinted at it when he wrote, "Ye receive no witness until after the trial of your faith." (Ether 12:6.) This weakening of self and circumstances gives way to the strength that comes when the power of God is made manifest in our lives.

We look up to the sons of Mosiah for their courageous missionary service, which extended at least fourteen years. Ammon stated that their road to success was not always over smooth ground: "When our hearts were depressed, and we were about to turn back, behold, the Lord comforted us, and said: . . . Bear with patience thine afflictions, and I will give unto you success." (Alma 26:27.) Anyone who has served a successful full-time mission has felt this same process.

Elder John B. Dickson spoke to the Saints about accepting our weaknesses without either giving up or giving in to them:

"As some of you have noticed, I only have one arm. . . . I want you to know that having one arm for nearly thirty years has been one of the greatest blessings of my life. . . . It has been a great teacher to me, teaching me to be more patient and tolerant with others as I have had to learn to be more patient with myself. It has helped me to understand the necessity of our having challenges in life to help develop our character and stamina, helping us to become what the Lord ultimately wants us to become. Our challenges may be physical, spiritual, economic, or emotional, but if we will treat them as opportunities and stepping-stones in our progress, rather than barriers and stumbling blocks, our lives and growth will be wonderful." (*Ensign*, Nov. 1992, p. 45.)

It is in this context that the fifth principle of the gospel, enduring to the end, is better understood.

PREMORTAL DECISIONS

I was once asked a very thought-provoking question by a student when we were discussing this concept of "weaknesses to strengths." His question went something like this: "How much of what we experience here on earth did we know about before we were born?"

Once again, the Book of Mormon, in company with Latter-day

prophets, gives us insight. Long before Christ's birth, the prophet Nephi knew many of the challenges the Savior would face in mortality: "He cometh . . . in six hundred years from the time my father left Jerusalem. And the world, shall . . . scourge him, . . . and . . . smite him, . . . spit upon him, . . . and . . . [he] yieldeth himself, . . . to be lifted up, . . . to be crucified, . . . and to be buried in a sepulchre." (1 Nephi 19:8–10.) If Nephi knew that much about the Savior's life in mortality, hundreds of years before his birth, then it is reasonable that the Savior knew as well. The logical extension in this line of reasoning would be to inquire if we knew just as much concerning our own mortality prior to our birth.

As commentary to this concept, President Joseph F. Smith wrote, "I believe that our Savior . . . possessed a foreknowledge of all the vicissitudes through which he would have to pass in the mortal taber-nacle. . . . *If Christ knew beforehand, so did we. But in coming here, we forgot all, that our agency might be free indeed, to choose good or evil.*" (*Gospel Doctrine*, p. 13; italics added.) President Smith's words remind us that we understood and accepted many of the circumstances of our mortality before we were born.

The words of President Spencer W. Kimball add witness to this truth: "God does nothing by chance, but always by design as a loving father. . . . The manner of our coming into the world, our parents, the time, and other circumstances of our birth and condition, are all according to the eternal purposes, direction, and appointment of divine Providence." (*Ensign*, Dec. 1974, p. 5.) The scriptures tell us that before our own birth, when we contemplated our mortal condition, we "shouted for joy." (Job 38:7.)

The Book of Mormon states that this understanding of our mortal condition before we were born involved the priesthood as well: "This is the manner after which they were ordained—being called and prepared from the foundation of the world according to the foreknowledge of God, . . . thus *this holy calling being prepared from the foundation of the world* for such as would not harden their hearts." (Alma 13:3, 5; italics added.)

Elder Henry D. Moyle reminded us that we accepted many of our mortal conditions before we came to earth: "We had our own free agency in our pre-mortal existence, and whatever we are today is likely the result of that which we willed to be heretofore. We unquestionably knew before we elected to come to this earth the conditions under which we would here exist. . . . I have a conviction deep down in my heart that we are exactly what we should be, each one of us, except as we may have altered that pattern by deviating from the laws of God here in mortality." (Conference Report, Oct. 1952, pp. 71–72.)

This doctrine doesn't take away our agency; it serves to reinforce the truth that many of our weaknesses as well as our strengths here in mortality are not just a matter of mortal genetics or environment. One day while serving as a counselor to the inmates at the Utah State Prison, I was meeting in a Sunday School setting with a group of inmates who had been convicted of rape or child abuse. I was sharing this quotation from Elder Moyle, and when I read the words, "We unquestionably knew before we elected to come to this earth the conditions under which we would here exist . . . ," one of the inmates jumped to his feet and cried out, "That's not true! If I had known before I was born that I was going to be a rapist, I never would have come!"

As calmly as I could, I asked him to sit down and listen to the rest of the quotation. When I came to the words, "I have a conviction deep down in my heart that we are exactly what we should be, . . . except as we may have altered that pattern by deviating from the laws of God here in mortality," he leaned forward and put his head in his hands. Slowly lifting his head, he spoke to himself as much as to the rest of us, "That's true. The first time I raped I was standing outside the girl's dorm at Fresno State College thinking about doing it, and words came into my mind that I know weren't from me. I was told that if I did this act today, I would find myself on a path that would destroy my life and injure many people." He continued, "I know I was not sent to this earth to rape." His eyes stared straight ahead as he contemplated the consequences of his decision to commit that terrible deed so long ago.

Because this inmate had not followed the Savior's invitation to face our weaknesses with humility and faith in Christ (see Ether 12:27), he had placed himself on a road that did not allow the Savior to do for him what Christ has the ability to do. As the inmate stared at the wall in front of him, he realized, perhaps for the first time, that he alone had derailed himself from his divine destiny. He was getting a glimpse of the truth expressed in the words of Elder Neal A. Maxwell: "God, who knows our capacity perfectly, placed us here to succeed. No one was foreordained to fail or to be wicked. . . . Let us remember that we were measured before and we were found equal to our tasks; and therefore . . . when we feel overwhelmed, let us recall the assurance that *God will not overprogram us; he will not press upon us more than we can bear.*" (*1978 Devotional Speeches of the Year*, p. 156; italics added.)

Conclusion

I'm not sure how or why it happened, but as a boy growing up in northern California I had a problem with my ability to learn. As I viewed my peers in a classroom setting, it always seemed as if they were understanding at a much higher level than I was. I don't know exactly when it happened, but somewhere in my youth I began to see myself as a "dummy." Each day my attendance at school did nothing to work against this negative view I had accepted about myself. After all, a boy can only be on the bottom end of the grading curve so long before he begins to doubt his intellect. After being held back in the third grade and expelled periodically through junior high and high school, I was confident the reason I was given a diploma stating I had graduated from high school was just to get rid of me. Looking back on it now, I think the only reason I didn't drop out altogether was that I wanted to play sports and be with my friends.

With a track record like mine, I never gave much thought to life after high school. Fortunately for me, the Lord graciously called me on a full-time mission for the Church. As I boarded the plane carrying me to England, I believed the tears of joy in my parents' eyes were mingled with feelings of relief that I had made it that far.

However, something happened to me soon after my arrival in the mission field, something that slowly changed my life for the better. The desire to be a good missionary grew every day, and I quickly threw my whole heart into the work. As I made this transition, another change began to take place. For the first time in my life, I began to respect myself. I liked this feeling and did not want to do anything to lose the change that had come over me like a refreshing breeze. I liked the way I was treated by the other missionaries, as well as by people in general. However, there was still that little voice calling from my past insecurities, like a shadow hanging over my head, and I still felt like a "dummy." I feared that over a period of time, the people around me would inevitably begin to see me as an impostor.

Apparently the mission president thought more highly of me than I did, because after nine weeks in England he assigned me to a brand new elder fresh from the MTC. On the very day that I lost my senior companion and became a senior companion myself, we were scheduled to teach a third discussion. Because of my learning problem, I had not memorized that discussion yet. In those days the MTC for English-speaking missionaries lasted less than a week, so I knew that the new elder I would be picking up that morning wouldn't be any help teaching a third discussion. I also knew that it was important for me to be the kind of missionary in whom my new companion would have confidence, so I couldn't very well go to him and say, "Guess what, Elder, we have a third discussion tonight, and I haven't learned it yet!"

I was so scared that I considered taping the third discussion inside my scriptures and using it as a "cheat sheet." The thought of that made me sick to my stomach, because it reminded me so much of the kind of hide-and-seek mentality that had been such a part of my life before my mission, and I was determined not to be that kind of person ever again. No, there was only one answer: I had to learn the discussion in a day. That seemed an impossible task, because we were required to spend the time working in our area.

As we tracted all day, I was unable to tell my new companion that I didn't know my discussions. I continually called "time out" and ran into the public restroom nearby to study. Naturally, I couldn't stay too long or my companion would get worried, so in the limited time I had, I took out my third discussion and tried my best to memorize it. As I reviewed the dialog, I prayed with all my heart that Heavenly Father would help me overcome my inabilities and help me learn that discussion. After several trips to the public restroom, my companion expressed his fears regarding my health. Mumbling something about the English food, I assured him all was well.

As we cycled home to our apartment for dinner, my heart pounded so hard with the extra burden of my fears that it seemed to be trying to come up through my throat. I had a discussion to teach in about two hours, and I just knew I couldn't do it. As we entered our home, I asked my companion if he would prepare dinner while I studied what I would be teaching that evening. He agreed, and I took my discussion and disappeared into the bathroom. I tried to study, but the words became a blur as I was continually blinded by my insecurities. I had taken counsel from my fears for so long that I just could not find the confidence within myself to do the task that lay ahead.

Having no place else to turn, I summoned all my faith. Without knowing it, I was doing as the Lord suggested in Ether 12:27: I had become humble enough to take my weaknesses to the Lord in the hope that he would turn them into strengths. Tears flowed freely as I poured out my fears to the Lord. After a few minutes, I raised my head and attempted, as best I could, to regain my composure. I didn't want my companion to see that I had been crying, and besides, the clock was reminding me that it was time to face my fears. With the moment of truth drawing near, I knew that I would either stand that night as a servant of God, or I would tremble before our investigators like the Cowardly Lion in *The Wizard of Oz*.

I returned to the kitchen, trying to present myself with the kind of demeanor that gave the impression that this was "just another night" in the mission field. After finishing our dinner, we climbed on our bicycles and headed for our appointment. Once again my heart began trying to separate itself from my chest.

My stomach was full of butterflies as we entered our investigator's home; I could hardly remember how to get things started. Then something totally new to me took place during the opening prayer. It is odd that what was so spiritually profound to me was done in the presence of my companion and our investigators, who were totally unaware of what was taking place. As the prayer was being offered by my companion, I became completely immersed in the Spirit. The emotion of fear that had been with me all day was replaced with a peace and a calm that was foreign to me up to that point in my life. I knew that the Lord was mindful of me and that my weakness could be replaced by his strength.

With the help of the Holy Ghost, I had a total recollection of the things I had studied throughout the day. (See John 14:26.) Something else was happening that I had never experienced—I was teaching with an effectiveness that was absolutely foreign to me. It was as if all I had to do was open my mouth and the Lord did the rest. The Lord had done for me what he had promised in the Book of Mormon: "The weakness of their words will I make strong." (2 Nephi 3:21.) I was aware, even as I was teaching, that in this particular discussion more than one lesson was being taught. While I was teaching them, the Lord was teaching me what I was capable of doing when his Spirit was present.

Following the discussion, we climbed on our bikes and headed for home. I road ahead of my companion so he would not see my face. As I celebrated my private victory, tears streamed down my face, and I whispered words that my heart had waited so long to exclaim: "I'm not a dummy! I'm not a dummy!" Repeating the words had the effect of purging myself of a great weight that I had carried as long as I could remember.

In the days that followed, during my gospel study as well as in learning my discussions, the dark cloud of insecurity was taken from me. I had read Ether 12:27 before, but the Lord had personalized it for me in such a way as to lift my confidence in myself and elevate my praise for him. My weakness had truly become a strength. For some reason, in my youth I had accepted the label of "dummy," and the world had been all too willing to reinforce it, but now the Lord had told me it was a lie. I was living proof of his words: "He that loseth his life for my sake shall find it." (Matthew 10:39.)

This experience is not unique to me—it is the same one my young student Phil faced. It is available for all who humble themselves and take their weaknesses with them to Gethsemane and place them at the Savior's feet, allowing him to do for each of us what only a Savior could do—change our weaknesses into strengths.

CHAPTER 9

How the Lord Deals with Us during Adversity

K. DOUGLAS BASSETT

The traditional approach to the topic of adversity is to answer the question, "Why do bad things happen to good people?" As valuable as this focus is, I will approach the topic from a somewhat different perspective as outlined in the Book of Mormon. The scriptures as well as the Latter-day prophets affirm that the Lord's dealings with us during times of trials and adversity have a great deal to do with our own attitude in the process. The Lord is the same yesterday, today, and forever—he is the great constant. It is often we who become the variables in this earthly experience of adversity. An analogy given by Elder Joseph B. Wirthlin illustrates this point:

> There is a story about a young builder who had just gone into business for himself. A wealthy friend of his father came to him and said: "To get you started right, I am going to have you build a ranch house for me. Here are the plans. Don't skimp on anything. I want the very finest materials used, and I want flawless workmanship. Forget the cost. Just send me the bills."
>
> The young builder became obsessed with the desire to enrich himself through this generous and unrestricted offer. Instead of employing top-grade labor and buying the finest

materials, he shortchanged his benefactor in every way possible. Finally, the last secondhand nail was driven into the last
flimsy wall, and the builder handed over the keys and bills . . .
to his father's old friend. That gentleman wrote a check in full
for the structure and then handed the keys back to the builder.
"The home you have just built, my boy," he said with a pleas-
ant smile, "is my present to you. May you live in it in great
happiness!" (Conference Report, Apr. 1982, p. 33.)

Just as the young builder in Elder Wirthlin's story had a definite
role in the blessing he received from his father's friend, the same is true
for us in how the Lord is able to work with us in times of trial here in
mortality.

Elder Dennis B. Neuenschwander said, "Whatever happens in the
life of a person, *if his attitude is right,* the Lord will work that experience
for that person's good." (Faculty Inservice, Orem Institute of Religion,
Dec. 14, 1996; italics added.)

We can better understand this "attitude" spoken of by Elder
Neuenschwander by viewing a contrast between two opposing attitudes
in working with our Heavenly Father: There is "my will," a selfish view
of the world, and "thy will," the desire of a person to understand and
follow God's will during times of trial and adversity. This "my will–thy
will" comparison is not meant to be a categorization of people but a
description of attitudes that all of us have from time to time, depending
on our spiritual perspective.

A person with the "my will" attitude in working with the Lord during life's challenges may view each of life's adversities, trials, or
tragedies as a painful obstacle, an insurmountable wall, with God's role
in the process being to remove this negative intrusion from the path.
In the "my will" approach to prayer, Heavenly Father is viewed as a
kind of spiritual Santa Claus. Just as St. Nick is called upon only in one
particular season each year, so the "my will" attitude approaches God
only in the season of affliction. Once the trial has passed, the person

carries on with life, approaching God only when the brick wall of adversity looms again in the path.

Many children understand that each yuletide season, the key to receiving Santa's richest blessings is to be able to sit on his lap and say, "I've been good." Santa gives his gifts based on whether a child has been *naughty* or *nice*. The "my will" approach to opposition assumes that the person's role is to keep the commandments, and that God's gift for those who have been obedient (or "nice" in Santa terminology) is simply to make "it" (meaning adversity) go away.

When taken to the extreme, this spiritually warped view assumes that a spiritual Santa's greatest gifts come in the packages called health, wealth, worldly success, business security, and the total acceptance and appreciation of others. If this were true, then people such as Jesus Christ and Joseph Smith received few blessings from their Father in Heaven.

President Ezra Taft Benson referred to this self-agenda in general conference: "We pit our will against God's. When we direct our pride toward God, it is in the spirit of '*my will and not thine be done.*' . . . The proud wish God would agree with them." (*Ensign*, May 1989, p. 4; italics added.)

On the same subject, Elder Erastus Snow said, "If our spirits are inclined to be stiff and refractory, and we desire continually the gratification of our own will to the extent that this feeling prevails in us, the Spirit of the Lord is held at a distance from us; or, in other words, *the Father withholds his Spirit from us in proportion as we desire the gratification of our own will.*" (*Journal of Discourses*, 7:352; italics added.)

The positive side of this two-sided coin could be termed the "thy will" approach in working with our Heavenly Father regarding life's opposition. This consecrated attitude is similar to the "my will" attitude only in that adversity, trials, or tragedies may also be seen as walls looming in the path ahead. The difference for the "thy will" person is that, with the Lord's help, the wall is not identified as being insurmountable. The view of the "thy will" person is proactive or solution oriented as opposed to the reactive nature of the "my will" mentality. But the basic difference is in a person's willingness to scale or even endure the obstacle with the help of the Lord. Any event of opposition or tragedy is dealt with by approaching Heavenly Father for strength and understanding, always seeking to recognize his will in the process. This view accepts that God's role is that of the trusted Father in Heaven, who will allow us to be tested in our best interest, with the promise that we will not be tested more than we are able to bear. (See 1 Corinthians 10:13.)

The "thy will" view of life's challenges and even tragedies assumes that growth often comes in the midst of the struggle, and that inner peace in mortality is obtained through commitment and consecration. However, this perspective does not rob us of initiative or agency.

The fundamental difference in this attitude, as compared to the "my will" perspective, is the willingness on the part of the person to place total trust in our Heavenly Father and his timing. The "thy will" view sees life as being more than just life here in mortality, and while the Lord may see fit to make an obstacle in life's path *just go away*, that is the Lord's option rather than the constant expectation on the part of the individual.

Incorporated in this concept is the doctrine of enduring to the end, which assumes the notion of being "willing to submit to all things which the Lord seeth fit to inflict upon him, even as a child doth submit to his father." (Mosiah 3:19.)

Elder Robert D. Hales spoke of this "thy will" mentality concerning our prayers: "Gratitude is a divine principle: 'Thou shalt thank the Lord thy God in all things.' (D&C 59:7.) This scripture means that we express thankfulness for what happens, not only for the good things in life but also for the opposition and challenges of life that add to our experience and faith. We put our lives in His hands, realizing that all that transpires will be for our experience. When in prayer we say, 'Thy *will be done,'* we are really expressing faith and gratitude and acknowledging that we will accept whatever happens in our lives." (*Ensign*, May 1992, p. 65; italics added.)

Elder Graham W. Doxey spoke of the peace that can come from the Lord to us when we are truly consecrated: "We must learn to pray with meaning, 'Not my will, but Thy will be done.' When you are able to do this, his whisperings to you will be loud and clear. The Prophet Joseph Smith, after five months of extreme suffering in the dungeon of Liberty Jail, experienced it, and he said, 'When the heart is *sufficiently contrite*, then the voice of inspiration steals along and whispers, My son, peace be unto thy soul' (*History of the Church*, 3:293.)" (Conference Report, Oct. 1991, p. 34; italics in original.)

Somewhere during those months in the Liberty Jail, with so little to eat and so much time to ponder, the Prophet digested these words given to him by the Savior: "The Son of Man hath descended below them all. Art thou greater than he?" (D&C 122:8.) For Joseph and for all who are taken to the limits of adversity, accepting this theme during those times when suffering seems so undeserved can help them carry on with a "thy will" perspective.

President James E. Faust referred to the practical application of the "thy will" attitude: "Recently I met with a family who had lost a precious son through an unfortunate automobile accident. They wondered when the comforting spirit of the Holy Ghost would envelop them to sustain them. My counsel was that when they were prepared to say to the Lord, '*Thy will be done*,' then would come the sweet peace which the Savior promised. This willing submission to the Father is what the Savior exemplified in the Garden of Gethsemane." (*Ensign*, Nov. 1996, p. 96; italics added.)

During those times, when we are able to maintain a "thy will" perspective, even tragic events are often accompanied by a feeling of peace as we discover a strength that lifts us beyond our own capacities.

Let us look to the Book of Mormon to illustrate the two contrasting attitudes of which I have been speaking. At a particular point in the recorded history of this scriptural text, there were two groups of Nephites in bondage to the Lamanites. One of the groups, which could be referred to as the "my will" group, was led by Limhi. These people were not humbled by the words of Abinadi or Alma. They seemed to exhibit the kind of humility that would bring them to prayer only when they were humbled by *circumstance*. At this time, the *circumstance* was their being held captive by the Lamanites. Only then did they turn to the Lord; in their season of adversity they cried out for a spiritual Santa Claus for a present of deliverance.

The contrasting "thy will" group was led by the prophet Alma. This group of Saints was initially humbled by the words of Abinadi or Alma. They gave up many of their worldly possessions, including their homes, in order to follow the prophet Alma. They even submitted themselves to be hunted by the wicked King Noah in order to follow the "thy will" path that lay before them. Though their circumstances were humbling, their humility was born of a change of heart, not of their circumstances. Eventually, they were captured by the Lamanites, who placed the wicked former priests of Noah over them as their guards.

So now we find two groups of Nephites in bondage. What a marvelous opportunity to observe how God deals with his children, which has a great deal to do with the level of their spiritual preparation. Notice how the Lord dealt with these two groups differently, based upon the "my will" or "thy will" attitude of those seeking his assistance. In one particular episode, Limhi's "my will" group went to battle with the Lamanites three times without the spiritual preparation that had been typical of the Nephites during times of righteousness. (See Mosiah 21:7–12.) The result of each of their attacks was that "they were driven back . . . , suffering much loss." (Mosiah 21:11.)

Because of the circumstances they found themselves in, and with no *arm of flesh* left at their disposal, they turned to the Lord in the season of their grief: "They did humble themselves even in the depths of humility; and they did cry mightily to God." (Mosiah 21:14.) In the best interest of these "my will" Nephites, "the Lord was slow to hear their cry." (Mosiah 21:15.)

To their greatest benefit, their burdens were not quickly removed by their Father in Heaven: "The Lord did not see fit to deliver them out of bondage . . . , [although] they began to prosper by degrees." (Mosiah 21:15–16.) If the Lord would have instantly removed the obstacle of adversity from their path, he might have been seen by Limhi's group as a spiritual Santa Claus, with the people enjoying their blessing of deliverance for a season but eventually returning to their old ways, and returning to their God only when another emergency arose.

The reason the Lord prospered Limhi's people by degrees rather than immediately delivering them is expressed by the prophet Mormon: "At the very time when he doth prosper his people, . . . and delivers them out of the hands of their enemies; . . . yea, then is the time that they do harden their hearts, and do forget the Lord their God." (Helaman 12:2.) To help Limhi's people progress from a "my will" attitude to a "thy will" perspective, the Lord worked with them carefully over a period of time so that they would not return to their former mentality of not wanting "that he should be their guide." (Helaman 12:6.)

In the contrasting story of Alma's people, we are given a magnificent example of God's dealings with his children based upon their spiritual attitude. The fact that Alma's people had consistently maintained a "thy will" approach to their lives set the stage for the Lord to deal with their deliverance in a much different manner than he did for Limhi's group. In the midst of their prayers, the Lord stated, "I will also ease the burdens which are put upon your shoulders, that even you cannot feel them upon your backs." (Mosiah 24:14.)

The casual reader might falsely assume that this meant the Lord was going to quickly remove the obstacle of bondage of the Lamanites from their path. Such was not the case. The Lord chose to do something for Alma's group that he did not do for Limhi's group. Their burdens became light not because the Lord removed them, but because "*the Lord did strengthen them* that they could bear up their burdens with ease." (Mosiah 24:15; italics added.) The "thy will" attitude of Alma's people allowed the Lord to do something for them that Limhi's people were completely unprepared to receive. Alma's group was strengthened to bear the weight of adversity, while Limhi's group had their burdens removed by degrees. While both groups were eventually relieved from the oppressive hand of their captors, the manner in which the Lord dealt with these two groups, throughout the process, was completely different, based upon their faith and spiritual preparation. (See Bassett, *Latter-day Commentary on the Book of Mormon*, p. 232.)

We can see this "thy will" perspective in the life of the Prophet Joseph Smith, in his writings from the Liberty Jail. In that time of anguish and deep suffering for the gospel's sake, he wrote the following message to the Saints: "Dear brethren, do not think that our hearts faint, as though some strange thing had happened unto us, for we have seen and been assured of all these things beforehand, and have an assurance of a better hope than that of our persecutors. *Therefore God hath made broad our shoulders for the burden.* We glory in our tribulation, because we know that God is with us, that He is our friend." (*Teachings of the Prophet Joseph Smith*, p. 123; italics added.) Just like Alma's group, the Prophet Joseph was experiencing the attitude adjustment that accompanies this "broadening of the shoulders": He "could bear up [his] burdens with ease, and . . . did submit cheerfully and with patience to all the will of the Lord." (Mosiah 24:15.)

This concept of broadening our shoulders to carry life's burdens has also been spoken of by President Thomas S. Monson: "When we are on the Lord's errand, we are entitled to the Lord's help. Remember that *the Lord will shape the back to bear the burden placed upon it.*" (*Ensign*, May 1992, p. 48; italics added.)

If we take the experience of Limhi and Alma and liken it to a training or weight room in our day, we might find an interesting perspective. It is as if each of us here in mortality is in a weight room filled with all the equipment used to strengthen and build physical as well as spiritual muscle. Someone who wants to be strong and grow must be willing to submit to the work required for growth in this arena. Those who have consistently worked hard can see themselves progress and grow. As they approach the weights, they have a completely different attitude than the weekend warrior who only occasionally enters this workout arena.

Limhi's people stood before the long, round, steel bar of adversity with its weights fastened on both ends. Unprepared to lift the weight, they asked God to remove the weight from the bar so that it could be lifted easily. In the past, they had not been willing to place themselves in the hands of their instructor (Heavenly Father) in an effort to develop the kind of strength that would be needed to lift the weight. Suddenly, they found themselves in a position where the only way for the bar to be lifted was to take the weights off both ends so it could be lighter. This is the concept of "prosper by degrees." (Mosiah 21:16.) The result was that the bar could be lifted only by taking the weights off, little by little.

But the growth to the participants was minimal compared to Alma's people, who had developed a working relationship with their divine Instructor. The Instructor was willing and able to do so much more for Limhi and his people, but he was handicapped by the lack of preparation and spiritual work ethic of this group of Nephites.

In Alma's people we find a group who had been in the spiritual weight room for some time. They had been continually working with their Instructor, so that when the seemingly overwhelming weight of adversity was placed before them, they turned once again to their Instructor, who was able to strengthen their backs so that they were able to lift the bar. This is in contrast to Limhi's people, who could lift the bar of adversity only when the weight had been removed by degrees. The muscles on the backs of Alma's people were strengthened because of their faith in their Instructor and their desire to do whatever was asked of them by him, even to the extent that they were able to "submit cheerfully and with patience." (Mosiah 24:15.)

The only people I have seen in a typical weight room who are cheerful and patient are those who have been built up physically to the point where their backs have been strengthened—even under the burden of some very heavy weights. This is just as true in the spiritual weight rooms, where the weights of adversity, pain, affliction, and opposition become a great test here in mortality. The Lord may choose to remove the weight, even for people with a "thy will" perspective. The point is that they understand that this is his decision rather than theirs. The "thy will" perspective is willing to do whatever is necessary to accomplish the will of the Lord. The eternal irony to this weight-room analogy is that the Savior has already lifted all the weights we will carry, in that lonely place called Gethsemane, where the weight of our adversities was lifted by his blood.

In our weakest moments, each of us may blame God or lose faith in his influence in our lives. At these times we are all at a "my will"–"thy will" crossroads, and how we deal with those feelings can set a spiritual course that allows us to work hand in hand with our Heavenly Father or places us at a distance from his assistance. As latter-day Nephites, it is for us to decide if we will mirror Limhi's or Alma's manner of discipleship. The test is in our willingness to pay the consistent price necessary to work with the Lord in the process of lifting the weight of life's adversities.

To those who question their own resolve to endure in this weight room of affliction, I encourage you to reflect on these words from President Ezra Taft Benson: "There are times when you simply have to righteously hang on and outlast the devil until his depressive spirit leaves you. . . . To press on in noble endeavors, even while surrounded by a cloud of depression, will eventually bring you out on top into the sunshine." (*Ensign*, Nov. 1974, p. 67.)

The Divine Therapist

Because of circumstances in my family that began shortly after the birth of our first child, we have spent many days in the hospital over the past twenty-six years. In this setting we have experienced a number of events that have deeply affected our lives. One of these was not directly connected to our children, but it gave me a greater understanding of the "thy will" perspective we would need in dealing with our own circumstances.

During the long and difficult hours spent with our children at the hospital, I have tried to be productive by reading, writing, or just about anything I can think of to pass the time in a valuable way. As hard as I try, sometimes I just get tired of sitting and am forced to get up and move around to keep from going "stir crazy." On many of those occasions, I have found it helpful just to go for a walk to clear my head. In the old University of Utah Hospital, many times these walks took me to the burn unit and rehabilitation area located nearby.

Often I witnessed pain that gave me an appreciation for the much greater suffering in Gethsemane by our Lord. I saw doctors and nurses bring in people who were burned so badly that I could not immediately tell if they were lying face up or face down. At first glance, I couldn't tell if they were male or female, black or white, or where their clothes stopped and their skin began. They would often "air vac" these poor souls in by helicopter and hurry them down a hallway to a room that was used for washing their wounds and removing the burned skin, which was of no use to them. In fact, without being placed in a vat of liquid and going through the process of removal and cleansing of the skin, many of these people would not have survived.

As the hospital professionals worked with these victims, their screams of pain were such that at times the sounds seemed to be coming from animals rather than humans. Between these shrieks of agony, a few of the patients would verbally strike out against their nurses and caregivers, even to the point of making threats against them. In their agony they would misunderstand the role of this person before them as being the cause of their pain. I once heard a man cry out from the depths of his soul that he would somehow find the strength to recover, and with that strength he would return to the hospital and give the same pain to his therapist. In the agony of the moment, without thinking it through, he had lashed out at the person who was closest to his pain.

While it was true that the hospital employees were connected to the pain, they were actually tied to the solution of the pain rather than its source. The patience and empathy of these good people toward the burn victims was admirable. I'm sure there were exceptions, but I never saw these professionals take the verbal abuse in a personal way. Experience had taught them that even though the patient could die without going through the process, it is only natural for a burn victim to resist anything that brings such tremendous pain.

In many ways the prolonged, agonizing process of recovery is more painful for the burn victim than the actual event of being burned. I have seen a few of these burn victims give up on themselves, but as long as there was a chance of recovery, I never saw a burn-unit worker give up on a patient.

The most severely burned people would have to go through a process that could take years. Sometimes there were not many parts of their body that were not burned. Even then, the skin grafts would have to come from their own bodies. Therefore, when a portion of unburned skin was taken from one part of the body to be grafted onto another part, the patients would have to wait for a long time for enough skin to grow back to be grafted again.

During this time, the patients spent a great deal of time in bed. This inactivity caused the muscles and joints to atrophy. Therefore, therapists would be assigned to strengthen them and help them extend their range of motion. A burned arm or leg needed to be able to go through its maximum possible range of motion before the skin graft could be performed.

Prior to the skin grafts, therapists would come in and assist patients in the always painful and often excruciating process of exercising the joints, as well as the rest of the limbs, in order to obtain maximum mobility. To do this, the therapist would have to push the patient's arm or leg beyond what the atrophied limb, as well as the overworked burn victim, was willing to do by himself. Periodically, the verbal rebellion of the patient that accompanied this exercise would be directed toward the therapist. With few exceptions, the therapists seemed to exercise compassion and charity as they did what was necessary in their patient's behalf. In the midst of all the pain, it would have been easy to see the therapist as part of the problem rather than the solution. Yet, as time passed and the patients began to see the progression in their recovery, many of these patients looked toward their therapist as a kind of savior.

Over the course of their recovery, they were able to leave the hospital. On their return visits, it was obvious by the way they treated the professionals—toward whom they might once have directed their deepest anger—that more than just their burns had been healed. They had gained a fuller appreciation for those who would not give up on them in their darkest hour. As they walked through the doors of the hospital, they were hailed by many people they had known during their most difficult times. But their deepest thanks was saved for those who pushed them beyond their pain so that they might live again. I have seen a former patient fall into the arms of the very person he had once promised to come back and punish for the pain he had needed to endure.

We can easily liken the roles of patient and therapist to ourselves and the Savior. With all the physical and spiritual pain and suffering of so many people, their greatest error would be to see Jesus Christ as the problem rather than the solution. His arm is stretched out continually in our behalf. (See 2 Nephi 28:32.) The question is how we deal with his stretched out arm. Just as with the burn victims, there is often pain associated with growth and recovery. To adopt the "my will" attitude of not being willing to submit and endure is to handicap the Therapist's ability to assist.

I have a feeling that when each of us meet again with our Therapist on the other side of the veil and have the opportunity to see mortality with full clarity, we will thank the Lord for many of the things that brought us the most pain in mortality. In that setting, we won't thank him for cars, houses, or much of anything that brought us worldly security, but we will thank him for the things that brought us to our knees, and eventually to him. Only as we ponder adversity and trials with a "my will" perspective are we able to gain a view of the big picture that stretches even beyond mortality. In this setting we may experience the peace that distills upon the soul like a healing balm.

The "thy-will" strengthening from the Lord is the reason why even death becomes sweet for those who die unto him. (See D&C 42:46.) This sweetness comes from the fact that when a person's shoulders have been broadened and strengthened for the burden placed upon them, there is a peace and a calm that not only empowers the person but also acts like a spiritual anesthesia against the pain of the moment. This is true even for those loved ones who are left behind to live with the loss.

This sweetness became a part of my family a number of years before I was born. My father contracted a rare form of bone cancer during World War II, when he was nearly twenty years old. When he was a young man, just out of his teens, the cancer found a home in his hips. He went from being an athlete to a spectator during the time he spent serving his country. He carried this burden for some thirty-five more years before death finally released him from the earthly prison of his body. I never knew a time when he did not suffer from this terrible disease.

Gradually, over a period of years, the marrow in his hips was destroyed. His frame was so weakened that from time to time his hips would dislocate as he walked.

One morning when I was eighteen years old, my father was working alone in the backyard. His pain grew with such intensity that he needed to go to the hospital right away. Without taking time to shave and freshen up, he decided to drive himself to the emergency room, where he could receive the necessary medication.

As fate would have it, the car ran out of gas shortly after his departure. The nearest service station was about a quarter of a mile away. Even though his body was racked with pain, there was nothing left to do but walk with gas can in hand to obtain fuel. As he pressed forward toward his goal, his hips dislocated. In agony, he collapsed helplessly to the ground.

One by one the cars passed by until a group of teenage boys stopped their vehicle off the road between my father and the view of the passing cars. I'm sure his grubby work coveralls and general appearance gave the boys the impression that he was a homeless man. They made the quick decision to do what only cowards would do. Like vultures preying on the wounded, they taunted and jeered him. When they grew tired of this sport, they hurled rocks in his direction. When they became bored at his lack of resistance, they climbed into their car and drove away from the sight of the crime.

As my father lay there, a car passed that happened to contain a good Samaritan. Sensing Dad's plight, he pulled his car over to offer assistance. Helping his wounded passenger into his car, he drove to the hospital so that my father could obtain the pain medication he needed to carry on. This kind man then drove to the gas station and purchased a can full of fuel. Returning to my father's car, he poured it into the vehicle and, as quickly as he had entered my dad's life, he departed, with no thought of recognition. To this day we don't even know his name.

I arrived home shortly after Dad's ordeal. I found him seated in his overstuffed chair with his face buried in his hands. I can't adequately describe the frustration I felt as he related his experience to me. His face reflected the feelings of a man who had been sorely tormented.

I have never been to Gethsemane, and I'm not sure I will ever fully appreciate in mortality the agony that caused the Savior to bleed at every pore. However, I do have a sense of what it might be like to witness someone carrying a cross, for the expression I saw on my father's face that day was that of a man trying to bear up under a heavy load. Growing up, I saw it more than once before the Lord relieved my father of the burden his body had become. He carried his body courageously and without asking for pity, but as the years progressed it became a kind of cross to bear. Like my father, each one of us will be asked to carry a cross from time to time in this life. In the most difficult times in my own life, it helps to remember my father—I learned courage from him.

Shortly before he passed away, I was visiting with him in a casual setting. He said something to me that I have grown to appreciate more and more with the passage of time: "Of all the gifts that God has given to me, the one I'm most thankful for at this point in my life is cancer."

The stunned look on my face begged for an explanation. He continued, "I am a proud and stubborn man. If it hadn't been for cancer slowing me down as a young married man, I'm not sure I ever would have been humble enough to join the Church and remain true and faithful. Because I did, I know I will have my family forever. I'm willing to lose a few years in this life to gain eternal life with my family."

I witnessed the "thy will" consecration I have written about in this chapter first in my father before I became acquainted with it in the scriptures.

Conclusion

I am reminded of the experience in the New Testament when Jesus fed the five thousand with just five loaves and two fishes. (See Matthew 14:17–21.) There is a subtle message within this miracle that speaks to our potential when we work with the Lord in a "thy will" partnership. While it may have been true that the disciples could not have fed five thousand people with five loaves and two fishes, they discovered what could happen when they gave the best they had and then put it into the hands of the Lord.

They could have contended with the Savior by saying, "I'm sorry, but there isn't enough here to feed a multitude. We'll just have to send most of them home hungry."

There is nothing in the text to indicate that this took place. They gave the best they had with faith that the Lord would do the rest. Is this not what the Lord requires of us? It is his work, and he takes our meager best when presented with a consecrated "thy will" heart. And as the New Testament disciples learned, he makes up the difference.

We see this miracle happening every day in places like the Missionary Training Center, where hundreds of missionaries are asked to do things they know are as impossible as feeding five thousand people with five loaves and two fishes. And yet when they leave that boot-camp for missionaries, they know that the Lord has taken their meager best and will use it to feed the multitudes throughout the world.

They come like trembling children on the first day of kindergarten and leave a short time later with a glimpse of what the Savior can do with them if their attitude is right. And if they understand this all the way down to their souls, it becomes a great gift they can take home with them at the conclusion of their missions. Students, married couples, Primary teachers, honest business people—all can see their meager five loaves and two fishes turn into a miracle through totally placing their lives into the Lord's hands.

The scriptures encourage us to press forward, endure, and even change a "my will" attitude in order to fully appreciate life—even life's challenges. In our best moments, have not all of us had a glimpse of what life could be like if we could only maintain a consistent "thy will" perspective? I am convinced that by placing total trust in the Lord as the divine Therapist, each of us may witness his hand in our lives until we eventually kneel at his feet and, as did the Nephites of old, feel the prints of the nails in his hands and feet. (See 3 Nephi 11:15.)

CHAPTER 10

SUPPORTING
CHURCH LEADERS:
A CELESTIAL STRATEGY

K. DOUGLAS BASSETT

Many years ago I was doing research for a presentation I was asked to give on the importance of supporting our leaders in the Church. After studying for a few hours, I started getting tired and began losing my concentration. I felt I needed to focus on something else for a while; then I could return to my studies with renewed efforts. My eyes wandered about the room, eventually resting on a magazine with a picture of the granite faces of Mount Rushmore on its cover. Picking it up, I began to read about this marvelous achievement. I finished the article and set it down with the expectation of returning to my research on supporting our leaders. However, the thought occurred to me that the principle I had been studying all morning had application in what I had been reading about Mount Rushmore. So I sat down and wrote a story, almost as a parable, based on the facts I had read concerning this monument at Mount Rushmore. The following account is that story:

In my youth, one of the more memorable vacations our family took was to the Black Hills of South Dakota. As we stood at the base of Mount Rushmore, gazing into the granite faces of Washington, Jefferson, Roosevelt, and Lincoln, it was easy to get caught up in the majesty of the moment. The spirits of those four great presidents seemed to be looking out across the Black Hills like watchmen over America. The work and dedication of their creator, Guton Borglum, made the faces of these four men seem as timeless as the pyramids of Egypt. Our moment of awestruck wonder was interrupted by a workman who had been eavesdropping on our conversation.

"What ya lookin' at?" he asked.

Our first reaction was one of laughter at the odd nature of the question. But the expression on his face let us know he was completely serious. Our smiles were quickly replaced with a query of our own. "We're enjoying the faces of these great men. Is there something wrong with that?"

Stealing a glance back at the faces on the mountain, he said, "If you knew what I did about those four guys up there, you would be enjoying a vacation at Disneyland instead of wasting your time here."

Now that he had captured our complete attention, he began to share his evidence with us: "Why, there ain't a day goes by that I don't have to rappel my way up and down their faces repairing cracks of one sort or another." Pointing toward the granite faces, he continued, "From where you stand it looks like those men are made of solid rock. But that just ain't so. Take it from someone who spends his time filling in those cracks with cement; there's more faults in those faces than you'd ever believe."

The dazed expression on our faces was evidence that he had left us speechless. He used our silence as license to continue his discourse. "In fact, if you look real close, you can see that we had to give Thomas Jefferson a new lip—the old one had so much soft mineral in it that we thought the bottom half of his face would fall off. And look up there at Abe Lincoln's nose. He used to have a bush growing out of it till we took care of that problem."

He was on a roll and was going to take full advantage of the audience he had gained. "Ya see George Washington's lapel? If you look real hard, you can see the stumps we left in it from the pine trees that were sticking out. If you could see what I see every day, up close, you'd know that the granite is turning a greenish-brown color. Those guys have so much cement filling up the cracks in their faces it would make you sick."

Stopping just long enough to make sure we hadn't walked away, he turned back toward the monument and continued his speech. "Well, from my vantage point, it's hard to see why anyone would want to go out of their way to stand here all day gawking up like they was gettin' a glimpse into heaven." With a shrug of his shoulders he said, "Well, maybe I've said too much; anyhow, we'll see you around." Without even a glance at our stunned faces, he walked away.

As quickly as he had come into our lives, he was gone. Try as we might, we couldn't gaze up with the same wondering awe we had experienced just moments before. In fact, we spent the next half hour trying to locate the flaws that had been pointed out to us by this self-proclaimed authority on the four faces in the sky. In this new frame of mind, it wasn't long before our hunger for Rushmore was satisfied. With nothing left to do here, we decided to conclude our vacation a day early.

The first thirty minutes of our drive home was filled with silence. I felt cheated, and from the look on everyone else's faces, they felt the same way. It was as if we had all sat down together to have a Thanksgiving feast, with all the trimmings, but instead the trip to Rushmore had turned out to be more like reservations at McDonalds's.

Our brooding was interrupted by Dad's laughter. He said, "I can't believe we fell for it. What a bunch of stooges we are.

Even if everything that guy said was true, it doesn't change a thing. Those are still the faces of four great men, and they don't have to be perfect to be appreciated. All that guy's negative words still can't replace the decade of sweat and effort it took to bring the beauty out of those granite hills." Confirming our original feelings, he continued, "It was spectacular, and nothing that detractor said will ever change that. In fact, I'm turning this car around, and we're going to drive back to Mount Rushmore and stay overnight at a motel. In the morning we're going to return and enjoy the sculpture along with everything it stands for."

That night at the motel, Dad read to us some literature he had picked up at the gift shop about the Mount Rushmore monument and all the sacrifice that had gone into it. We then spent the rest of the evening talking about the four great men represented in stone and their contribution to this wonderful nation. Sure enough, at daybreak the mountain monument had returned to its former luster, looking every bit as glorious as it had before. Even though we were no longer blind to its flaws, we all agreed it could not have been more beautiful.

The parallel between this fictional account and the experience of supporting our leaders within the Church is apparent. Whether it be a bishop, stake president, or even the prophet, there will always be people like the employee at Rushmore saying that if we only knew the real man, we would not support him so religiously. There are always those who are willing to point out the cracks in a particular leader's character or to share what they perceive as the flaws of his past. Their critical words are used like cement to fill in the crevices in the imperfect lives of those in authority over them.

The conclusion finally reached by the family in the story mirrors the words of President Gordon B. Hinckley: "I have worked with seven Presidents of this Church. I have recognized that all have been human.

But I have never been concerned over this. They may have had some weaknesses. But this has never troubled me. I know that the God of heaven has used mortal men throughout history to accomplish His divine purposes. They were the very best available to Him, and they were wonderful." (*Ensign*, May 1992, p. 53.)

Just as the feelings of the family members were at a low ebb as they drove away from the monument after digesting the words of the Rushmore employee, those who have accepted a negative opinion of their leaders place themselves on that same dark road.

The father in the story had the right idea when he stopped the car, as well as the negative conversation, and returned to the motel where they began studying that which was positive about the granite faces of Rushmore. As they studied the monument with the right perspective, they were uplifted and inspired. Is that not how we as members of the Church should view those who have been called to lead us within the Church?

With a testimony that this is the true church of Christ, we can safely assume that God will supplement the weakness of our leaders with his strength. It is through our support that we become a part of that process. In the end, how we view our leaders and how we express ourselves regarding them may reveal more about us than it does them. In the final analysis, the test is not whether the Church is true but whether or not we are true to the teachings of the Church. How we sustain our leaders has a great deal to do with whether or not we pass the exam.

Standing by Our Leaders

Some of the most wonderful blessings from our Father in Heaven are connected to the principle of sustaining our leaders. President Ezra Taft Benson said, "If you want to be close to the Lord, if you want to have His favor and Spirit to be with you, follow the counsel of those who have been called to preside over you." (*Teachings of Ezra Taft*

Benson, p. 334.) On another occasion President Benson taught, "If we complain against the Lord's servants, the heavens are offended." (Ibid., p. 332.)

President James E. Faust reinforced this when he said, "God will not ennoble a person, man or woman, who refuses to uphold . . . those whom God has called and ordained to preside over [him or her]." (*Ensign*, May 1998, p. 97.)

Just prior to Lehi's sons' traveling back to Jerusalem to obtain the brass plates, Lehi said to Nephi, "Thy brothers murmur, saying it is a hard thing which I have required of them . . . [but] thou shalt be *favored of the Lord, because thou hast not murmured.*" (1 Nephi 3:5–6; italics added.) Notice that Nephi was favored of the Lord (unlike his brothers) because he refused to murmur against his father. Nephi's story is evidence that "if our lips are closed to murmuring, then our eyes can be opened." (Neal A. Maxwell, *Ensign*, Nov. 1989, p. 85.) This principle runs from beginning to end in the Book of Mormon and continues to our day.

Elder Dallin H. Oaks stated the doctrine plainly: "Rejection of or murmuring against the counsel of the Lord's servants amounts to actions against the Lord himself. How could it be otherwise? The Lord acts through his servants. . . . His servants are not perfect. . . . But if we murmur against the Lord's servants, we are working against the Lord." Elder Oaks then bore witness to the cost of murmuring: "We . . . will soon find ourselves without the companionship of his Spirit." (*Ensign*, Feb. 1987, p. 71.)

On the occasion when the bows were broken in the desert and his family was faced with starvation, even Lehi "began to murmur against the Lord." (1 Nephi 16:20.) Nephi continued to support authority by asking his father, "Whither shall I go to obtain food?" (1 Nephi 16:23.) Why did Nephi do such a thing when his father was wavering? This worthy son was not only giving heed to the sixth commandment to honor his father but, being a prophet himself, he was aware that "individual members of the Church may not receive spiritual instruction for those higher in authority. . . . Those who claim direct revelation from God for the Church outside the established order and channel of the priesthood are misguided." (James E. Faust, *Ensign*, May 1996, p. 7.)

This concept of support for authority is illustrated in Helaman's letters to Captain Moroni. In these epistles he recounted his military adventures with the 2,000 stripling warriors who volunteered to fight against the Lamanites so that their fathers could maintain the oath they had previously taken to "never . . . use weapons again for the shedding of man's blood." (Alma 24:18.)

Helaman wrote these words regarding those 2,000 young men: "They had been taught by their mothers, that if *they did not doubt*, God would deliver them. And they rehearsed unto me the words of their mothers, saying: We do not doubt our mothers knew it." (Alma 56:47–48; italics added.)

Notice that this promise was predicated on the challenge "that if they did not doubt, God would deliver them." So there was more involved than just keeping the commandments of God, though all would have been lost if they had not done that. So what else were they not to doubt? A closer look at the scriptural text indicates that it implies more than just not doubting their mothers' words. In the chapters following this promise, it is easy to see that the promise was connected to total obedience to their new military leaders. This became the ultimate test of obedience for them—to show their allegiance to a perfect and infallible God by how they obeyed those less than perfect who were called to lead them in battle.

For example, nothing up to this point in the Book of Mormon indicates Helaman had extensive experience as a military leader; on the contrary, our exposure to him is in his service as a missionary to the Zoramites and his interaction with his father, Alma. Yet, in the heat of battle, when the Nephite army was "about to give way before the Lamanites" (Alma 57:20), it was these young men who saved the day through their obedience to their military leaders, one of whom was this Helaman. This missionary-turned-military-leader wrote to Captain Moroni of the experience: "They did obey and observe to perform every word of command with exactness." (Alma 57:21.) In other words, in the heat of the battle they "did not doubt" (Alma 56:47) the word of the leaders. It was by supporting their leaders "with exactness" that the promise of deliverance given them by their mothers was made complete, or, as the scriptures say, "it was done unto them." (Alma 57:21.) This promise would have been closed to them had they tried to "fill in the crevices on the faces of their leaders" by murmuring.

In the late 1970s, as an instructor at the Missionary Training Center, I sat at the feet of Elder Marion D. Hanks while he gave commentary on this concept of obeying with exactness by standing by our leaders. He related a true story shared with him by Elder Hugh B. Brown shortly before the passing of this great apostle, who had served in the Canadian military:

> The story is of a young officer in the First World War. He was second-in-command of a cavalry unit. His commanding officer was killed, and he was then summoned and asked if he could follow orders. He responded that he could. The query was repeated twice, and he answered affirmatively and with some impatience. Of course he could follow orders.
>
> He was then told to lead his troops to the top of a long hillcrest overlooking a deep ravine on the other side. At the crest of the hill he was to turn his troops to the left and at hard gallop proceed for ten minutes by the clock. Nothing was to interfere, no diversions were to distract him; he was to lead his troops without fail at full gallop for ten minutes. He assured the general over the field telephone that he could do this.
>
> The order was given, the troops mounted, the mission begun. At the crest of the hill the young major turned his troops to the left, ordered full gallop, and began the maneuver.

Just as he began, he noticed a peculiar sight in a ravine to their right. Some of the bushes seemed to be moving. He paused, took the field glasses, and was electrified to see the enemy in great numbers infiltrating in camouflage up the ravine.

He was a soldier; there was the enemy; the action was plain. His repeated promise to follow orders was forgotten. He stopped his troops, turned them to the right, ordered them to draw sabers, and at full gallop charged his cavalry unit down the ravine to meet the enemy. At exactly ten minutes from the time when he was supposed to begin his full gallop away from the scene, his troops were engaged in a fierce battle with an enemy force. At that moment his own artillery, far back of the lines, opened up on the spot and killed every man in the ravine, his own soldiers as well as the enemy.

Allied intelligence had informed the army of enemy infiltration. The major and his cavalry unit were to be the diversion that would keep the enemy coming. They were to be clear of the scene when the artillery delivered its payload and the strong unit of the enemy would be wiped out. As it was, not only that unit but also the young officer along with his men paid the price of his not being able to obey with exactness. (This story was recorded by Elder Hanks's secretary and sent to me in January 1991.)

Elder Hanks did not use this story to illustrate that every order, in every situation, given by every leader, in every army must be obeyed with exactness in order to have the Lord's approval. But he used it to show that the need for total obedience to authority by the sons of Helaman was directly connected to the promise of deliverance given them by their mothers. Deliverance for these young warriors, as well as ourselves, is directly tied to our obedience to those called to preside over us.

Helaman understood the principle that the Lord stands by us as we stand by those in authority over us. He continued his letter to Moroni by asking why the government had not sent the requested assistance. Then, almost as an apology for being negative, he wrote, "We do not desire to murmur." (Alma 58:35.) Notice how Helaman shared an unpleasant truth in a manner that would still allow the lines of communication to remain open. His sensitivity to his leaders, as well as his subordinates, is commendable. His was not the expression of a weak-kneed foot soldier trying not to be responsible for the bad news he had born. While he was not blind to the problem, he chose to relate the details to Moroni and at the same time reinforce his own support. He once again illustrated his total allegiance to his leaders, recognizing full well that he could not expect God to stand by him if he didn't stand by his leaders. He concluded his letter by reaffirming his testimony of the source of his small army's strength: "We trust God will deliver us, notwithstanding the weakness of our armies, yea, and deliver us out of the hands of our enemies." (Alma 58:37.) It is apparent that he believed that the blessings of deliverance were in direct correlation with his support of those who presided over him.

Elder Ted E. Brewerton shared an experience in South America that reinforces this principle:

> In the Brazil São Paulo South Mission there was an Elder Malheiros who entered into the field not being able to read or write very proficiently. He was even a little fearful of giving a prayer in public. But this young man . . . became one of the very greatest missionaries imaginable. The [mission] president asked him toward the end of his mission how he had turned into such a dynamic, very successful missionary. (He had baptized more than two hundred people and had baptized every week for fifty-two consecutive weeks.) In a very humble-manner Elder Malheiros answered, "Well, president, I never doubted you. You said one could baptize every week, so I knew

I could baptize every week. I never doubted. It was not always easy, *but I tried to obey.*" . . .

In Alma 57 we read about the 2,060 sons of Helaman who fought valiantly in many wars. . . . Yet not one lost his life because they knew "that if they did not doubt, God would deliver them." (Alma 56:47.)

In Alma 57:21 we read: "Yea, and they did *obey and observe to perform every word of command with exactness.*" *They were totally obedient.* Hence, they had unbelievable protection and success. (*Ensign*, May 1981, p. 69.)

Leadership without discipleship does not complete the celestial strategy the Lord has in place to bless the members of the Church. When worthy leadership is accompanied by true discipleship, the Lord places his stamp of approval by allowing the Holy Ghost to be our guide. But we are reminded in the story of the broken bow that the Lord makes up for the weaknesses of leaders when true discipleship is present.

THE CUSTOM OF SUPPORTING LEADERS

It's fascinating to look within the armed services at the customs we use to show allegiance to our country. For example, the flag is to be handled only in a manner that shows total reverence and allegiance to that for which it stands. The way in which it is flown, taken down, folded, and stored—all must be done in a fashion that shows total loyalty to the flag. Even the manner in which it is saluted is important—always using the right hand, with all the participants standing at attention. Often a verbal recitation is given—pledging allegiance to the flag by those wearing uniforms upon which rest visual emblems of support for the things the flag represents. The music that is played and even the way the soldiers march are all a part of an effort to show loyalty and support for the flag and the country it represents.

Many of these elements extend beyond the military to other

programs within our society, such as Scouting, all in an effort to develop patriotism and a sense of duty in the hearts of our youth. Tradition calls for many athletic contests, from Little League to professional events, to be preceded by a ceremony of allegiance to the flag. All of these customs are in place to show loyalty to the flag that symbolizes our country, as well as the causes for which its patriotic citizens accept as a united body.

It is interesting how this idea shines forth in the Book of Mormon through the customs of the Nephites. In reading Alma 46, I have been intrigued by the drawing power of a torn coat known as the title of liberty. Even though our culture has traditions that show great respect for the flag, the custom Captain Moroni chose to rally his people is one that Americans would be hard pressed to relate to. Each country and each culture throughout history has had its own unique customs and purposes that strengthen its people's loyalty. In this story, the prophet Mormon introduces us to a custom from long ago with roots in a land far from our own.

It would be difficult to envision a military leader in our time, marching about in any city in America, dressed in full battle array, waving a shredded portion of a coat on which is written a message of freedom. Added to this improbable latter-day scene would be his parading through town giving a patriotic speech in a loud voice, while waving this homemade banner. (See Alma 46:19.) In our society, this behavior would probably draw more laughter than patriotism from those witnessing the performance. In fact, even though someone in our day might have full military authority, he might find himself trading his pole and flag for a pair of handcuffs and a ride in a police car.

In Alma 46, the reaction of the Nephites to Moroni's title of liberty was much different than if today's chief commander over the American armed services performed the same scenario in front of the citizens in our nation's capital. The Book of Mormon account says that "the people came running together with their armor girded about their loins." (Alma 46:21.) The scriptures don't even hint that the Nephites questioned Captain Moroni's behavior. Not only did they not see his behavior as extreme, they mirrored it to the extent of dressing in like manner and "rending" or tearing their clothing as a token of support. (See Alma 46:21.) These Nephites identified with a custom Moroni was not inventing but was using to arouse the feelings of patriotism among the citizens of Zarahemla. Their spontaneous response as a group is evidence that they were reacting to some behavior on Moroni's part that was not only understood but also accepted by them. It would be similar to the immediate expectation within our culture for every patriot to stand when hearing the "Star Spangled Banner" or to instantly place the hand over the heart during the recitation of the Pledge of Allegiance.

As a teacher, I have struggled to satisfactorily explain the background of Moroni's title of liberty, which was obviously not a part of Joseph Smith's America, or our own, for that matter. However, in 1990 while teaching at BYU, I had an experience that opened the door of understanding for me.

With my limited background, I was teaching Alma 46 to a Book of Mormon class. Sensing my lack of cultural understanding on the subject, an Iranian student who was not of our faith and who had never before been exposed to the Book of Mormon raised his hand and said that he understood what Captain Moroni had done and why the people reacted the way they did.

He related to the class that he had demonstrated many times during the Iranian Revolution of 1979 using this custom we were calling the title of liberty. I invited him to come forward and share with the class his understanding of the custom. He began by drawing what looked like a wagon wheel on the board, fully equipped with a hub and spokes extending from the middle, tied to a rim surrounding the spokes. He then told the class that this was an aerial view of the city of Isfahas, which is laid out with streets that resemble a wagon wheel, with all major streets intersecting in the middle of the wheel, and extending to a major street that circled the city like the rim of the wagon wheel. The hub of the wheel is known as the government gate or city square. He explained that the outskirts of the city extended about one mile in all directions from the hub or city square.

He told how he and his companions made a cloth banner, approximately fifteen feet by three feet, and attached it to poles on both ends to be held overhead as these protesters marched through the streets. The purpose of this march was to protest Pahlavi, the Iranian Shah. A group of about fifty people divided into four to seven processions and marched from the outskirts of town down the streets that connected to the city square. Carrying a banner, each procession walked the one-mile distance in approximately an hour and a half. He indicated that with the use of these banners they typically gathered a group of 100,000 to 150,000 to the city square.

He explained that the purpose of the poles was not just to hold the banner, but this custom of "raising the pole" was used to gather an army. I asked him why then was there a need for a banner. "To state the cause," he responded.

I inquired, "What was written on these banners that would bring so many people together in such a short time?"

"Liberty," was his simple reply.

He paused as all of us recognized the obvious similarity between the word he chose and its tie to the title of liberty. He continued, "We would write in the Persian language; Liberty, Independence, and Islamic Law."

I then asked, "What is the origin of the custom?"

He responded, "I don't know; it is a widely understood custom among my people." He continued, "My grandfather used the same custom to gather people to demonstrate four decades earlier."

Though I have lost touch with this student over the years, I have often thought of the relevance of the actual title of liberty to our day in this church. As President Ezra Taft Benson said, "We should constantly ask ourselves, 'Why did the Lord inspire Mormon (or Moroni or Alma) to include that in his record? What lesson can I learn from that to help me live in this day and age?'" (Conference Report, Oct. 1986, p. 5.)

Obviously, from a strictly military standpoint it is difficult to generalize this custom to the rituals that are encompassed within our faith. However, the application becomes clearer when viewed in a spiritual perspective. Are we not gathered together as members of the Church in a spiritual army through the symbolic act of raising our right arm to the square as a united body in support of our leaders? Elder Angel Abrea said, "The raised hand becomes a symbol of the covenant we make to support [our leaders]. Each time we criticize or condemn them, we become literally covenant breakers." (Ensign, Nov. 1981, p. 24.)

The followers of Captain Moroni showed their allegiance by mirroring his appearance and his behavior, with the exception that rather than placing their torn cloaks on a pole they "cast their [torn] garments at the feet of Moroni." (Alma 46:22.) By doing these things they were illustrating to Moroni, each other, and their God that they had given total allegiance to Moroni and his cause. From this point on, each time they criticized or condemned Moroni, they literally became covenant breakers.

John Taylor said, "What is meant by sustaining a person? . . . For instance, if a man be a teacher, and I vote that I will sustain him in his position. . . . I will do everything I can to sustain him. . . . And then if anybody in my presence were to whisper something about him disparaging to his reputation, I would say, look here! are you a Saint? Yes. Did you not hold up your hand to sustain him? Yes. Then why do you not do it? . . . When we vote for men in the solemn way in which we do, shall we abide by our covenants? or shall we violate them? If we violate them we become covenant-breakers." (Journal of Discourses, 21:207–8.)

The title of liberty would have been of little use to Moroni if he had witnessed the kind of support spoken of by President Heber J. Grant: "I have traveled six solid weeks at a time in different settlements and heard 'We Thank Thee, O God, for a Prophet' sung in every one of them. And I have thought time and time again that there were any number of Latter-day Saints who ought to put a postscript on it and say, 'We thank thee, O God, for a prophet to guide us in these latter days provided he guides us in the way we want to be guided.'" (*Gospel Standards*, p. 172.) Our support for our leaders within the Church today begins with the raising of the right arm when they are presented before the body of the Church for sustaining. A celestial strategy is set in place when our thoughts, words, and deeds reflect our continued support of all Church leaders.

WHY LEADERS ARE CALLED

It is only natural to assume that everyone who is called to leadership positions within the Church is the *best* the Lord has available to him. However, Robert Millet, former dean of religious education at BYU, explained a flaw in this assumption: "People are not necessarily called to positions of responsibility because they are the most qualified, the most talented, or the most gifted gospel scholars. Our challenge is to sustain—that is give our full loyalty and support to—people who are often less than perfect, even people that we might feel to be less capable than ourselves." (*Selected Writings of Robert L. Millet*, pp. 380–81.)

Elder Henry B. Eyring expressed a similar sentiment: "So why should a Sunday School teacher who seems to us weak and simple and less experienced be called by inspiration to teach us? One reason is that it requires humility on our part. It requires a humble heart to believe that you can be taught by someone who apparently knows a good deal less than you do, and perhaps seems less likely to get revelation." (*To Draw Closer to God*, pp. 11–12.)

Based on this logic, we understand that among the many reasons leaders are called in this church is this: They are called to test us. And what is the manner of the test?

The explanation is founded in the celestial strategy identified throughout this chapter: The way the Lord deals with us has much to do with how we deal with those who are called to lead us. Our blessings from the Lord are derived not only from the quality of mortal leadership over us but also, to a great degree, from the quality of our own discipleship. Even a wonderful leader can do little to serve those who are unwilling to heed his direction.

This can be illustrated in no better way than in the mission field when a young elder holds his first mission president in such high regard that he would do anything he counsels; and through this obedience, he is blessed in his labors. Then, halfway through this elder's mission his president completes his own mission and is replaced by a new president. Instantly, the missionary begins to see a new style of leadership and different programs instituted that seem contrary to his first president. It may feel wrong for him to be loyal to this new man who seems to be changing almost everything his old mission president had established. The elder begins to struggle for a season; and his success as a missionary, along with the companionship of the Spirit, diminishes for a period of time. If he is wise he will eventually recognize that his drought as a missionary has not come about because of a lack of leadership from his new mission president but due to his own lack of discipleship.

As President David O. McKay said many years ago, "The bishop may be a humble man. Some of you may think you are superior to him, and you may be, but he is given authority direct from our Father in heaven. You recognize it. Seek his advice. . . . *Recognition of authority is an important principle.*" (Conference Report, Oct. 1965, p. 105; italics added.) Just why then is "recognition of authority . . . an important principle"? Not only because the kingdom moves forward more efficiently, but also because therein lies the test of our discipleship.

As Elder George Q. Cannon stated, "It is better to carry out a plan that is not so wise, if you are united on it. Speaking generally, a plan or a policy that may be inferior in some respects is more effective if men are united upon it than a better plan would be upon which they were divided. . . . When they carry that counsel out unitedly . . . God will supplement [their] weakness by His strength." (*Gospel Truth*, pp. 207–8.)

THE SPIRIT OF PAHORAN

In Helaman's letter to Captain Moroni, he hinted that Pahoran, the chief governor, was not sending men and supplies to his assistance. (See Alma 58:34–37.) Uncharacteristically, Moroni sent a scathing letter to Pahoran. In this appeal for Pahoran to do his duty Moroni accused him of "neglect" (Alma 60:5) and of sitting on his political backside "in a state of thoughtless stupor" (Alma 60:7). He made accusations to Pahoran that because of his wickedness "the blood of thousands shall come upon your heads for vengeance." (Alma 60:10.)

This is a fascinating letter for a number of reasons. First and foremost is that Captain Moroni was totally wrong in his assessment of Pahoran and his situation. The truth was that Pahoran had been expelled from the capital city and was in hiding. He was not in a position to satisfactorily defend himself, much less to send supplies and reinforcements to the men under Moroni's command.

Another interesting sidelight is that Mormon chose to include in his abridgement this letter from the man whom he had previously praised in the highest terms: "If all men had been, and were, and ever would be, like unto Moroni, behold, the very powers of hell would have been shaken forever; yea, the devil would never have power over the hearts of the children of men." (Alma 48:17.) Mormon was so impressed by Captain Moroni that he not only used a substantial portion of his text to include information about this military leader, but he also named his own son after him.

This being the case, why did Mormon choose to include in his record something that could be seen as derogatory toward this man whom he obviously admired very deeply? Perhaps the reason is that without this letter illustrating Moroni's blunder, we would not receive the full impact of Pahoran's letter of reply to his captain.

Few people would have scorned Pahoran for writing a return message to Moroni that was filled with rage at Moroni's overzealous epistle. On the contrary, rather than attacking Moroni or defending himself, the spirit of Pahoran's reply is captured in his use of the phrase "my beloved brother" in reference to his captain (Alma 61:14, 21). Elder Neal A. Maxwell wrote, "Moroni was not . . . the first underinformed Church leader to conclude erroneously that another leader was not doing enough. (See Alma 60.) Nor was Pahoran's sweet, generous response to his 'beloved brother,' Moroni, the last such that will be needed. (Alma 61.)" (*Notwithstanding My Weakness*, p. 8.)

The following words of Pahoran to Moroni illustrate the spirit in which we should deal with each other during moments of conflict: "You have censured me, but it mattereth not; I am not angry, but do rejoice in the greatness of your heart" (Alma 61:9), and "I do joy in receiving your epistle." (Alma 61:19.) In taking this approach he was able to secure in their relationship "the Spirit of God, which is also the spirit of freedom." (Alma 61:15.) In the spirit of unity between themselves and their God, Pahoran then encouraged Moroni to send the message to the Nephites that "God will deliver them." (Alma 61:21.)

Notice how Pahoran dealt with Moroni when the captain was in error. He sought first for unity rather than stooping down to attack Moroni or defend himself. In doing this, he felt confident the Spirit of the Lord would abide their cause.

This then becomes the same spirit in which we should resolve conflicts between ourselves and our leaders within the Church. Conflicts, after all, are inevitable and not necessarily bad on their face. Elder Dallin H. Oaks wrote:

> What do we do if we feel that our Relief Society president

or our bishop or a General Authority is in transgression or pursuing a policy of which we disapprove? Is there no remedy? . . .

There are remedies, but they are not the same remedies or procedures that are used with leaders in other organizations.

Our Father in Heaven has not compelled us to think the same way on every subject or procedure. As we week to accomplish our life's purposes, we will inevitably have differences with those around us—including some of those we sustain as our leaders. The question is not *whether* we have such differences, but *how we manage them.* . . . We should conduct ourselves in such a way that our thoughts and actions do not cause us to lose the companionship of the Spirit of the Lord.

The first principle in the gospel procedure for managing differences is to keep our personal differences private and not allow them to be a source of contention. In this we have worthy examples to follow. Every student of Church history knows that there have been differences of opinion among Church leaders since the Church was organized. Each of us has experienced such differences in our work in auxiliaries, quorums, wards, stakes, and missions of the Church. We know that such differences are discussed, but they are not discussed in public. . . . Counselors acquiesce in the decisions of their president. Teachers follow the direction of their presidency. Members are loyal to the counsel of their bishop. All of this is done quietly and loyally, even by members who would have adopted a different policy if they had been in the position of authority.

Why aren't these differences discussed in public? Public debate—the means of resolving differences in a democratic government—is not appropriate in the government of the Church. We are all subject to the authority of the called and sustained servants of the Lord. They and we are all governed by the direction of the Spirit of the Lord, and that Spirit functions only in an atmosphere of unity. That is why personal differences about Church doctrine, policy, or procedure need to be worked out privately. There is nothing inappropriate about private communications concerning such differences, provided they are carried on in a spirit of love." (*The Lord's Way*, pp. 200–201.)

CONCLUSION

The focus of this chapter has been the responsibility of discipleship in maintaining the spirit of unity within the Church. The celestial strategy I have identified assumes that in order to fully participate in the gospel we must have an assurance that this work is the Lord's. Realizing this basic fact, we are free to accept as truth the words of his prophets. The prophet Joseph F. Smith said, "While the commandments of God are to all the world, there are some special commandments that are applicable to the Latter-day Saints only. . . . One of these commandments is, that we shall honor those who preside over us. . . . For [a] man to say, 'I oppose the bishop because I don't like him' or 'because I haven't faith in him,' is proof by that very act that he does not understand the principle of government and submission to divine authority. He therefore becomes obstreperous, unyielding, ungovernable, undesirable, and worthy to be dealt with according to his merits or demerits." (*Teachings of Presidents of the Church: Joseph F. Smith,* pp. 212, 217.)

President James E. Faust said, "I have always tried to follow . . . counsel [from priesthood leaders], whether I agreed with it or not. I have come to know that most of the time they were in tune with the Spirit and I was not. The safe course is to sustain our priesthood leaders and let God judge their actions. . . . I advocate being more in tune with the Spirit so we may feel a confirming witness of the truthfulness of the direction we receive from our priesthood leaders. There is great safety and peace in supporting our priesthood leaders in their decisions." (*Ensign*, May 1997, pp. 42–43.)

The challenge for many people is that when the blessings of

discipleship are not immediately rewarded, they feel that they are no longer obligated to sustain their leaders. The prophet Joseph F. Smith exemplified the long-term discipleship that is needed in the kingdom:

"I was called on a mission after I had served four years on a homestead and it was only necessary for me to remain one year more to prove up and get my title to the land; but President Young said he wanted me to go to Europe on a mission. . . . I did not say to him, 'Brother Brigham, I cannot go; I have got a homestead on my hands, and if I go I will forfeit it.' I said to Brother Brigham, 'All right, President Young; whenever you want me to go I will go; I am on hand to obey the call of my file leader.' And I went. I lost the homestead, and yet I never complained about it; I never charged Brother Brigham with having robbed me because of this. I felt that I was engaged in a bigger work than securing 160 acres of land. I was sent to declare the message of salvation to the nations of the earth. I was called by the authority of God on the earth, and I did not stop to consider myself and my little personal rights and privileges; I went as I was called, and *God sustained and blessed me in it.*" (*Teachings of Presidents of the Church: Joseph F. Smith*, p. 210.)

The Brethren as well as the Book of Mormon remind us that the Lord stands by those who stand by their leaders. It requires little wisdom to be critical of those who have been called to guide us in this church. It takes no intellect or insight to continually look for cracks in the character of our leaders like the employee at Mt. Rushmore. But to follow in the Lord's way requires humility and a desire to obtain a testimony of this work, to be followed by a spirit of cooperation in whatever positions we are called to. It is not possible to lead others in this church unless we can follow those same people when they are called to lead us. What a marvelous sifting tool the Lord has set in place to aid us in our progression. We may be called to lead from time to time, but there will never be a season of our activity in the Church where we will not be required to follow.

CHAPTER 11

THE UNFORGIVING HEART

K. DOUGLAS BASSETT

Over the years I have discovered that if there are fifty students in my classroom, my lesson will likely be perceived in fifty different ways. In a real sense, we don't see the world as it is, but we do view the world as we are. With this truth extended over a period of years, it becomes clear that it is our attitudes that determine our physical circumstances. The places we call heaven and hell are but an extension of the way we have lived here in mortality. Any visit through a prison supplies ready evidence that some inmates don't have to die to go to hell. President David O. McKay wrote of the connection between attitude and circumstance:

> In ancient days in Japan, there was a scholar who went out of the gates and came in at nights and gave a lecture to the workmen whom he met. One day as he started out to get his lessons from nature, a man approached him and said, "Will you please bring me tonight a rose that I may see the lessons you mentioned last evening?"
>
> "Yes, I will bring you a rose."
>
> A second one accosted him and said, "Will you bring a twig such as you used to illustrate your lecture of last evening?"
>
> "Yes, I will bring you a twig."

And a third, "Will you bring me a lily that I may study the lesson of purity you gave?"

And he promised to bring the lily. At sundown, after work, the three laborers were there to meet the educator, philosopher. To the first he gave the rose, to the second the twig, and to the third the lily.

Suddenly the one with the rose exclaimed, "Why, here is a thorn clinging to the stem of my rose."

The second said, "And here is a dead leaf on my twig."

Encouraged by the remarks, the third man said, "And here is dirt clinging to the roots of my lily."

"Let me see." And the educator took from the first the rose, from the second the twig, and from the third the lily. From the rose he plucked the thorn, and keeping the flower, handed the thorn to the first. He took the dead leaf from the twig and gave it to the second, took the dirt from the roots of the lily and handed it to the third.

"There," he said, "each of you has what attracted him first. You looked for the thorn and found it. I left it there. I left the dead leaf and you saw that first. You have it. You saw the dirt clinging to the roots of your lily, and I have placed that in your hand. I will keep the rose, the twig, and the lily, for the beauty I see in them." (*Pathways to Happiness,* pp. 108–9.)

In President McKay's story, the rewards given to the three men were but a reflection of the way they each chose to view the world. At the Judgment Day, more than a few of God's children may be surprised to discover the Savior will deal in a like manner.

OUR BEHAVIOR AS VIEWED BY THE SAVIOR

The scriptures remind us that the Savior accepts our behavior toward our fellowman as if it were directed toward him. It is amazing how many times this concept is reinforced in the scriptures. In the New

Testament the Lord taught that, "Inasmuch as ye have done it unto one of the least of these my brethren, *ye have done it unto me.*" (Matthew 25:40; italics added.)

King Benjamin admonished the Nephites, "When ye are in the service of your fellow beings *ye are only in the service of your God.*" (Mosiah 2:17; italics added.) Elder Theodore M. Burton said, "You can repay Jesus for his mercy to you by being kind, thoughtful, considerate, and helpful to those around you. By such service to others, you can gradually pay back your indebtedness to your Savior." (*1984–85 Devotional and Fireside Speeches*, p. 99.)

When the Savior visited the Nephites he taught them that the degree of mercy he extends to each of us at our own judgment day has a great deal to do with the level of mercy we have extended to our fellowman here in mortality: "If ye forgive men their trespasses your heavenly Father will also forgive you; But if ye forgive not men their trespasses neither will your Father forgive your trespasses." (3 Nephi 13:14–15.)

Notice how often on the very first day of his visit to the Nephites he reinforced this doctrine:

"Forgive us our debts, as we forgive our debtors." (3 Nephi 13:11.) "Judge not, that ye be not judged. For with what judgment ye judge, ye shall be judged." (3 Nephi 14:1–2.) "Blessed are the merciful, for they shall obtain mercy." (3 Nephi 12:7.) Many people see these verses as indicating that the way we treat others is an invitation for them to treat us in like manner. However, by looking at the Savior's teachings in a broader perspective, it becomes apparent that the mercy we give others in this life has a direct effect on the level of mercy we will obtain at the judgment. Therefore, we may rightfully assume that to separate ourselves from our fellow beings in terms of our giving service and compassion is to distance ourselves from the Savior and his mercy.

In the Doctrine and Covenants, the Savior echoed the same testimony: that not only will he judge us according to our works generally in this life but he will also specifically "measure to every man according to the measure which he has measured to his fellow man." (D&C 1:10.)

He said, "Inasmuch as you have forgiven one another your trespasses, even so I, the Lord, forgive you." (D&C 82:1.) In the same section he admonished, "Leave judgment alone with me, for it is mine and I will repay." (D&C 82:23.)

Elder Robert L. Simpson wrote: "How can you love God and hate your neighbor? You cannot! So forgive right now, today. That is the beginning of love, for *forgiveness is indeed that prime ingredient of love.*" (*Proven Paths*, p. 85; italics added.)

The Lord admonished the Nephites, "Love your enemies, bless them that curse you, do good to them that hate you, and pray for them who despitefully use you and persecute you." (3 Nephi 12:44.) When a person is able to achieve this level of spirituality, the Savior taught all of us that we "may be the children of your Father who is in heaven." (3 Nephi 12:45.) It is amazing that he accepts personally our treatment of others—even those who hate us. In this context, it may take more than singing "I am a child of God" to qualify as being one.

INNOCENT ALLIES

In my role as a teacher for the past thirty years I have observed that the results of our behavior toward all people are unconsciously mirrored by those who look to us for guidance. When our general behavior is inappropriate, the resulting effect on those we love—especially our children—can be devastating, even when our attitude and behavior were never consciously directed toward them.

Many years ago, just before a new school year was to start, a female student came into my office to introduce herself. At first she was very enthusiastic, obviously trying to make a positive impression. Her appearance was most appealing, and my initial thought was that she was happy and well adjusted, with a bright outlook on life.

However, as the time passed, I began to notice an attitude that illustrated she had some kind of chip on her shoulder, a type of negativity that didn't seem to be directed toward anyone or anything in particular. It was just a kind of invisible cloud that seemed to hang over her, directing her outlook and thought processes. As she spent more time around me, her everyday behavior began to come through, and it became obvious that something was not right.

I didn't think too much about it until I met her brother, whose enthusiasm and appearance also made for a good first impression. Over time, however, the same negative outlook on life began to surface, especially when the two of them were together. They seemed to be feeding off each other—reinforcing their negativity. They were obviously "at home" when they were jointly criticizing or negatively dissecting something or someone.

I did not choose to confront or openly question their behavior at this time because it had not yet affected those around them in the classroom. I could not discern why they were so dark in their perspective. Their physical health was good, they were not living in poverty, they were not persecuted by their peers, their grades were solid, and their faith did not appear to be in crisis. There were no immediate clues I as their teacher could see that might reinforce the attitude that encompassed them; and then I met their father.

Once again, the same pattern began to surface: The positive physical appearance, supported by the cheerful and outgoing first impression. Then, over a period of time, as he became more comfortable with me, the chip on his shoulder began to reveal itself. I began to wonder what could be at the root of such a self-destructive attitude.

As the school year progressed, I had a few occasions to visit with their father about various seminary activities, and our paths crossed periodically in the normal comings and goings of everyday life. On one occasion we happened to be visiting in my office, and the conversation turned to more serious matters. He shared with me an experience that helped me understand the negativity I had discerned in him, as well as in his son and daughter.

He related that many years ago, before these two children were born, he had a son who had been the love of his life. Just mentioning the boy brought his emotions to the surface. When the child was but a few years of age, he was joyfully playing in the front yard of their rural home. A drunk driver had misdirected his vehicle through the front fence at a high rate of speed, violently striking the boy. The car continued forward until it slammed against the house.

This good man ran frantically to the aid of his son. Recognizing that the child was in critical need of medical attention, he jumped into his car. He laid his unconscious child across the front seat with the lad's head resting on his lap. As he sped to the nearest hospital, the intoxicated driver of the vehicle that had hit his boy rested comfortably—passed out—still behind the wheel, totally unaware of the deed he had just committed.

My friend arrived at the emergency room within minutes. Clutching his wounded son, he ran through the entrance of the hospital. The waiting room was filled with people due to a serious accident that had just occurred on the freeway. The patients were stranded (some in great distress) because of the minimal numbers of professionals in this small-town emergency room. In this chaos this man stood holding his wounded son, while the doctors and nurses worked as fast as they could.

Frantically, my friend tried to obtain the necessary attention his son needed right away. It did not take him long to decide that the needs of his son were greater than the number of doctors and nurses available. Instinctively, without full consideration of the consequences, he ran to his car, holding fast to his injured son.

He quickly decided that by driving to another hospital on the other side of town, his son might receive the attention he so desperately needed. At this point, he had no way of knowing how seriously injured the boy really was. Even though his son had not been conscious since the accident and could give no feedback, he felt it was a chance he had to take. As he raced against time, he continually glanced down at his son. Bruised and possibly broken, he appeared to be sleeping. He had no way of knowing what was really happening inside his son's body.

The hospital he was racing toward sat on a small hill. As he approached from a distance his hopes soared. He had taken a chance and everything seemed to be working. Then he noticed the railroad tracks as he approached the base of the hill; as tragic luck would have it, a long train was passing by. Frantically he reasoned, "How could this be? I've never seen a train on these tracks!"

The minutes passed as he sat helpless, his heart beating like never before. He glanced down to see his son had stopped breathing—he was dead!

The telling of his story had ended, but what happened next told another story which bore testimony to the negativity I had witnessed in his daughters. As I looked into his face I could see a transformation. The tears of mourning for his son were replaced with another kind of emotion. Physically it was just a continuation of the same tears he had been crying, but emotionally and spiritually he began to cry in a different manner. The change in his face began ever so slightly until it engulfed his whole facial expression. His face became hardened; the pain of loss was replaced with the agony of anger and bitterness, almost revenge.

He looked at me and said, "I hate that drunk driver." He continued, "I hate the doctors and nurses in the emergency room." Then he bowed his head and lamented, "I even hate the conductor of the train."

It is ironic that more than one person on that hate list never even knew of their role in his life on that fateful day. Elder Marion D. Hanks said that forgiving others can "relieve the one aggrieved of the destructive burden that resentment and anger can lay upon us." (Conference Report, Oct. 1973, p. 15.)

It was apparent that this father had found little *relief* regarding his son's passing. He was definitely engulfed in "the destructive burden that resentment and anger can cause."

This good man felt that by directing his anger toward these people, he could be relieved of his terrible burden. He seemed blind to the fact that his pain could be completely relieved only by forgiveness. What a simple remedy to define, and so terribly difficult for this brother, as well as the rest of us, to master.

If only he could have found the strength to do as Nephi did with his brothers Laman and Lemuel following their attempt to kill him: "I did frankly forgive them all that they had done." (1 Nephi 7:21.) Think of the wasted energy Nephi would have expended if he had spent himself by seeking revenge against his brothers. His promised land certainly would not have been nearly as "promising." The wasted time and effort, as well as the erosion of peace Nephi spared himself, had taken a terrible toll on my friend.

Now I was in a better position to understand the chip this man's teenage children carried on their shoulders. It reminded me of the painting by the famous western artist Charles M. Russell, *The Innocent Allies*. The title refers to the horses in the painting, which stand dutifully nearby a stagecoach that is being robbed by their riders.

In their formative years these children had stood by as "innocent allies," witnessing the hatred of their father's unforgiving heart. Their father's attitude had become a part of them, and they were now entering a position in which they could rob their own stagecoaches. As they matured they would need to learn to use their own agency in choosing a better way. As with all of us, there would come a point in which they could no longer be "innocent allies" but would need to be responsible for their own attitudes.

The Greater Sin

The fruits that come forth from the negative nurturing of an unforgiving heart can turn out to be something we might never suspect. The

Doctrine and Covenants states, "For he that forgiveth not his brother his trespasses standeth condemned before the Lord; for there remaineth in him the greater sin." (D&C 64:9.) When I first read this scripture I wondered how this could be possible. I just couldn't understand how the "greater sin" could lie with the victim! How is it possible that the "greater sin" would rest with this good brother rather than the drunk driver, simply through his choice of not forgiving?

As he related his tragic experience, I began to sense how the "greater sin" could lie with the victim. He had identified the parties responsible for his son's death with the resolve that he could not, and would not, forgive them of the deed. What he had not understood is that an unforgiving heart, like its companions hatred and revenge, are not a laser beam to be directed solely toward those who offend us. Hatred is a double-edged sword that, while it will never fully repay the person who has offended, always sinks its blade deep into the heart of the one holding the weapon.

The proof of this was in his hatred of the employees in the emergency room as well as the conductor of the train—who would probably never be aware of this father's enmity toward them. The sword of the unforgiving heart cut him to the soul without even making contact with those for whom he had ill will.

He had not only become blinded by the damage he had inflicted on himself but was also totally unaware of what he had done to those for which he had no ill will—his own children. He had planted the seed from his unforgiving heart, and in just a few years it had grown into a family tree that had unwittingly tied him to his innocent children. They had grown up in close proximity to their father's temperament, and in that environment they had learned to love their friends and hate their enemies. The fruits of this negative family tree are identified as the "greater sin."

Like "innocent allies," these children had initially been cut by the sword of hatred just by their mere proximity to their dad, even though his unresolved feelings regarding his son's accident were never consciously directed toward them. These cuts were the emotional scars I had initially sensed in his son and daughter, sending the unmistakable message to everyone to keep their distance. When they spoke negatively about the events and people around them, it was their voices I heard, but the echoing stamp of approval came from their father's example.

By our not forgiving, the "greater sin" becomes a cancer that spreads from one generation to another until its effects are more damaging than the initial transgression, originally committed by someone who is often long forgotten. It's not hard to calculate that the sum total of the unforgiving hearts between this father and his children could be more damaging than what the drunk driver had done to the man's son. What I had seen in these two teens was their father's anger carried on to the next generation—and when would it end? Which generation would have the will to terminate such a negative tradition? Therein would lie the "greater sin," spreading like a weed, choking out the promise of charity, service, and faith, and the joys of living. These virtues never receive a full chance to grow when they become overtaken by the weeds of hatred and revenge rooted in an unforgiving heart. This "greater sin" may take multiple generations to achieve; but rest assured, the *fallout* from one individual's unforgiving heart can create the "greater sin" over a period of years.

Perhaps this is one of the reasons that Lehi blessed his grandchildren (who were the children of Laman and Lemuel) that their sins would "be answered upon the heads of [their] parents." (2 Nephi 4:6.) Though Laman and Lemuel had not been sinned against, they still had unforgiving hearts planted deep within their breasts, and this begrudging attitude extended through many generations.

Another reason that there is a "greater sin" in the unforgiving heart is that it actively works against the repentance process. If, for example, the drunk driver in the story had any desire to repent, it could have been facilitated by the forgiving heart of a grieving father. An unforgiving heart, however, becomes hardened and unwilling to let the light of repentance seep in anywhere.

In a 1994 general conference address, Elder James E. Faust illustrated the far-reaching power of forgiving those who have sinned against us:

> Jeff and Joyce Underwood of Pocatello, Idaho, are the parents of Jeralee and five other children. . . . One day in July 1993, their daughter Jeralee, age eleven, was going door-to-door collecting money for her newspaper route. Jeralee never returned home—not that day, nor the next day, nor the next, nor ever. . . .
>
> . . . It was learned that Jeralee had been abducted and brutally murdered by an evil man. When her body was found, the whole city was horrified and shocked. All segments of the community reached out to Joyce and Jeff in love and sympathy. Some became angry and wanted to take vengeance.
>
> After Jeralee's body was found, Jeff and Joyce appeared with great composure before the television cameras and other media. . . . Joyce said, . . . "I have learned a lot about love this week, and I also know there is a lot of hate. I have looked at the love and want to feel that love, and not the hate. We can forgive."
>
> Elder Joe J. Christensen and I, representing the General Authorities, were among the thousands privileged to attend Jeralee's funeral service. The Holy Spirit blessed that gathering in a remarkable way and spoke peace to the souls of all who attended. Later, President Kert W. Howard, Jeralee's stake president, wrote, "The Underwoods have received letters from people both in and out of the Church stating that they prayed for Jeralee, and they hadn't prayed in years, and because of this, they had a renewed desire to return to the Church." President Howard continued, "We will never know

the extent of activation and rededication this single event has caused. Who knows the far-reaching effects Jeralee's life will have for generations untold." Many have come into the Church because they wanted to know what kind of a religion could give the Underwoods their spiritual strength. (*Finding Light in a Dark World*, pp. 47–48.)

The final explanation for the "greater sin" comes in the role of the person who has been sinned against. By not forgiving those who have hurt us we become a judge—taking on the role of Christ, and condemning our enemies before their actual day of judgment. Along this line of reasoning, Elder Neal A. Maxwell said that refusing to forgive others is "to hold hostage" those whom the Lord would wish to set free. (*Ensign*, Nov. 1991, p. 32.)

In this country, as well as in the rest of the world, we are witnessing the "greater sin" that arrives when the Holy Ghost is replaced by a need for revenge and a complete lack of forgiveness. We need look no further than the Book of Mormon to see the "greater sin" in a people who had become so stricken with terminal spiritual heart disease that they were blinded to their own sins, blinded to the point that they committed things which would have been unthinkable in better times: "For behold, many of the daughters of the Lamanites have they taken prisoners; and after depriving them of that which was most dear and precious above all things, which is chastity and virtue . . . they . . . tortur[ed] their bodies even unto death; and after they [did] this, they devour[ed] their flesh like unto wild beasts." (Moroni 9:9–10.)

Truly, the Nephites at the end of the Book of Mormon are evidence of where the path of the "greater sin" eventually leads. Are we not witnessing in America today acts that would have been unthinkable at other times in our history? Parents kill their own children (before and after their birth). Children shoot their classmates at school. Bombings like the one in Oklahoma City kill more and more of our innocent children. As a nation, are we becoming more like the

Nephites, our hearts growing colder and colder until eventually there may be the living death known in the Book of Mormon as being "past feeling"? (1 Nephi 17:45; Moroni 9:20.) When a nation is more concerned with individual rights than personal responsibilities, it is not difficult to see the fruits of an unforgiving heart. Selfishness is so closely connected to the unforgiving heart that it is rare to see one without seeing the other.

The Lord said, "Of you it is required to forgive all men. And ye ought to say in your hearts—let God judge between me and thee, and reward thee according to thy deeds." (D&C 64:10–11.) We need to have sufficient faith in God in order to trust him with our griefs; even to the point of giving to him our grievances regarding others. In actuality, we cannot forgive; that is the role of Christ. All we can do is recover by leaving all our grievances in his hands. "To forgive is to turn over to God the ultimate right to judge." (Madison U. Sowell, *Brigham Young University 1996–97 Speeches*, p. 51.) Only then can we obtain a degree of freedom from the effects of sin against us.

Perhaps it is hardest to forgive when the person who has sinned against us does not seek forgiveness, as was true of the drunk driver. President Spencer W. Kimball said: "Remember that we must forgive even if our offender did not repent and ask forgiveness. . . . The offended one treasures in his heart the offense, adding to it such other things as might give fuel to the fire and justify his conclusions. . . . To the disciples in Judea [the Lord] said: 'Therefore if thou bring thy gift to the altar, and there rememberest that thy brother hath ought against thee; Leave there thy gift before the altar, and go thy way; first be reconciled to thy brother, and then come and offer thy gift.' (Matt. 5:23–24.)

"Do we follow that commandment or do we sulk in our bitterness, waiting for our offender to learn of it and to kneel to us in remorse? . . . No bitterness of past frictions can be held in memory if we forgive with all our hearts." (Conference Report, Oct. 1949, pp. 132–33.)

By not giving to Christ all the emotional baggage associated with the tragedy of his son's passing, my friend was then obligated to carry it himself. What I had witnessed with his daughters was the inheritance of that baggage unconsciously willed to the next generation. He was such a good man, and to see him suffer from this spiritual cancer was painful to witness. In truth, we forgive for our own sake—to help us free ourselves of the past, to move forward without baggage.

Of course when we don't extend mercy, we don't have to wait until the Judgment Day to discover that we are not experiencing all the Savior is willing to give us. Madison U. Sowell said: "As a young adult ward bishop, . . . I realized that many individuals who had gone through the formal steps of repentance still did not feel forgiven. In many cases the only reason for their not feeling forgiven stemmed from their not having forgiven others their trespasses." (*Brigham Young University 1996–97 Speeches*, p. 51.) What an awesome injunction: The level of mercy we give others has an effect on the level of mercy the Savior extends to us!

DIAGNOSING AN UNFORGIVING HEART

A chronic medical condition called constrictive pericarditis has application in trying to diagnose spiritual heart problems:

> A normal heart is encased in a well-lubricated sac called the pericardium. This sac has several functions, one of the most important of which is to allow the heart to expand and contract freely as it pumps blood throughout the body. Another function is to protect it from irritation on the outside, to lubricate the outside of the heart muscle (the heart is really a large bundle of hard-working muscle fibers) so that its movement will not be hindered by friction. This sac also gives a general extra covering to the heart, similar to a layer of plastic wrap, but it permits sliding and slipping in any direction to accommodate each contraction.

But occasionally the sac itself becomes irritated and infected. When this happens, the inflammation causes a thickening of the sac's layers, eventually permitting the sac to become glued to the heart muscle itself. The result is a thick, scarred, unwieldy layer of inelastic fibrous tissue that does just the opposite of what it was originally intended to do. Instead of aiding, it restricts the movement of the heart.

Instead of allowing the heart to expand freely, progression of the disease process begins to contract and constrict the heart. This constrictive narrowing of this leathery encasement works like a vise as it causes irregularity of the beat, ineffectiveness of the stroke of the heart, and ultimately heart failure. The heart is actually squeezed to a smaller size and is therefore less able to do its job of pumping blood to the body. . . .

Sometimes a similar process takes place spiritually. . . . We wrap a tight, inflexible layer of selfishness around our heart that restricts it from caring about others who are in need. If not treated . . . the heart becomes totally nonfunctioning as far as spiritual things are concerned. (Lindsay R. Curtis, *Parables for Teaching*, pp. 16–17.)

The unforgiving heart can be stricken with a form of spiritual constrictive pericarditis that if left untreated will surely lead to spiritual death. This process of constrictive pericarditis is connected to what the Book of Mormon calls "hard heartedness." (See Book of Mormon Index, p. 144.)

Those with an unforgiving heart digest a poisonous attitude that becomes too much for their hearts to bear. Many in the medical profession are finally realizing that "ill will" is a major contributor to ill health. I believe that many people don't understand the connection between their physical health and the spiritual doctrine of forgiveness and letting go of the past.

Elder George Q. Cannon said, "A crust of bread eaten with a

cheerful heart will do us more good than the choicest food partaken of in sullenness or wrath." (*Gospel Truth*, p. 442.) If the bodily function of digestion is enhanced or decreased by our attitude at mealtime, then it stands to reason that a negative attitude will also affect the entire body's ability to function normally. Even a healthy heart eventually can become overloaded by the burden of wrong thinking.

An unforgiving *spiritual* heart places stress on the *physical* heart, as well as the other organs of the body. This may help to explain the dilemma written about by Dr. Paul Pearsall: "We hear much about the major risk factors for developing heart disease, including high cholesterol, obesity, smoking, and high blood pressure, yet about half of those who suffer their first heart attack have none of these common risk factors, more than eight out of ten people with three of these risk factors never suffer a heart attack, and most people who do have heart attacks do not have most of the risk factors." (*The Heart's Code*, p. 36.)

It is the damage to the spiritual heart that may explain some of the immeasurable negatives that affect the physical heart. We don't have to look for heart disease to diagnose the effects of not forgiving others. An unforgiving heart planted deep inside an individual initiates a slow death—a kind of suicide that gradually snuffs out the vitality within that person long before he breathes his last sigh in mortality. As the spiritual light diminishes, the body responds in like manner, often introducing illness within the physical system as well. Those who have "given up" spiritually by harboring an unforgiving heart may never recognize its connection to their physical heart, until it has given up the ghost as well. It is a certainty that if spiritual constrictive pericarditis is not treated with divine medicine the results will prove fatal.

It has been said that we all recognize a fool when we see one, but few recognize a fool when we are one. Similarly, it is much easier to see an unforgiving heart in others than to recognize it in ourselves. We can easily recognize the "mote" in our brother's eye, but find it so difficult to identify the "beam" in our own eye. (See 3 Nephi 14:1–5.) This is especially true of the person with an unforgiving heart.

As a side note for those who have been sinned against to the point where legal action seems appropriate: Do not assume that this chapter encouraging forgiveness is suggesting that the sinner should not be accountable before the law. The manner in which this should be done is given by Elder Richard G. Scott: "When anguish comes from evil acts of others, there should be punishment and corrective action taken, but the offended is not the one to initiate that action. Leave it to others who have that responsibility. Learn to forgive; though terribly hard, it will release you and open the way to a newness of life. Time devoted by one injured to ensure the offender is punished is time wasted in the healing process." (*Ensign*, May 1994, p. 9.)

Even if my friend had been asked to participate in prosecuting the drunk driver, his motive should not be connected to revenge. He still needed to forgive—for his own well-being, if for no other reason. The driver should have been required to suffer the legal consequences of the law he had broken—if for no other reason than to protect future victims. If my friend chose to participate in the legal process, he would need to move forward with a heart empty of the need for revenge.

Here is a list of attitudes and behaviors that may help to diagnose an unforgiving heart. This list is not inclusive, and its purpose is solely as an aid in looking within rather than trying to diagnose problems in others:

- An unforgiving heart is not free and easy with people.
- An unforgiving heart is defensive and not open and accepting of others.
- An unforgiving heart finds that negative conversation may become more a part of everyday life than ever before.
- An unforgiving heart does not lift and inspire those around her.
- An unforgiving heart finds that sarcasm and humor directed at

the weakness of others has become a part of normal conversation.

- An unforgiving heart chooses those friends who will join him in negative conversation. (But these friendships eventually end, when it is sensed that these friends may not be trusted.)
- An unforgiving heart wishes to be alone rather than around those she could be serving.
- An unforgiving heart may continue to attend church but places little value in the service of others, while becoming more and more concerned with personal growth independent of others.
- An unforgiving heart may take on the role of "spiritual commentator" for the ward, feeling a greater obligation to give personal observations rather than personal service and sacrifice.
- An unforgiving heart may lose the belief in the divine potential of man. He no longer believes that people are basically good.
- An unforgiving heart may be hampered in her ability to express love, even the simple expressions of love that come so naturally to us when our hearts are pure.
- An unforgiving heart cannot forgive himself.
- An unforgiving heart eventually loses trust in Heavenly Father, especially in his timing. (While the individual still may believe in God, she no longer feels God's love and eventually takes on the view that the Lord has forsaken her, when in fact, it is she who has forsaken the Lord.)
- An unforgiving heart compares circumstances with those around her and begins to feel cheated by God. (This kind of mentality is always destructive. In this mind-set, spiritual thought processes become warped into the false assumption that hardship and struggle should only follow disobedience rather than obedience.)

- An unforgiving heart has an unhealthy preoccupation with the past.
- An unforgiving heart is easily angered. (He has become so blind that he doesn't realize that he has been harboring grudges—keeping score for and against his fellowman.)
- An unforgiving heart finds it difficult—almost impossible to say, "I'm sorry," or, "I was wrong."
- An unforgiving heart has no desire to repent.
- An unforgiving heart does not forgive others.

Members of the Church with unforgiving hearts can easily become "knife and fork" Mormons—eating the meal, but lacking the ability to taste, always being where they are supposed to be, but not with the level of consecration needed to enjoy the flavor that comes with the companionship of the Holy Ghost. For some people who find themselves in this place, it may be just a season of healing. However, for others, it can extend for many years and eventually lead to the "greater sin."

The reader may rightfully ask, "How can a person have an unforgiving heart and not know it?" Partly because an unforgiving heart is not a goal in and of itself—it is just the result of wrong thinking. To compound the problem, the longer an individual carries this disposition the more blinded she becomes to her own sins. This path continues to the point that eventually she ceases to feel the need to repent of anything at all because she has become focused on self-defense and self-preservation, as opposed to spiritual progression.

Most of us who are traveling the path of the unforgiving heart are unaware that we have detoured from the straight and narrow path. With vision blurred, we are unable to recognize the direction of these "strange roads." (See 1 Nephi 8:32.)

The scriptures define the person traveling on this path of the unforgiving heart as one who "walketh in darkness, and knoweth not whither he goeth, because that darkness hath blinded his eyes." (1 John 2:11.)

Those with an unforgiving heart are under the false assumption that they are correctly moving forward, but they are actually like the driver moving down the road with his eyes firmly fixed on the rearview mirror. With eyes focused on the past, they unknowingly set the stage for future accidents. Over and over again, an unforgiving heart creates these kinds of accidental self-fulfilling prophecies. While they may personally feel they are "not looking back, and refusing to let yesterday hold tomorrow hostage," they are only fooling themselves. (Neal A. Maxwell, *Ensign*, Nov. 1998, p. 63.)

CURING AN UNFORGIVING HEART

Once an individual has recognized that he possesses an unforgiving heart, he is in a better position to move forward. The cure for an unforgiving heart is not nearly as difficult to identify as it is to implement. It requires concentrated faith as well as courage to begin transforming the unforgiving heart into a spiritually healthy heart.

Would it be too basic to say that the solution is to simply repent of our own sins, and to forgive those who have hurt us—to stop clinging to the past like a child clinging fast to a pacifier? It sounds so simple, but it is true. Only when we totally let go of the past do our hearts begin the process of healing. This seems like an impossible task for so many people. Certainly we must learn from the past and remember just enough of it to be profitable; but to hang on to it to the point that our todays and our tomorrows are handicapped is sad indeed.

Elder Robert L. Simpson said: "There are no shortcuts in the kingdom of God. We repent, we forgive, we progress; . . . it all starts with our own willingness to forgive one another. . . . First forgive and then stand eligible in the sight of God to be forgiven. . . . In so doing, we guarantee forgiveness for our own weaknesses." (*Proven Paths*, pp. 82–83.) In the New Testament, Matthew advises us to "first be reconciled to thy brother, and then come and offer thy gift." (Matthew 5:24.) Notice, before a gift is acceptable before the altar of the Lord, we must first have forgiveness in our hearts toward our fellowman.

The Savior said, "Ye ought to say in your hearts—let God judge between me and thee, and reward thee according to thy deeds." (D&C 64:11.) The strength to do this is achieved oftentimes only as a gift from the Lord for those who diligently seek it.

Even the prophet Nephi, who once had the ability to "frankly forgive" (1 Nephi 7:21), eventually exclaimed "O wretched man that I am," when his ability to extend mercy to his brothers was replaced by anger. (See 2 Nephi 4:17, 27.) Nephi struggled to obtain this gift of the Lord that had once come so easily to him.

The Savior can change hearts for those who are willing—even grieving hearts to be once again childlike, full of life, hope, and trust in a loving Heavenly Father. The Savior took the first step in Gethsemane, but the next step begins with us. This effort on our part must begin with the sincere desire and heartfelt need to change—to recognize something is wrong within ourselves. I can best illustrate this by sharing the true story of Corrie ten Boom, who, with her sister Betsie, was arrested by the Nazis for hiding Jews during World War II and sent to the concentration camp at Ravensbruck. She survived the experience and went on to spend years speaking about Christianity and the healing balm of the Savior. The following experience took place at one of her speaking engagements:

It was in a church in Munich that I saw him—a balding, heavyset man in a gray overcoat, a brown felt hat clutched between his hands. People were filing out of the basement room where I had just spoken, moving along the rows of wooden chairs to the door at the rear. It was 1947 and I had come from Holland to defeated Germany with a message that God forgives.

It was the truth they needed most to hear in that bitter,

bombed-out land, and I gave them my favorite mental picture. Maybe because the sea is not far from a Hollander's mind, I liked to think that that's where forgiven sins were thrown. "When we confess our sins," I said, "God casts them into the deepest ocean, gone forever. . . ."

The solemn faces stared back at me, not quite daring to believe. There were never questions after a talk in Germany in 1947. People stood up in silence, in silence collected their wraps, in silence left the room.

And that's when I saw him, working his way forward against the others. One moment I saw the overcoat and brown hat; the next, a blue uniform and visored cap with its skull and crossbones. It came back with a rush: the huge room with its harsh overhead lights; the pathetic pile of dresses and shoes in the center of the floor; the shame of walking naked past this man. I could see my frail sister's form ahead of me, ribs sharp beneath the parchment skin. *Betsie, how thin you were!*

[Betsie and I had been arrested for concealing Jews in our home during the Nazi occupation of Holland; this man had been a guard at Ravensbruck concentration camp where we were sent.]

Now he was in front of me, hand thrust out: "A fine message, Fräulein! How good it is to know that, as you say, our sins are at the bottom of the sea."

And I, who had spoken so glibly of forgiveness, fumbled in my pocketbook rather than take that hand. He would not remember me, of course—how could he remember one prisoner among those thousands of women?

But I remembered him and the leather crop swinging from his belt. I was face to face with one of my captors, and my blood seemed to freeze.

"You mentioned Ravensbruck in your talk," he was saying. "I was a guard there." No, he did not remember me.

"But since that time," he went on, "I have become a Christian. I know that God has forgiven me for the cruel things I did there, but I would like to hear it from your lips as well. Fräulein,"—again the hand came out—"will you forgive me?"

And I stood there—I whose sins had again and again to be forgiven—and could not forgive. Betsie had died in that place—could he erase her slow terrible death simply for the asking?

It could not have been many seconds he stood there— hand held out—but to me it seemed hours as I wrestled with the most difficult thing I had ever had to do.

For I had to do it—I knew that. The message that God forgives has a prior condition: that we forgive those who have injured us. "If you do not forgive men their trespasses," Jesus says, "neither will your Father in heaven forgive your trespasses."

I knew it not only as a commandment of God, but as daily experience. Since the end of the war I had had a home in Holland for victims of Nazi brutality. Those who were able to forgive their former enemies were able to return to the outside world and rebuild their lives, no matter what the physical scars. Those who nursed their bitterness remained invalids. It was as simple and horrible as that.

And I stood there with coldness clutching my heart. But forgiveness is not an emotion—I knew that too. Forgiveness is an act of the will, and the will can function regardless of the temperature of the heart. "Jesus, help!" I prayed silently. "I can lift my hand. I can do that much. You supply the feeling."

And so woodenly, mechanically, I thrust my hand into the one stretched out to me. And as I did, an incredible thing took place. The current started in my shoulder, raced down my arm, sprang into our joined hands. And then this healing warmth seemed to flood my whole being, bringing tears to my eyes.

"I forgive you, brother!" I cried. "With all my heart!"

For a long moment we grasped each other's hands, the former guard and the former prisoner. I had never known God's love so intensely as I did then. ("I'm Still Learning to Forgive," *Guideposts*, November 1972. Used with permission.)

As the unforgiving heart heals, day-to-day life takes on a freshness and joy, even a kind of hope that the person may not have experienced in a long time. Spencer W. Kimball said, "When you do not worry or concern yourself too much with what other people do and believe and say, there will come to you a new freedom." (*Teachings of Spencer W. Kimball*, p. 236.) Those whose hearts have been healed have a refreshing taste of that "freedom" because they have separated themselves from the negative elements of the past. Once again, relationships with people become rewarding because the person who was once intent on survival has become less preoccupied with self-protection. Once again, she is reaching out from her heart to others without fear or defense. To a greater degree than ever before, she understands the "change of heart" spoken of so much in the Book of Mormon. (See Mosiah 5:1–7; 27:24–26; Alma 5:7, 12–14, 26.)

CONCLUSION

There are many people in the world today who are trying to find themselves. In truth, there is no finding ourselves; it is the Lord who identifies us to ourselves, if we only let him. As we come to know him, we begin to realize who we really are. Perhaps this is what the Savior meant when he said, "He that loseth his life for my sake shall find it." (Matthew 10:39.) In today's preoccupation with self-discovery, men are "ever learning, and never able to come to the knowledge of the truth" about who they really are. (2 Timothy 3:7.) Forgiveness then becomes part of this miracle of losing self in order to find self. It is a major link in the process of progression. Elder Robert L. Simpson wrote: "As we forgive, we achieve the right to be forgiven. As we forgive, we increase our capacity for light and understanding. As we forgive, we live beyond the power of the adversary. As we forgive, our capacity for love expands toward heaven. And as we forgive, we approach the ability to stand one day in the midst of oppressors who do their ugly deeds out of ignorance and misdirection with the capacity to say, 'Father, forgive them; for they know not what they do.' (Luke 23:34.)" (*Proven Paths*, pp. 85–86.)

As the world struggles to find answers, a living prophet defines the way to peace. President Gordon B. Hinckley has said, "Is there a virtue more in need of application in our time than the virtue of forgiving and forgetting? . . . There is no peace in the nursing of a grudge. . . . There is peace only in repentance and forgiveness." (*Ensign*, Nov. 1980, pp. 62–63.)

In President Hinckley's book *Standing for Something*, he sends this message to America as well as the rest of the world: "Hatred always fails and bitterness always destroys. Are there virtues more in need of application in our day, a time marked by litigious proceedings and heated exchanges, than those of forgiving, forgetting, and extending mercy to those who may have wronged us or let us down?" (p. 69.)

In a game of catch, it is impossible for the person facing you to catch the ball unless you throw it with such effort that it is no longer a part of you. In like manner, the Savior cannot completely take hold of those sins committed against us unless we have the faith to throw them from our wounded hearts to the hands which were once wounded for our sakes. Even in his resurrected state the Lord has kept the appearance of those wounds just to remind us of what he is capable of doing for us. (See 3 Nephi 11:15.)

The ability to give our burdens to Christ is one of the Lord's greatest gifts. Faith, hope, charity, as well as all other divine attributes are enhanced by a heart that has been healed spiritually. On our day of judgment, each one of us will account for how we lived and the influence we had on those around us. To be repentant and to be found with the kind of heart capable of forgiving is to invite the highest level of mercy the Savior is able to give at our day of reckoning. To gain his approval is to be like him. In the words of William Shakespeare: "Wilt thou draw near the nature of the gods? Draw near them then in being merciful. Sweet mercy is nobility's true badge." (*Titus Andronicus*, Act 1, sc. 1, l.117–119.) A forgiving heart is nobility's truest badge.

CHAPTER 12

Maintaining a
Spiritual Pace

K. DOUGLAS BASSETT

The 1865 pocket billiard championship of the world is an unexpected place to find a teaching moment. The large group that crowded into the Washington Hall ballroom in Rochester, New York, received more than the anticipated show of cue-ball wizardry. None could have predicted the end result of the match between Louis Fox and John Deery, who were playing for a purse of over $40,000.

As the game progressed Louis Fox displayed his magic by running up 300 points while giving no indication of losing his hold of the green felt table. A passerby may have mistaken the silent hush of the crowd as religious reverence as the spectators viewed Fox's skill in silent fascination. With a few balls left to dispose of, his victory was a forgone conclusion.

Fox, a handsome man, looked the part of a champion as he dominated the slate table. His confidence was contrasted by his opponent, who sat, dejected, near the crowd, anticipating his defeat.

With Fox leaning across the table to put away the last few balls, the moment was interrupted by a common housefly that just happened to choose the most important moment in Fox's life to land on the cue ball. As the crowd quietly looked on, he sent the intruder on its way with a gracious wave of his hand over the white ball.

Totally in control he leaned over the table to finish off the match. Like a boomerang, the fly circled back and landed atop the cue ball. A fleet murmur of laughter spread through the crowd as the champion, still in command, shoed his unwanted companion away from the table.

But the crowd abandoned restraint as the fly returned the third time. Unnerved at having to share the spotlight with this uninvited creature, Louis Fox lost his composure and stabbed at the fly with his cue stick. With the skill of a surgeon he accomplished his goal of getting rid of the pest, but in the process he nicked the ivory ball just enough to move it one quarter of an inch. His haste had cost him his turn at the table.

While his opponent, John Deery, stepped up and took advantage of his rebirth, Fox staggered away from center stage and leaned against the wall like a despondent statue. Making the most of his chance, Deery gathered his skills and strung together a superb display of shots, enough to run out the match and capture the championship and the lion's share of $40,000.

Louis Fox never stroked a cue stick again. He left the ballroom that night like a man drunken in despair. The next day his corpse was discovered floating in the river, Fox having succeeded in an apparent suicide attempt. His life had been perfectly focused on the goal of the world championship, but his dream was thwarted by an opponent for which he was totally unprepared—a common housefly. This tiny fly had helped decide the billiard championship of the world and had cost the life of the man who lost it. (See Mac Davis, *Sports Shorts*, pp. 1–2.)

Size has often been compared to influence; for example, the larger the size, the greater the influence. David proved this a myth as he confronted Goliath. Alma pointed this out to his son Helaman when he said, "By small and simple things are great things brought to pass." (Alma 37:6.)

Perhaps the best example of this would be the influence of the Holy Ghost. While it has been described as a still, small voice, we must not be fooled by the word *small*. This still, small voice has the power to transform a natural man to a child of God (see Mosiah 3:19); when it is withdrawn from a missionary, he is stripped of power (see Mormon 1:14–16); a strong army is left helpless at its departure (see Mormon 2:26); and when a nation has lost its influence that nation is ripe for destruction (see Helaman 13:8).

Just as Louis Fox had never considered the influence of a fly in his life because of its comparative size, the average man can go an entire lifetime without recognizing the influence of this still, small voice. Unlike the fly in the life of Louis Fox, the Holy Ghost will not interrupt our lives to the point of challenging our agency. We will find it when we seek it, and as the people of the Book of Mormon discovered, it has the ability to pierce us to the very center and cause our hearts to burn, ultimately bringing our souls to Christ. (See 3 Nephi 11:3–5.)

RUNNING TOO FAST

Many years ago I had an enlightening conversation with one of my students. He was a very sharp and sober-minded young man in his mid-twenties. He shared with me this personal observation: "In my early years growing up in the Church I had a perception that if I kept myself worthy I would automatically recognize the promptings from the Holy Ghost. I believed that by serving a worthy mission and by being married properly in the temple I would understand the workings of the Spirit better than I do. But sometimes I really don't know the difference between my own thoughts and the promptings of the Spirit."

My immediate response was to reinforce that worthiness is merely the foundation in gaining a relationship with the Spirit. His misunderstanding regarding the companionship of the Spirit came from the fact that he did not see that his personal responsibility extended beyond just being clean.

I referred him to the Book of Mormon prophet Jacob, who was preparing to teach the allegory of Zenos when he stated, "I will unfold this mystery unto you; if I do not, by any means, get *shaken from my firmness in the Spirit, and stumble because of my over anxiety.*" (Jacob 4:18; italics added.) Here was a prophet in the temple preaching the doctrines of the kingdom, and he was concerned about losing the Spirit over something as simple as anxiety. Even in his role as prophet, Jacob could not be in tune to the promptings of the Spirit when anxiety was a part of his life.

I asked my friend if he had adopted any negative attitudes or emotions, which although they may not be sins in and of themselves, still might cause him to be insensitive to the whisperings of this still, small voice. We reviewed a number of the circumstances and adverse emotions that might distance him from the Spirit. He was surprised to learn that things such as stress from the relentless demands of the clock, pressures to compete, insecurity, worry, fear of failure, academics, excessive workload, and many other things, all can distance us from recognizing the whisperings of the still, small voice.

Gradually he began to see that he had been under the false assumption that his sole responsibility was to avoid major sin so the Holy Ghost would naturally integrate itself into his life. I tried to help him understand that it takes more than being repulsed by sin, we also need to be proactive toward the Spirit, even down to the very pace of our lives. Only then can we trust that our feelings are in tune with the Holy Ghost.

To illustrate this idea of pace, my student and I looked at a portion of King Benjamin's marvelous discourse to the Nephites in the latter stages of his life. He gave them a key to traveling through life at a pace that would allow the Spirit to be their companion: "And see that all these things are done in wisdom and order; for it is not requisite that a man should run faster than he has strength. And again, it is expedient that he should be diligent, that thereby he might win the prize; therefore, all things must be done in order." (Mosiah 4:27.)

We gave special attention to the dynamics of what this prophet was saying to the Nephites, as well as to ourselves. It was not enough for my friend to do what was right, he also needed to conduct his life at a pace that was "diligent" and at the same time did not cause him to "run faster than he [had] strength."

There is a pace to living that allows the Lord to be our guide as we keep the commandments. It is ironic to me that so many of us may be able to answer all the temple recommend questions in a positive way and be worthy to enter the temple, yet the very pace of our lives distances us from the daily companionship of that Spirit we so desire. This was certainly true of my young friend. I used King Benjamin's words to remind him that life's race is not a sprint but a long-distance run. Unlike a sprinter, a long distance runner must be mindful of a pace that allows him to finish strong, or, as the scriptures say, "endure unto the end." (1 Nephi 13:37.)

I shared with him the Lord's counsel to Joseph Smith following the loss of the 116 page manuscript: "Do not run faster or labor more than you have strength." (D&C 10:4.)

My young friend responded, "What about President Spencer W. Kimball's encouragement to 'lengthen our stride'?"

I reminded him that even a long-distance runner must lengthen his stride; he just doesn't do it so early in the race that he has no second wind and thus exhausts himself and cannot finish the race. We opened the New Testament and read, "Let us run with *patience* the race that is set before us." (Hebrews 12:1; italics added.) I reviewed with him that patience is not required in a sprint.

I asked my young friend to join me in the basketball gym so I could make a point regarding this idea of spiritual pace. I stood on the baseline under the basket and had him do the same on the opposite end of the court under the opposing basket. I then had him sprint from where he was to the baseline where I was standing. I asked him to give his very best effort, to which he complied. I recorded the time of his mad dash using a stopwatch. Next, I had him repeat the procedure with one notable exception—this time he was to try to run just as fast as he had before, while at the same time dribbling a basketball.

The first few attempts ended when he lost control of the ball by "running faster than he was able" to maintain his companionship with the basketball. He had to repeat the sprint a few times in order to complete the task. As hard as he tried in his efforts at dribbling the ball, he was not able to duplicate his time recorded on his first sprint without the ball.

I reviewed with him the fact that his desire for speed rather than control was not only the cause of his losing the ball, but also possibly the cause of his lack of oneness with the Holy Ghost. Speed at the expense of control is not a realistic goal in basketball or in life. I identified how the task of dribbling a ball down the court is made more difficult when there is an opposing team present, with the desire to strip the ball from him. In life this opposing team, led by Satan, is trying just as hard to strip us of the companionship of the Spirit.

This is easy to recognize by observing young players dribbling the ball. They rarely succeed in controlling the ball because they repeatedly try to shove it into the floor rather than master the art of control. There is an ideal rhythm in bouncing the ball off the floor. In a sense it is the ball that dictates the pace in which we master the art of dribbling down the floor. With head down, totally unaware of his surroundings, the ineffective dribbler tries to plow through the opposition. If he does not lose control of the ball on his own, the opposition will surely accomplish the task. I asked my friend if this was not a little like his approach to life. I reminded him that like the effective dribbler, we must be in control of ourselves in order to be at one with the Spirit. The ball has its own pace, and an effective player must conform to it, in order to have the ball as his companion. And in life, it is the individual who must conform to the Spirit, not the other way around.

We read these words of Elder Henry B. Eyring, which were presented to the students of BYU: "[The still, small voice] is so quiet that if you are noisy inside, you won't hear it." (*1988–89 Devotional and Fireside Speeches*, p. 16.) What a challenge—to learn how to give 100 percent of our energies and at the same time conduct ourselves at a pace in which we can feel the whisperings of the still, small voice. It is so easy to have an accelerated pace in life that leaves us both exhausted and inefficient. On another occasion Elder Eyring said, "Now, I testify it is a small voice. It whispers, not shouts." (*Ensign*, May 1991, p. 67.)

I'm not sure if I communicated with my young friend as effectively as I had hoped, but at the very least it was a good reminder of the need to be in control of the pace of life in order to be sensitive to the whisperings of the still, small voice. I am convinced that if Satan can't influence us to sin outright, the next best thing he can do is fill our lives with so much clutter that he becomes our silent partner, so silent that too often we are unaware of his influence in speeding up the pace of our lives and camouflaging our priorities.

Running Too Fast in the Kingdom

An experience related by President Harold B. Lee illustrates why our *spiritual pace* is so important:

> A few weeks ago, President McKay related to the Twelve an interesting experience, . . . He said it is a great thing to be responsive to the whisperings of the Spirit, and we know that when these whisperings come it is a gift and our privilege to have them. *They come when we are relaxed and not under pressure of appointments.* I want you to mark that down. The President then took occasion to relate an experience in the life of Bishop Wells, former member of the Presiding Bishopric. A son of Bishop Wells was killed in Emigration Canyon on a railroad track. . . . His boy was run over by a freight train. Sister Wells was inconsolable. She mourned during the three days prior to the funeral, received no comfort at the funeral, and

was in a rather serious state of mind. One day soon after the funeral services while she was lying on her bed *relaxed*, still mourning, she says that her son appeared to her and said, "Mother, do not mourn, do not cry. I am alright." He told her that she did not understand how the accident happened and explained that he had given the signal to the engineer to move on, and then made the usual effort to catch the railing on the freight train, but as he attempted to do so his foot caught on a root and he failed to catch the hand rail, and his body fell under the train. It was clearly an accident. Now listen. He said that as soon as he realized that he was in another environment he tried to see his father, but couldn't reach him. *His father was so busy with the duties in his office he could not respond to his call.* Therefore, he had come to his mother. He said to her, "You tell father that all is well with me, and I want you not to mourn anymore." (In Bassett, *Latter-day Commentary on the Book of Mormon*, p. 210.)

Bishop Wells coped with the death of his son by going back to work. Even though this was the Lord's work, apparently this good man could not be reached by his departed son because of the *anxious* pace of his life. On the other hand, his wife was alone in the attitude of pondering and was able to be visited by her son. Is there not a lesson in this for each of us regarding the proper pace in our own lives? We cannot excuse "running faster than we are able" with the explanation that we are doing the Lord's work. How can we be doing the Lord's work without the companionship of the Spirit? Elder Boyd K. Packer said: "Too many of us are like those whom the Lord said '. . . were baptized with fire and with the Holy Ghost, *and they knew it not.*' (3 Nephi 9:20; italics added.) Imagine that. 'And they knew it not.' It is not unusual for one to have received the gift [of the Holy Ghost] and not really know it. I fear this supernal gift is being obscured by programs and activities and schedules and so many meetings. There are so many places to go, so many things to do in this noisy world. We can be too busy to pay attention to the promptings of the Spirit. The voice of the Spirit is a still, small voice—a voice that is *felt* rather than heard. It is a spiritual voice that comes into the mind as a thought put into your heart." (*Ensign*, May 2000, p. 8.)

I am reminded of the story of an elderly man who rested by the side of a much-traveled path. A much younger man stopped for a minute next to the old gentleman. In the course of conversation the younger man asked, "How has life in America changed most?"

The old man replied simply, "Speed." Pausing for a moment to think, he continued, "It's killing us. You have to make a part of your life in which you slow down. The world won't do it for you."

Once again, we can look to the Book of Mormon for evidence of the need for an appropriate spiritual pace to our lives. After the Nephites had established themselves in the land of Zarahemla, Zeniff and a group of men were sent to spy on the Lamanites who occupied the Land of Nephi, which had been vacated by the Nephites. To this point in the Book of Mormon, the Nephites and Lamanites had never lived together in harmony. Even the efforts of the Nephites to preach the gospel to them had failed. (See Jacob 7:24; Enos 1:20.)

Zeniff introduces himself to us by referring to himself as being "over-zealous." (See Mosiah 9:3.) In this same verse, he gives us a hint of what this word means: "We were slow to remember the Lord our God." For our purposes, and in the context of Zeniff's experience, we may define over-zealous as making decisions too quickly without approval of those in authority and without full consideration of the consequences of our actions. An over-zealous person is quick to do his own will and slow to consider the Lord's will.

After some turbulent moments as a spy, Zeniff proved to be an over-zealous colonizer by gathering a group of Nephites to travel back to the land of Nephi to live adjacent to the Lamanites. (See Mosiah 9:1–3.) The Book of Mormon gives no hint that Zeniff sought out the will of the Lord in prayer or even a visit with his spiritual leaders concerning this risky decision to move. It is not hard for anyone who has a sense of the relationship between the Nephites and Lamanites at that point in history to see the potential downside in his decision to move to the land of the Lamanites without seeking appropriate confirmation. But without consideration of the consequences of such a move, Zeniff and his colony moved forward.

It took Zeniff twelve years to wake up to the realization that his over-zealous choice was about to bear bitter fruit, like a marriage without the proper foundation. In the first battle between Zeniff's people and the Lamanites, 3,043 of the Lamanites were killed, while 279 Nephites lost their lives. (See Mosiah 9:19.) Following the second recorded battle, Zeniff wrote that there were so many dead among the Lamanites that "we did not number them." (Mosiah 10:20.) All of this because one man and his followers were in the wrong place at the wrong time. This sadness continued for almost two more generations, until these Nephites were able to return to Zarahemla.

Compare this over-zealous decision-making to that of the sons of Mosiah. These sons wanted to preach the gospel to the Lamanites who lived in this same land of Nephi that Zeniff's colony had been in turmoil with for many years. The scriptures tell us that these missionaries "plead with their father many days that they might go up to the land of Nephi." (Mosiah 28:5.) I'm sure Mosiah had the kind of fears that Zeniff should have had regarding this venture. He did not consent to their journey until he "inquired of the Lord if he should let his sons go." (Mosiah 28:6.) The Lord gave his approval and promised, "I will deliver thy sons out of the hands of the Lamanites." (Mosiah 28:7.) Only then the prophet "granted that they might go." (Mosiah 28:8.) What a difference between the manner in which these sons made their decision to go to the land of Nephi and Zeniff's earlier decision! The former choice resulted in thousands of deaths while the latter resulted in thousands of converts. Zeniff's over-zealous adventures stand as proof that the hardest thing to have faith in is the Lord's timing. Note also that the sons of Mosiah went to the Lamanites with a much different mission in mind than did Zeniff.

There is much for us to learn from Zeniff about making sure that the decisions of our lives are made at a time when we are operating within a pace that has wisdom and order, in which we are not over-zealously running faster than we are able. (See Mosiah 4:27.)

To consider the consequences of over-zealous choices, we need to look no further than a young man on his way to the temple to be sealed to his sweetheart. His things-to-do list of the morning has made him late for his appointed time in the temple. Is he worthy? Yes. Is his over-zealous attempt at beating the clock accompanied by the Spirit? Not likely. His over-zealousness leads to hasty decisions and over-corrections, which potentially could lead to an accident, and even the loss of life. As he is pulled over by a police officer, his worthiness for the temple cannot be used as a trump card against his over-zealous driving. Overwhelmed with the stresses of life, his decision making behind the wheel leaves the officer no other choice than to categorize him as a speeder.

Once again we are reminded of one of the great truths regarding the Holy Ghost: Speed is not a worthy substitute for control. There is little doubt that Zeniff grew in righteousness as he was humbled by the Lamanites (see Mosiah 9:17–18; 10:10–11, 19); but the sad tragedy in his story comes from those moments when his decisions were flawed simply due to his running too fast.

As a missionary in southern England, I once read a story of a champion boxer named Hammering Hank Armstrong. He had the reputation of being relentless, literally hammering his opponent until he wore him down. He was asked by a reporter how he had developed this style of fighting. He said his fighting style had its roots in an experience that occurred many years earlier when he was a child growing up in poverty.

Hank had many older brothers and sisters, and a mother who

disciplined with a stern but loving hand. His mother had a Bantam rooster that had become a pet, almost a companion to her. All the children knew the rule was "hands off" concerning that squawking bird.

One day little Hank found it just too irresistible to avoid tormenting the rooster. He began chasing the bird, not knowing what he would do if he ever caught up to it. The rooster ran around the outside of the house shrieking and flapping its wings with little Henry Armstrong in hot pursuit, all the while his brothers and sisters forming an audience at the front window. As Hank continually passed in front of them, they observed the chase with great interest due to the fact that their mother was standing behind them, with arms folded, in a manner that could only mean trouble for Hank.

The chase eventually reached its climax when the bird collapsed in a dead heap at the young victor's feet. This unexpected conclusion to the event brought total silence rather than cheers from the youthful onlookers. Past experience had taught them that the best part of the show—the fireworks display known as Mom's temper—was about to begin. They were all aware of the "hands off" rule, and were anxiously anticipating that momma was going to let Henry have it real good.

Sure enough, their mother slowly approached the dead fowl with Hank standing next to it in frozen fear. She picked up the pet and then held her hand firmly to the back of her guilty son's shirt. All of this was accomplished in total silence.

Turning to the rest of her children, she broke the silence. "Hank deserves a woopin' and you're hopin' he gets it. But there's a greater lesson to be learned here." She continued, "I want to tell each of you that if you want to be successful in life—if you truly wish to rise up out of the ghetto—set goals and then go after them just like little Hank did this rooster."

She had her audience and she took full advantage of their attention. "Get after whatever you want in this world with a passion, until it lies at your feet like my Bantam rooster."

This was one of those rare teaching moments in parenting where everyone—oldest to youngest—received the message and understood it fully.

Referring back to the experience, Hank Armstrong said, "That is how I developed the name Hammering Hank. I just pursued my opponent in the ring the way I pursued the rooster, and true to my momma's words, they eventually wound up at my feet."

As a missionary, this story meant a great deal to me and motivated me to continue tracting when the weather raged and the harvest seemed empty. But as the years have progressed the lesson from this story has been tempered for me just a bit. Once again we can look to the Book of Mormon for application: In situations when we relentlessly pursue unworthy goals, we can become over-zealous like Zeniff. He acquired his dream of living in the land of his choice with the same energy that little Hank attacked the rooster, only to find that his dream became a nightmare when he realized that he was chasing the wrong "rooster." It is well for us to take the time to know we are pursuing the right "rooster" before we begin moving our feet. Zeniff represents those who follow the approach of shooting a gun with the over-zealous attitude we'll call "ready, fire, aim." It is easy to see how lives can be tragically altered or even ended with this approach. Such was the case for Zeniff. I have learned by my own mistakes that the relentless approach to life's challenges must be tempered with the counsel of "wisdom and order" given by King Benjamin. (Mosiah 4:27.) We must be willing to fight life's battles with all our efforts, but it is well to make sure our energy is not used up in the first round, or even worse, wasted on unworthy battles.

Chasing life's roosters may drop the rooster, as Hank Armstrong discovered; but life is filled with one rooster after another, and if we run at full speed all the time, eventually it will be we, rather than the rooster, who will drop. Time and experience teach us that our best efforts are required in all worthwhile endeavors, but planning and expending appropriate energy, accompanied by a clear head and a heart at peace with itself, allow us to defeat our roosters without defeating ourselves. It is interesting how the virtue of relentless pursuit can turn so quickly to the vice of over-zealousness by running so fast we cannot endure to the end.

CONCLUSION

President Thomas S. Monson has spoken many times to the Saints regarding the purpose of the Holy Ghost and the need for each of us to have its companionship. Many years ago he wrote these words to the members of the Church:

> Those of you who have been in the service know that sonar is the device that warns of an impending vehicle, ship, or other obstacle. Sound waves are monitored. The operator becomes accustomed to listening for a repetitive beep. When it follows other than the normal pattern, he knows danger is at hand and can warn the ship's officers so that the course can be altered.
>
> When I was in school, many young men had white side-wall tires on their automobiles. These automobiles were equipped with what we called whiskers—a little metal device attached to the fender of the car. As the car pulled in against the curb, those whiskers would hit the curb and vibrate, echoing inside the car; and they warned the driver he could not go any closer to the curb without damaging his tires.
>
> If man can invent sonar to warn against disaster, and if he can invent whiskers to put on automobile fenders for the protection of white sidewall tires, doesn't it seem reasonable that the Lord would place a warning device within his precious children, to warn them when they are on a detour from his pathway? . . . I refer to the still, small voice, the Holy Ghost. (BYU Speeches of the Year, 1963, p. 4.)

As a young boy I had the wonderful privilege of sharing a bedroom with my older brother Bob. He was in high school and introduced me to many new things that made bunking with him a wonderful adventure. Among his many talents was that of being a great auto mechanic. At the age of sixteen he took an old wreck and made it into what seemed to me to be the perfect car. Just like the car in Elder Monson's story, this car had whitewall tires with a whisker just off the lower end of the right front fender. When I asked him what the whisker was for, he told me to get into the car and he would show me. He thought he was teaching me about the car, but neither he nor I realized at the time that he was teaching me something of much greater significance.

He drove the car for a few blocks then said, "Stop talking and listen." He then reached over and turned off the radio. Slowing the car down, he began to ease the car toward the curb on the right side of the road. When we heard the sound of the whisker scraping against the curb, he then straightened the direction of the car so that it parked parallel to the curb.

As time has passed, I have been able to see the spiritual application of the whisker, as compared to the whisperings of the still, small voice of the Spirit. Of what value is the whisker if you are driving so fast you cannot maneuver the car in such a way as to save the whitewall tires? Of what value is the whisker if the music and the commotion in the car is such that the still, small sound of the whisker cannot be heard? The proper preparation for the function of the whisker is to slow down, turn down the volume in the car, and listen. Is there not an obvious connection with this and the listening to the still, small voice of the Spirit?

Can we not see the same connection with sonar and the submarine? A submarine is blind; the operators within it maneuver the craft safely by responding to the rhythm of the beeps given off by sonar. When the pattern is not within the normal range, the operator knows to slow down and make the necessary corrections in order to have the craft move safely through the water. Of what value is sonar if there is too much noise and commotion within the submarine? Also, of what value is sonar if the submarine is moving so fast or out of control that the craft cannot safely adjust in time to the warning beeps of the sonar?

Once again, the application to the Holy Ghost is obvious. The still, small voice of the Spirit is ever-present, but is the pace and the noise in our lives conducive to responding in a timely manner to its promptings?

Any discussion about the companionship of the Holy Ghost must begin with the foundation of worthiness. But we must also speak of having control of those things which, left unchecked, would only serve to clutter and bring unnecessary noise into our lives. In this manner Satan becomes our silent partner in blocking the signals given to us by the still, small whisperings of the Holy Ghost.

CHAPTER 13

SPIRITUAL WAGES

K. DOUGLAS BASSETT

At 6:25 A.M. on Sunday, June 17, 1984, Swale, the 1984 Kentucky
Derby and Belmont winner, went for a routine gallop around Belmont
Park. His exercise rider, Ron McKenzie, said, "He went just the way he
always did, kind and willing."

After the run, Swale returned to the backstretch where, as usual,
he was watered down. Suddenly the black colt reared and fell back-
ward. Within moments the horse was dead. It was a shocking development, and one that was never completely explained. A three-hour
autopsy revealed no clue as to the cause of death. The colt, by all
appearances, seemed to be sound and healthy.

I love horses; but I don't follow horse racing closely and I hadn't
heard of this champion until I read the paper the day after his death. My
interest in the thoroughbred actually had nothing to do with the fact
that he was one of the most famous and valuable horses in the world.

My interest arose when I read about the response of Swale's owner
to news of his death. The owner showed little remorse and reportedly
said, "It's not every day a person discovers he has made five million dollars." (According to the Phoenix *Gazette*, Swale was insured for closer
to ten million dollars.)

While reading this seemingly callous reply, I couldn't help being staggered by the dollar signs. As I pondered the value of Swale to its owner, I wondered if others who had worked directly with the horse saw his worth as more than just the wages he brought to them.

As I continued thinking about this, I sadly came to the conclusion that the world believes much the same as Swale's owner—that the worth of an individual can be measured in dollars and cents. Indeed, when many of us think of wages—or the rewards our property and ownership bring to us—we naturally accept that those wages will come in the form of money.

A careful study of the Book of Mormon, however, teaches us that there is a lot more to the word *wages* than money. The Nephite scriptural text demonstrates that *wages* can also be considered an increase from a spiritual source.

Mormon added an interesting insight in his commentary regarding the death of thousands during the battles between the Nephites and the Lamanites. He indicated that their eternal reward was given "according to the spirit which they listed to obey, whether it be a good spirit or a bad one. For every man receiveth *wages of him whom he listeth to obey.*" (Alma 3:26–27; italics added; see also D&C 29:45.)

Alma reminded the Nephites that if they chose to "bringeth forth evil works, . . . [they] must receive [the devil's] *wages.*" (Alma 5:41–42; italics added.) This concept of receiving wages from a spiritual source is found numerous times in the Bible as well as the Nephite text.

Jesus taught that those who harvest souls "receiveth wages." (John 4:36.) Peter wrote of a wicked man who "loved the wages of unrighteousness." (2 Peter 2:15.) And Paul wrote that "the wages of sin is death; but the gift of God is eternal life through Jesus Christ our Lord." (Romans 6:23.)

ANGELS

In the Book of Mormon a portion of the spiritual wages received by those who were righteous was the companionship and the ministering of angels in their lives. The prophet Nephi (named after the son of Lehi) had such great faith that "angels did minister unto him daily." (3 Nephi 7:18.) The prophet Mormon's words bear witness to this theme: "Angels [have not] ceased to minister unto the children of men." (Moroni 7:29.) On another occasion Alma preached that "angels are declaring [the gospel] unto many at this time in our land." (Alma 13:24.)

Referring to this subject, Elder Jeffrey R. Holland said, "One of the things that will become more important in our lives the longer we live is the reality of angels, their work and their ministry. I refer here not alone to the angel Moroni but also to those more personal ministering angels who are with us and around us, empowered to help us and who do exactly that. . . . Perhaps more of us could literally, or at least figuratively, behold the *angels around us* if we would but awaken from our stupor and hear the words God is trying to tell us. . . . . I believe we need to speak of and believe in and bear testimony of the *ministry of angels* more than we sometimes do. They constitute one of God's great methods of witnessing through the veil." (*Ensign*, Jan. 1996, pp. 16–17; italics added.)

In keeping with Elder Holland's counsel "to speak of and bear testimony of the ministry of angels," I carefully share the following experience involving my wife, Arlene. This is a portion of her journal involving the last few hours of our six-year-old son's mortal life:

> My heart was heavy thinking that Boyd would not be with us, yet I thrilled for Boyd that a more peaceful life was awaiting him.
>
> When I arrived at the hospital, Boyd was laboring much more in his breathing, but resting well. . . . I so wanted to talk to Boyd again! It had only been one night, but I already missed hearing his voice. Doug looked so tired, so I stayed with Boyd while he went home and showered.
>
> I sat by Boyd's bed and held his hand. His blanket was next

to him, but not clutched in his hand like I was used to seeing when he slept. I watched his breathing while my mind wandered. I saw myself pregnant with Boyd, and felt the excitement that Doug and I had had. I saw myself in the cold labor room and I recalled the delivery. The unquenchable joy of having a son. The early morning feedings and the struggles with keeping his food down. His being diagnosed with cystic fibrosis at two months and our tremendous feelings of remorse. I had given him life and then I could not provide milk and love for him to continue his life.

I saw his sweet countenance that won the hearts of everyone when he was very small. I saw his happy babyhood— crawling and scrambling when he was excited. I saw his sensitivity to others. Even as a child he showed great interest when his playmates were hurt or crying. . . . I saw him riding his little blue bike with the training wheels. He took such great pride in peddling with one foot. I saw the special times when we read stories. I recalled the times he asked if he could go play with his friend Jenni next door. How many times had he asked to go knock on her door? I wouldn't hear that again—I wouldn't hear his cute little voice again.

I saw him sewing little pillows and the many times he interrupted me to thread a needle or tie a knot. I never got impatient when he interrupted me to thread a needle, because I was so touched at the joy and pride he received from this activity.

My thoughts were broken as Boyd suddenly gasped for air. He continued to gasp deeply as if he were scratching for air. His chest was heaving more as I silently watched, with emotion swelling inside me. This was more than I could bear. Tears came quickly and I put my forehead in my hands and sobbed.

I felt my mother's spirit close to me like I have felt in so many important events in my life. [Arlene's mother passed away when she was nine years old.]

I spoke to her, "Mother, I didn't have the privilege of you raising me completely, but I have felt you helping me many times. Please, please come take care of my boy!"

Instantly, I felt completely calm and assured. The emotions of despair, crying out, and then calm had come so quickly that I knew there was more than just human involvement. I felt there were other spirits close. My mother, grandma, Doug's father, and perhaps others were giving support to Boyd and me. (See Bassett, *Kisses at the Window*, p. 61–63.)

This gathering of loved ones in an environment of comfort should not be surprising to members of the Church. The Prophet Joseph Smith spoke of events such as my wife's: "The spirits of the just . . . are not far from us, and know and understand our thoughts, feelings, and emotions, and are often pained therewith." (*Teachings of the Prophet Joseph Smith*, p. 326.)

One of the basic principles taught in the Book of Mormon is that those in the spirit world have a constant awareness of us in mortality. Elder Holland further taught: "I am convinced that one of the profound themes of the Book of Mormon is the role and prevalence and central participation of angels in the gospel story. . . . No document in all this world teaches that principle so clearly and so powerfully as does the Book of Mormon." (*Ensign*, Jan. 1996, pp. 16–17.)

It may be comforting to know that our relatives who have passed on are a part of the angels who minister to us from the other side of the veil. Referring to those angels, President Joseph F. Smith said, "They are not strangers, but from the ranks of our kindred, friends, and fellow-beings, and fellow-servants." (*Gospel Doctrine*, pp. 435–36.) On another occasion he said, "We move and have our being in the presence of heavenly messengers and of heavenly beings. We are not separate from them. . . . We are closely related to our kindred, to our ancestors, . . . who have preceded us into the spirit world. . . . They know us better than we know them. . . . I claim that *we live in their presence*, they see us, . . . they love us now more than ever." (Conference Report, Apr. 1916, pp. 2–3; italics added.)

Elder Parley P. Pratt wrote of occasions when angels minister to us, even while we sleep: "God has revealed many important instructions and warnings to men by means of dreams. . . . Their kindred spirits, their guardian angels then hover about them with the fondest affection, the most anxious solicitude. Spirit communes with spirit, thought meets thought, soul blends with soul. . . . *In this situation we frequently hold communication with our departed father, mother, brother, sister, . . .* whose affections for us, being rooted and grounded in the eternal elements, or issuing from under the sanctuary of Love's eternal fountain, can never be lessened or diminished by death, distance of space, or length of years." (*Key to the Science of Theology*, pp. 120–21; italics added.)

In her mid-teens, my niece Janae Howells was diagnosed with a rare form of leukemia. She was sent to the UCLA Hospital where a painful medical procedure was to take place. She would receive a bone marrow transplant from her one-year-old sister, Angela. Her mother, LaRue Howells, would accompany the two of them from their home in Salt Lake City.

On the morning of the transplant, LaRue's heart was ready to break in expectation of the day's events. Picture her dilemma—not only the natural concern regarding the procedure itself, but the fact that her daughters were in separate rooms until the event would take place, both needing her support, and the impossibility of being there for her daughters as completely as their needs required.

Her tender feelings overflowed into prayer, "Dear Father in Heaven, as you know, I lost my own mother when I was young. I have felt her support at many difficult times in my life. If it is possible, could you send her to my daughter Janae for comfort?"

The day progressed into a never-ending stream of needles, tubes, and discomfort—but as with all days, this one finally drew to a close. After tucking in her youngest daughter, LaRue walked down the hospital hall to see how Janae was feeling. She was surprised to find her in such good spirits.

"Mom, the most wonderful thing happened to me this morning. While waiting for the day's activities to begin, I was so nervous I got out of bed and washed my hair. I lay back down—still nervous as before."

She continued, "Suddenly I felt two hands stroking my hair. I looked around but I could see no one. The hands were so gentle I felt no fear. The stroking of my hair continued until I was completely calm. For the first time I was able to relax with no anxieties about the transplant. Immediately after I thanked this person who had brought me such comfort, the stroking of my hair stopped. Mom, do you have any idea who this person was?"

Their hearts were full as LaRue related the humble prayer she had uttered that morning. Her conversation with Janae reinforced her belief that those spirits on the other side of the veil who have been true to the covenants that bind families continue the work of strengthening their families through the veil.

It may be well to bring up a caution on this subject: Though departed loved ones are doing what they can in our behalf from the other side of the veil, I am in no way attempting to nurture a preoccupation with communicating with dead relatives. I also do not suggest that we have the right and responsibility to summon spirits through the veil. The Lord is concerned infinitely more with saving our souls than with séances. As Elder Bruce R. McConkie warned, this type of angelic support comes only in "specific instances . . . , [and] by special assignment." (*Mormon Doctrine*, pp. 341–42.)

The words of President Joseph Fielding Smith also place the con-cept of guardian angels in perspective: "We have often heard of guardian angels attending us and many patriarchs have spoken of such protection. There are times no doubt when some unseen power directs us and leads us from harm. However, the true guardian angel given to every man who comes into the world is the Light of Truth or Spirit of Christ." (*Doctrines of Salvation*, 1:54.)

WAGES FROM THE DEVIL

Alma taught his son Helaman to be very careful with the dark works that had been recorded about the secret combinations inspired by Satan: "Keep [them] from this people, that they know them not, lest peradventure they should fall into darkness also." (Alma 37:27.) I have discovered in my teaching over the past thirty years that there is a great danger in speaking of the works inspired by Satan. Without meaning to, we can tickle inquisitive minds that have not yet chosen their spiri-tual course and lead them into "forbidden paths" without meaning to. (See 1 Nephi 8:28.)

President Joseph F. Smith said, "It is not necessary that our young people should know of the wickedness carried on in any place. Such knowledge is not elevating and it is quite likely that more than one young man can trace the first step of his downfall to a curiosity which led him into questionable places." (*Gospel Doctrine*, pp. 373.)

With this caution, I will try to issue a warning without advertising the adversary or his supporting cast. King Benjamin admonished the Nephites: "Beware lest there shall arise contentions among you, and ye list to obey the evil spirit, . . . for if he listeth to obey him, . . . he receiveth . . . his *wages*." (Mosiah 2:32–33; italics added.)

Regarding the third of the host of heaven that followed Satan, Samuel the Lamanite said, "We are surrounded by demons, yea, we are encircled about by the angels of him who hath sought to destroy our souls." (Helaman 13:37.)

In the Doctrine and Covenants we find similar counsel: "Pray always, . . . that you may escape the hands of the servants of Satan that do uphold his work." (D&C 10:5.)

President Wilford Woodruff warned the Saints concerning these "servants of Satan": "They have not bodies only as they enter the tabernacles of men. . . . There are many evil spirits amongst us, . . . There never was a prophet in any age of the world but what the devil was continually at his elbow. This was the case with Jesus himself. The devil followed him continually trying to draw him from his purposes and to prevent him carrying out the great work of God. . . . This same character was with the disciples as well as with their Master. *He is with the Latter-day Saints; and he or his emissaries are with all men trying to lead them astray.*" (*The Discourses of Wilford Woodruff*, p. 238; italics added.)

A story regarding music speaks of a portion of the "wages" offered by Satan and the work of his angels on this side of the veil. The following experience was shared with me by the Zirker family from Mesa, Arizona, many years ago. (See Bassett, *Kisses at the Window*, pp. 75–77.)

> The life of ten-year-old Bobby Jenkins seemed to be filled with turmoil. His parents were divorced and a short time later his father remarried a fine woman, but she just couldn't take the place of Bobby's real mother. To make matters worse, his oldest brother joined the Army.
>
> This left him at home with his fifteen-year-old brother, Timothy. He was the one person Bobby could rely on. They had been through so much together. Even though Tim was five years older, they were as close as brothers could be.
>
> Then one day Bobby received news which caused the bottom of his world to drop out. Tim had drowned in a senseless accident while swimming in a canal. In such a short space of time his parents divorced, his father remarried, his oldest brother joined the military, and now Tim was dead.

During the funeral, Bobby seemed to go numb. He had been hurt so many times that he just didn't want to feel again. Upon returning home from the funeral he made a decision: except for school and other necessary activities, he would remain in his room. He felt that in the seclusion of his bedroom he could not be hurt again. He made the decision that he would remain there except when his parents forced him to go to school. He insulated his feelings by turning on the radio to the hardest rock music he could find. Hour after hour for the next few days the music blared—even while he slept. With its loud and constant beat, he didn't have to think or even feel—he was just numb. He could now separate himself from the world that had hurt him so deeply.

His parents made the decision to give him some space for a little while before they would step in to help. After a few days of this, the noise from the radio made it impossible for his stepmother to sleep. In the middle of the night, while Bobby slept, she tiptoed into his room and turned off the radio. Recognizing that this gesture might initiate a struggle with her stepson, she decided to go to the kitchen and make his favorite breakfast.

A few hours later, he poked his head into the kitchen and asked, "Did you turn off my radio last night?"

Expecting the worst, she gently replied, "Yes, I did."

What came next was not the confrontation she had expected. Instead, Bobby sat down at the table and softly shared the feelings of his heart. "This morning when I woke up, Timmy appeared in my room. He was standing next to my bed. He told me he was happy and not to worry. He said the Church was true and I should start reading the Book of Mormon. He told me lots of things which really made me happy."

Bobby stopped just long enough to gain his composure,

then continued. "He said this was the fourth time he had received permission to visit me, but *he couldn't come into my room because of the type of music I had on the radio.*" With a hint of emotion in his voice, this ten-year-old boy said, "Thanks, for turning off my radio."

Bobby had learned a very important truth. His own brother could not communicate beyond the veil because of the spirits which accompanied the kind of music he was listening to. The "wages" he was receiving while listening to uninspired music had kept the door closed on the peace the Lord wished to send to him.

Many parents teach their children about unworthy music simply by stating that a particular kind of music is not good, with little regard to the spiritual consequences of that music. It may be wise to communicate to our children of the Book of Mormon concept of receiving "wages" from the spirits we list to obey. When we have the companionship of the Holy Ghost we also invite the companionship of those spirits from the other side of the veil who wish the best for our souls. On the other hand, when we participate in music or any activity that invites the Holy Ghost to depart, there is a new spiritual invitation sent out. This invitation may be answered by those spirits who followed Satan to this earth and who do not have our best interests at heart.

Elder George Q. Cannon said, "Until we can learn to control and resist those evil influences that are now invisible, I think it would be unprofitable to have the administration of [the Lord's] angels personally or visibly unto us." (*Gospel Truth*, p. 56.)

Most young people who express rebellion through violation of the counsel of the Lord's servants regarding the Word of Wisdom, music, morality, and so on, feel they are expressing their freedom. If they could only see through the veil to the spirits they are keeping company with by such behavior, would they not run for their eternal lives just for the opportunity to hold fast to the safety of the "iron rod"? (See 1 Nephi 8:19, 24, 30.) Can we not see the counterfeit nature of Satan's music in the world today? Elder Boyd K. Packer taught that these angels of the devil are "persuading us through the same channels that were established in order that we could receive the blessings of the Holy Ghost." (Satellite Broadcast, Mar. 5, 2000, Utah Valley State College.) Surely, music is one of those channels.

It has been my experience in watching the youth of Zion the past thirty years that we need to do whatever we can to let them understand that their choices, even in entertainment, do affect the spiritual company they keep from the other side of the veil.

An interesting sidelight to the Spirit of the Lord and its connection to music was reinforced over three decades ago in my mission in southern England by Elder Loren C. Dunn, who was a visiting General Authority at a zone conference. As the meeting began, he asked the mission president for the opportunity to express some of the feelings he was experiencing at the moment.

He stood in front of the missionaries and said, "Would all of the Elders called to the position of district leader please stand." One by one each was asked, "What is your favorite hymn?"

Six different district leaders chose separate hymns. There were songs of reverence and reflection such as "I Stand All Amazed" and rousing and spirited ones like "Ye Elders of Israel."

Elder Dunn then turned his attention to the rest of the missionaries seated in the chapel: "When I give the signal, I want all of you to sing the song chosen by your district leader." He continued, "And I want all of you to sing the hymns at the same time."

The instructions had barely sunk in when Elder Dunn signaled for the singing to begin. Eighty missionaries, representing six different districts, sang their hymns of praise—all at the same time. When all the verses were complete, the room was filled with an uncomfortable silence, as all the missionaries gazed toward Elder Dunn with the same thought. "Why were we asked to do such a humiliating thing?"

He looked into the faces of the confused and embarrassed missionaries and said, "What you just felt while singing these hymns is the same spirit I felt coming from you as I entered the chapel. Some of you need to rededicate yourselves so that we can all be singing the same song of service to the Lord."

Elder Dunn had done something that had completely caught the missionaries off guard. He had used the sacred hymns of Zion to illustrate that it is not enough just to sing good music, or just to be in the right place; our hearts must also be united in order to obtain the "wages" which are promised through the Spirit of the Lord.

President Wilford Woodruff spoke of the third of the host of heaven who followed Satan, and the protection offered us if we are united in the Lord's work: "Where are they? . . . They are in every city and hamlet wherein the inhabitants of the earth dwell, and especially where there are any Latter-day Saints. And whether there are one hundred or not to every man, woman, and child, there are enough of them, at least, to labor for our overthrow. . . . We cannot escape it. What will they do to you? They will try to make us do anything and everything that is not right. These devils would be very glad to . . . divide us one against the other. . . . We should, therefore, watch ourselves well. . . . And *unless we are united together, as has been said before, we are not the Lord's.*" (*Discourses of Wilford Woodruff*, p. 239; italics added.)

SAVED AS BY FIRE

We don't normally think of being saved or protected by contact with fire. However, the gospel introduces another kind of fire. Elder Mark E. Petersen said: "In the midst of all these tribulations *God will send fire from heaven*, if necessary, to destroy our enemies while we carry forward our work. . . . You do not need to fear about anybody. Just serve the Lord and keep his commandments and build the Kingdom, and as you do so you will be protected in these last days. God will have his hand over you, and you can plan your lives in confidence." (Conference Report, Oct. 1960, p. 82; italics added.)

The Book of Mormon helps us to understand what is meant by this "fire from heaven." In the book of Helaman we are introduced to two great missionaries who were named after the original Nephi and Lehi who settled the promised land. As Nephi and Lehi were preaching to the Lamanites they were cast into prison. After many days the Lamanites "went forth into the prison . . . that they might slay them." (Helaman 5:22.)

Mormon tells us that "Nephi and Lehi were encircled about *as if* by fire." (Helaman 5:23; italics added.) Notice the words "as if"; meaning that it wasn't fire as we would normally define it, but fire was the closest word that would describe it. This fire protected them (see Helaman 5:24) and eventually surrounded the Lamanites, whose hearts "were filled as if with fire." (Helaman 5:45). This experience initiated the conversion of almost the entire Lamanite nation. (See Helaman 5:50.)

In these last days we have been promised similar protection by fire as a Church and a nation. President Ezra Taft Benson said: "Yes, it was here under a free government . . . that protection was provided for his restored Church. Now God will not permit his base of operations— America—to be destroyed. He has promised protection to this land if we will but serve the God of the land. He has also promised protection to the righteous even, if necessary, to send *fire from heaven* to destroy their enemies. (Ether 2:12; 1 Nephi 22:17.) No, God's base of operations will not be destroyed. But it may be weakened and made less effective." (Conference Report, Apr. 1962, p. 104; italics added.)

Nephi explained that a time would come that "the righteous . . . shall be saved, even if it so be *as by fire.*" (1 Nephi 22:17.) He appears to be speaking of the Second Coming. However, the Latter-day prophets have taught that this protective fire also includes our day. Elder Dallin H. Oaks related this scripture to an experience he had in

Chicago, when he and his wife were driving home a sister from their ward:

> I enjoyed that protection one warm summer night on the streets of Chicago. . . . I parked at the curb outside this sister's apartment house and accompanied her into the lobby and up the stairs to her door. June remained in the car on 61st Street. . . . By the light of a nearby streetlight, I could see that the street was deserted except for three young men walking by.
>
> As I came to the driver's side and paused for June to unlock the door, I saw one of these young men running back toward me. . . . There was no time to get into the car and drive away before he came within range. . . . The young man pushed [a] gun against my stomach and said, "Give me your money." I took the wallet out of my pocket and showed him it was empty. . . . "Give me your car keys," he demanded. . . . He jabbed me in the stomach with his gun and said, "Do it, or I'll kill you." . . .
>
> When I refused, the young robber repeated his demands, this time emphasizing them with an angrier tone and more motion with his gun. . . . His gun wavered from my stomach until its barrel pointed slightly to my left. My arm was already partly raised, and with a quick motion I could seize the gun and struggle with him without the likelihood of being shot. . . . Just as I was about to make my move, I had a unique experience. I did not see anything or hear anything, but I *knew* something. I knew what would happen if I grabbed that gun. We would struggle, and I would turn the gun into that young man's chest. It would fire, and he would die. . . .
>
> I relaxed, and . . . I followed an impulse to put my right hand on his shoulder and give him a lecture. June and I had some teenage children at that time, and giving lectures came naturally.

"Look here," I said. "This isn't right. What you're doing just isn't right. . . . you could get killed or sent to jail for this."

With the gun back in my stomach, the young robber replied to my lecture by going through his demands for the third time. But this time his voice was subdued. When he offered the final threat to kill me, he didn't sound persuasive. When I refused again, he hesitated for a moment and then stuck the gun in his pocket and ran away. June unlocked the door, and we drove off, uttering a prayer of thanks. . . .

I am grateful that the Lord gave me the vision and strength to refrain from trusting in the arm of flesh and to put my trust in the protecting care of our Heavenly Father. *I am grateful for the Book of Mormon promise to us of the last days that "the righteous need not fear," for the Lord "will preserve the righteous by his power."* (1 Nephi 22:17.) (*Ensign*, Nov. 1992, pp. 39–40; italics added.)

As those of us who have lived many years ponder this often unseen protective fire from heaven, does not the Spirit whisper of those occasions in our lives when we have enjoyed this same promise. In the same talk, Elder Oaks taught: "Faithful Latter-day Saints are protected from the powers of the evil one and his servants until they have finished their missions in mortality. For some the mortal mission is brief, as with some valiant young men who have lost their lives in missionary service. But for most of us the mortal journey is long, and we continue our course *with the protection of guardian angels.*" (*Ensign*, Nov. 1992, p. 39; italics added.)

Awesome are the wages promised to those who keep the commandments and carry forth the work of the Lord here on the earth. Even in the darkest of times, when the pioneers suffered hardships beyond belief, President Brigham Young taught, "God has been and is our helper, and is on our right and left, and round about us like a wall of fire to defend this people, if they serve him with an undivided heart." (*Journal of Discourses*, 8:172.)

CONCLUSION

A friend of mine named Mac Thompson shared an experience he had many years ago as a contractor. He had been hired by an insurance company to repair a home that had received substantial water damage. After completing the job, he was asked by the man of the house to install an extra door for which he would pay the small wage of eighteen dollars.

When the job was finished, Mac approached him for the money. The home owner laughed and said, "I'm not going to pay you the money. It's not enough money for you to take me to court, so there is really no way you can collect it."

His stance was that of a man who had just declared "checkmate" on his opponent in a chess match.

Realizing he had little recourse, Mac's next move left the dishonest fellow with something to think about. "Before I leave, let me ask you a question. Is that all your soul is worth to you?" He continued with another question: "Would you sell your soul for eighteen dollars?"

The puzzled expression on the man's face gave my friend every reason to believe his words had had about as much impact as a leaf settling quietly to the ground. Assuming he was wasting his time, Mac climbed into his truck and began the short drive home.

He had been home just long enough to make a sandwich and settle on the couch when the doorbell rang. To his surprise, the latter-day scrooge he had just left stood in the doorway. This same fellow who had been so smug not too long before seemed to be accompanied by a different spirit as he stood at the front door. Even the tone of his voice was more subdued. "Here's the money I owe you. I've done a little thinking since you left my home, and I want you to know something." He continued, "My soul is worth more than eighteen dollars to me."

Hesitating for a moment, he said, "Thank you for bringing this to my attention." He then handed the money to a rather stunned contractor and headed for his vehicle with no further conversation.

The gospel invites each of us to do what my contractor friend did for that home owner—to see beyond the dollars and cents of this world and look to the actual worth of the soul. Our worth is greatly enhanced by the company we keep through the veil.

In the Doctrine and Covenants we read, "Remember the worth of souls is great in the sight of God." (18:10.) Those who are willing to submit their souls to Satan's "wages" personally devalue the "great worth" spoken of by the Lord, even to the point identified by the apostle Paul when he wrote, "The wages of sin is death." (Romans 6:23.) What an unbelievable devaluation of divine potential when a person trades exaltation for that which leads to spiritual death!

On a much larger scale, when each of us begins to see our worth as more than just financial, or even physical, we are stepping on to a path that will take us on a very special journey. At that very moment we open the door to wages that include not only the companionship of the Holy Ghost but also the support of angels whose sole desire is to unite us once again with our God.

The Old Testament prophet Elisha tried to bolster the courage of his servant who was troubled by the sheer number of those against them: "Fear not: for they that be with us are more than they that be with them." (2 Kings 6:16.) Elisha prayed that the Lord would open the eyes of the servant to see through the veil. The result was that the young man beheld "the mountain was full of horses and chariots of fire round about Elisha." (2 Kings 6:17.)

May all of us believe and live in such a way as to feel the wages we are receiving through the veil from the Spirit we list to obey.

THE BOOK OF MORMON: BRINGING US CLOSER TO GOD

K. DOUGLAS BASSETT

As a boy growing up in northern California, I struggled in my desires to read the scriptures. Somehow I never seemed to get much further than the first few pages of the Book of Mormon before I began to lose interest. I recall the many times my father would bear his testimony to me about this church being the true church of Jesus Christ, and how he came to gain that testimony by diligent reading and praying concerning the Book of Mormon. He told me that the day would come in my life when I would hunger to know if this church is true; he wanted me to know that the way to my own personal sacred grove was through this book. I listened to his message respectfully but without much interest in testing his theory; I just did not feel the need to accept the challenge at that time. In the life I was leading at the moment it just didn't seem important. My father was in the category of those spoken of in the scripture: "To some it is given by the Holy Ghost to know." (D&C 46:13.) While I seemed to be in the group that fed off them: "To others it is given to believe on their words." (D&C 46:14.)

So I grew up believing but not knowing for myself the truth of my father's words. I knew that he was honest; he said the Church was true—and that seemed to be enough for me, at least for the moment. Elder Heber C. Kimball's words spoken to the Saints well over one hundred years ago applied directly to my circumstances: "The time will come when no man nor woman will be able to endure on borrowed light. Each will have to be guided by the light within himself. If you do not have it, how can you stand?" (Orson F. Whitney, *Life of Heber C. Kimball*, p. 449.)

That time came for me on the first day I went door contacting in England as a full-time missionary in May of 1971. I had been tracting little more than an hour when an elderly lady answered our knock on her door. She listened politely as I said the words of introduction I had learned at the Missionary Training Center. Then she interrupted my speech by saying, "I'm not interested; I have my own faith."

I had been taught at the MTC how to react in this situation and immediately followed with the appropriate response. I did my best to bear testimony that this was the true church of Jesus Christ on the earth today and invited her to take the time to listen to the missionaries when they knocked on her door again. I then turned to walk away, feeling rather good that I had done just what I had learned at the MTC. However, my departure was interrupted by her words, which were delivered like one of my high school coaches under stress, "Young man, come back here!" This was delivered as an order, not an invitation. She was obviously intent on making her point to me face to face.

She took a step toward me, placing a long, rather twisted finger close to my nose so there would not be any misunderstanding between us. She chose her words carefully and delivered them with the deliberate style of an authority figure laying down the law. "Before you go I want you to know something." She continued, "I know that the Methodist Church is the true church of Jesus Christ on the earth today."

Almost as quickly as the words left her mouth, she turned on her heels and marched into her home. I stood there in stunned silence. I had never heard anyone outside our faith bear testimony like that. Her words echoed within me, creating a tremendous sense of confusion. The time spoken of by Elder Kimball had now arrived for me. In my heart I knew my father's testimony wasn't enough for me to stand behind anymore. The day had arrived for me to stop living on "borrowed light."

That evening as I knelt in prayer I began the search for my own sacred grove. I knew the time had arrived for me to discover my own testimony. In an effort to communicate to the Lord regarding the intensity of my desire I committed myself completely to the work. I needed to know as badly as anything in my life that the religion of my youth was what it claimed to be.

From that time forth, whenever I had a free minute I read the Book of Mormon, all the while praying that I might receive the witness promised in the scriptures that would come to all those who search with a "sincere heart" and "real intent." (See Moroni 10:4.)

As I studied the Book of Mormon I learned the importance of fasting, and I practiced this as much as possible. A hunger deep inside me began to grow as I got a glimpse of just how my life would change if only I had the testimony of my father.

As I look back on this experience some thirty years later, I find it surprising that even though my quest lasted many months during my mission, I did not become discouraged. In fact, my faith grew and I had a quiet, simple feeling within me that in the Lord's time the promised witness would come. Looking back on it now, I recognize that this feeling in and of itself was part of that witness.

I initially had an expectation that Moroni's promise would happen while I was on my knees, or when I was reading the Book of Mormon. But I have come to understand that while it is each individual's choice to search for truth, it is the Lord who chooses the time and place, and even the manner, in which the witness comes to each individual. I have also learned that the witness promised by Moroni doesn't always come in a sacred grove event. This witness of the truth can come for many people "line upon line" over a period of time, rather than in a single moment. Elder Robert D. Hales said, "Generally, testimony emerges over time and through life's experiences." (*Ensign*, Nov. 1994, p. 22.)

For others, it just seems to have always been there. For example, Elder Bruce R. McConkie said, "I was born with a testimony, and from my earliest days have known with absolute certainty of the truth and divinity of his great latter-day work. Doubt and uncertainty have been as foreign to me as the gibberish of alien tongues." (*The Promised Messiah*, p. xvii.) I believe my wife has a witness and faith similar to Elder McConkie's, but for whatever reason such was not the case for me.

A number of months into my mission, my companion and I 'tracted out' a man whom we took to the visitors' center of the temple in Crawley, England. The visitors' center stood separate from the temple, and at that time was little bigger than a one-room schoolhouse. We walked in and sat down in a little theater with a movie screen in front, flanked on both sides by walls with pictures depicting the fundamental beliefs of the Church.

An elderly missionary couple showed us a short movie and then shared with our investigator the basic beliefs of our faith using the pictures on the walls. It was obvious that they were not from England, as they gave their presentation in a thick Texas drawl. Looking at the good brother making the presentation gave me a twinge of homesickness for America, as he stood there with his cowboy boots and his ornamented belt buckle.

As this humble man continued to speak, the spirit of the message became the dominant theme. There was a power in his message that I could see was having an impact on the investigator we had brought to this sacred place.

And then, something happened within me too, something that I still struggle to find the words to describe. It was a feeling I had never experienced before, but recognized unmistakably. As the elderly servant of God spoke, the Spirit branded into my heart the message that his words were true. I was engulfed in the Spirit; it extended through my entire being.

I found it odd that I wasn't reading or praying for a witness of the Spirit at the time; in fact, I wasn't even thinking about it. But that was the place the Lord chose to bless me with the testimony of my father. I could not doubt the message I had received was true, nor can I do so now, more than thirty years later. I hold that witness high among the greatest gifts I have received in my life. It is something I can feel and know to be true, but I cannot give to anyone else in a manner that they feel what I feel. Like my father before me, I cannot duplicate this experience, even for those I love the most; I can only show the pathway that leads to it. My father was right: The Book of Mormon placed me on the path; and like the iron rod that it is, it kept me moving in the right direction.

The elder from Texas concluded by bearing testimony and bid us and our investigator well. As my companion and our investigator stood to leave, they were surprised that I did not move. I'm sure they thought it odd that I was not in step with them in their departure. With a glance I could see that what I had experienced was unique to myself and had not been shared by anyone else in the room. Not even the old missionary from Texas was aware of what had happened to me while he was speaking.

I asked my companion if he would take our investigator into the foyer and told him I would join them in just a minute. My reason for this request was simple—my body was totally and completely exhausted. Even though what I had just experienced was not tearful or emotional, it had left me without the strength to even rise to my feet. Although I had not done anything requiring physical exertion, I was totally and completely drained to the point that it would have been impossible for me to stand at that moment.

I sat there alone for a minute, contemplating what had just

happened. Within a short time my strength returned to me and I joined my companion in the foyer.

From that day to this, I have had a hunger to read and study the Book of Mormon that has never been completely satisfied. Each time I open myself to its pages I get a little bit of the feeling that became a part of me on that day so many years ago in England. Reading it moves me forward while at the same time giving me a reunion with my own sacred grove so many years before. My exposure to the Book of Mormon has been much the same as so many people's: What began as an attempt to digest the book ended with my being digested by the power behind the book. I have been astounded many times over the years at the ability this book has to bring about change in the lives of those who are exposed to its pages. The Book of Mormon will feed a person only if that person comes to its pages hungry. While it is a thanksgiving feast to the individual who comes to its table with an overwhelming appetite for truth, it may actually appear to be meaningless and even boring to the person who does not approach its pages with a "sincere heart" and "real intent." (See Moroni 10:4.) In my own youth, this book seemed to be lifeless and void of flavor until I prepared myself to *sup* at its table. From that moment forward, its pages have fed me in ways I could never have imagined. I have seen the same process repeat itself in the lives of others, as well.

For example, there was a young college student who felt that his burden was much more than he could bear. In desperation, he decided the best alternative to his dilemma was to end his own life. He closed all the doors and windows of his garage with the intent of sitting in his car with the engine running. He had concluded that the result of such deliberate action would separate him from his troubles. After starting the vehicle, he settled into the front seat, waiting to expire.

For some reason, he looked down to his right between himself and the passenger seat. As he did so, his eyes fell upon a Book of Mormon that had been left there by one of his parents. He picked up this book that had been a stranger to him for so long. While it had always been around him, he had never been hungry enough to "sup" from its pages. He held it in his hands, letting it fall open without any textual destination in mind.

His eyes happened to fall upon one verse, which read, "And I will also ease the burdens which are put upon your shoulders, that even you cannot feel them upon your backs." (Mosiah 24:14.) His desire to end his life was replaced with a hunger to find out if this promise was true. He recognized that this verse presented a divine alternative to his problems.

Quickly, he pressed the button on the garage door opener and backed the car out of the driveway. After clearing out his lungs, he followed an impression to drive to the office of a good man who had been his teacher. As he walked into the building, his youthful strides took him through the doorway of his teacher's office unannounced. Laying the book on the teacher's desk, he exposed the scripture that had caught his own eyes just minutes before. Pointing to Mosiah 24:14 he said, "Will Jesus do that for me?"

Hesitating long enough to read the verse, the teacher looked up from his desk, and proclaimed, "He certainly will."

To which the young man responded, "Can you tell me how?"

Thus began a change of heart and lifestyle that connected this young man to Christ. The months and years that have followed in his life bear witness to the change that is brought about for those who avail themselves to the gospel of Jesus Christ through the power of the Book of Mormon.

It is not hard to imagine what may have happened if that Book of Mormon had not been in the right place at the right time; and if he had not been willing to read just a single verse. What began with just a nibble of the text at a critical time in his life turned into a feast that saved his soul.

This story bears witness to the words of President Heber J. Grant:

"There is a mark of divinity on this book; and I maintain that no man can read [it] . . . without receiving an impression of this kind." (Conference Report, Apr. 1908, p. 57.) Such was the experience of this young man. But what of those times he had read words from the book earlier in his life? The answer may be connected to the fact that this time he came to the table hungry. The Book of Mormon is a feast to those who hunger and thirst after the truth. For the first time in his life he was truly willing to do as Alma suggested: "Because ye have tried the experiment, and planted the seed, and it swelleth and sprouteth, and beginneth to grow, ye must needs know that the seed is good." (Alma 32:33.) In the most unlikely place and the most precarious time in his life, he "tried the experiment" with the seed explained by Alma.

As a young boy, my own son Jacob tried so hard to learn to read but had little success. We had him examined many times and took him for hundreds of hours of tutoring. While he was very sharp in many other academic areas, he just could not master the art of reading.

Brother Ed Pinegar, a former MTC president, and I were having lunch one day, when I brought up the subject of my son's dilemma. He interrupted my words by saying, "Brother Doug, I'm shocked at you." He continued, "You, who spend so much of your time in the Book of Mormon obviously don't understand what this book can do for your son."

I replied, "The Book of Mormon is not in a position to do anything for Jacob, because he can't read it."

He countered with, "Doesn't he read during family scripture study?"

My words were delivered in a defensive tone. "He can't read 'Run Dick, run Jane.' How in the world is he supposed to read 'I, Nephi, having been born of goodly parents'?"

Sensing my frustration, he simply said, "Just have him regularly read the book out loud; the rest will come."

Typical of Brother Ed, he then winked at me and said in his high-pitched voice, "I guess you don't know everything about the Book of Mormon." Chuckling to himself, he walked away, leaving me to ponder his words.

That night I went home and announced to my nine-year-old son that we were going to read the Book of Mormon. He struggled in his initial attempt, as I expected him to do. Then, over the next few weeks as he persisted, his reading became markedly improved. He was actually able to read the scriptures with greater ease than the more basic reading he was doing with his tutors. Over a period of time, as he continued reading the Book of Mormon, his reading in all subjects began to improve significantly. By age twelve his proficiency in reading was up to speed with that of his peers. Jacob had come to the table hungry, and the Book of Mormon was able to feed his "sincere heart" as he exercised "real intent."

PROMISES CONCERNING THE BOOK OF MORMON

The Prophet Joseph Smith taught that the Book of Mormon is "the most correct of any book on earth, and the keystone of our religion, and a man would get nearer to God by abiding by its precepts, than by any other book." (*History of the Church*, 4:461.) My own experience has proven this statement to be factual; for it placed me on a path that has brought joy and peace to my life that I never could have obtained in any other way.

But this is not all; consider the following promises from President Ezra Taft Benson to individuals as well as families in the Church:

- Greater power to resist temptation (*Ensign*, Nov. 1984, p. 7)
- Power to avoid deception (*Ensign*, Nov. 1984, p. 7)
- Life, in greater and greater abundance (*Ensign*, Nov. 1984, p. 7)
- Fortification against the evils of our day (*Ensign*, May 1986, p. 43)
- Spirituality (*Ensign*, May 1986, p. 43)

- An increase in the spirit of reverence in the home (*Ensign*, Nov. 1986, p. 7)
- Greater mutual respect and consideration for each other in the family (*Ensign*, Nov. 1986, p. 7)
- The departure of contention in the home (*Ensign*, Nov. 1986, p. 7)
- The ability to counsel your children with greater love and wisdom (*Ensign*, Nov. 1986, p. 7)
- Increased responsiveness and submissiveness of children to counsel from their parents (*Ensign*, Nov. 1986, p. 7)
- Success in righteousness (*Ensign*, May 1986, p. 82)
- Healing of the soul (*Ensign*, May 1986, p. 82)
- Continued blessings from God poured out upon each child of Zion and the Church (*Ensign*, May 1986, p. 82)

Elder Russell M. Nelson stated the following promises regarding the Book of Mormon to the saints in general conference (*Ensign*, Nov. 1999, p. 71):

- "A testimony of its divinity" to all who read it
- Help with personal problems, including ridding ourselves of bad habits
- Improved family relationships
- Increased spiritual capacity
- "A crown of eternal life" (D&C 20:14)

Elder Bruce R. McConkie made this promise regarding the power of the Book of Mormon: "It is the book that will save the world and prepare the sons of men for joy and peace here and now and everlasting life in eternity." (Conference Report, Oct. 1983, p. 107.)

These statements, and many others that have come from the Brethren since 1830 regarding the Book of Mormon, leave me wondering why a greater number of members are not seriously and carefully reading this marvelous work. Are there individuals, as well as families in this church, who are not in need of the blessings promised through studying this ancient scripture? The world may be able to hide behind the veil of ignorance, but what of us?

THE NATURE OF THE BOOK OF MORMON

As a student of the Book of Mormon, I have taken many moments to ponder the nature of this particular book of scripture—what allows it to fulfill such a bold agenda? I will not attempt at this time to give a comprehensive answer to this query, but I will take a little space to list a few concepts that allow the Book of Mormon to accomplish the promises I have just listed.

1. The divine editing of the text

President Benson spoke regarding this matter: "God, who knows the end from the beginning, told [Mormon] what to include in his abridgement that we would need for our day." (Conference Report, Apr. 1975, p. 94.)

Nephi bore similar testimony: "These words . . . are the words of Christ, and he hath given them unto me." (2 Nephi 33:10.) Nephi also recorded, "The Lord hath commanded me to make these plates for a wise purpose in him, which purpose I know not." (1 Nephi 9:5.)

Mormon, the man for whom the book was named, also spoke of the Savior's role in his writing: "The Lord . . . worketh in me to do according to his will." (Words of Mormon 1:7.) Later Mormon prefaced his words to the latter-day Gentiles by writing, "Jesus Christ . . . commanded me . . . that I should write." (3 Nephi 30:1.)

The Savior himself spoke to the Nephites regarding the record they had been keeping: "Other scriptures I would that ye should write, that ye have not." (3 Nephi 23:6.)

It is easy to see this book's ability to bring people to Christ when we recognize the Savior's personal role in the shaping of the text.

2. The role of Joseph Smith in the process of translation

I do not wish to elaborate on the intricacies of the Urim and Thummim or the manner of translation itself. That has been well documented in many other texts. Rather, I simply wish to identify the purity of this process as one of the reasons the Book of Mormon has such a great ability to draw people to Christ.

President Benson said, "Unlike the Bible, which passed through generations of copyists, translators, and corrupt religionists who tampered with the text, the Book of Mormon came from writer to reader in just one inspired step of translation. Therefore, its testimony of the Master is clear, undiluted, and *full of power.*" (*A Witness and a Warning*, p. 18; italics added.)

Elder Russell M. Nelson stated, "The King James Version of the Bible . . . was produced by 50 English scholars who accomplished their work in seven years, translating at the rate of *one* page per day. . . . In contrast, Joseph Smith translated the Book of Mormon at the rate of about 10 pages per day, completing the task in about 85 days!" (*Ensign*, Nov. 1999, p. 71.)

All of the other reasons that enable the Book of Mormon to accomplish its purposes would be diluted were it not for the purity of its translation. We need look no further than the manner in which the Bible was translated as evidence of this. The Savior spoke of his connection to the Prophet Joseph in this process: "[I] gave him power from on high, . . . to translate the Book of Mormon." (D&C 20:8.) We can clearly sense his role in the translation as well as in the authorship of the original text.

3. The teachings of the Book of Mormon

The Savior bore witness to the strength of the teachings within the Book of Mormon: "There are many things engraven upon the plates of Nephi which do throw greater views upon my gospel." (D&C 10:45.) For anyone who has studied the Book of Mormon, it is not hard to recognize its impact on our understanding of the following doctrines, as well as many other teachings:

- Christ's atoning sacrifice
- The fall of Adam
- The plan of salvation
- The Resurrection
- The spirit world
- The necessity of ordinances
- Grace and works
- The gathering of Israel

President Benson stated:

The Book of Mormon is the keystone in our witness of Jesus Christ. . . It bears witness of His reality with power and clarity. . . . Its testimony of the Master is clear. . . . Much of the Christian world today rejects the divinity of the Savior. They question His miraculous birth, His perfect life, and the reality of His glorious resurrection. The Book of Mormon teaches in plain and unmistakable terms about the truth of all of those. It also provides the most complete explanation of the doctrine of the Atonement. Truly, this divinely inspired book is a keystone in bearing witness to the world that Jesus is the Christ. (See title page of the Book of Mormon.)

The Book of Mormon is also the keystone of the doctrine of the resurrection. . . . [T]he Lord Himself has stated that the Book of Mormon contains the 'fulness of the gospel of Jesus Christ.' (D&C 20:9.) That does not mean it contains every teaching, every doctrine ever revealed. Rather, it means that in the Book of Mormon we will find the fulness of those doctrines required for our salvation. . . . The Book of Mormon offers so much that broadens our understanding of the doctrines of salvation. Without it, much of what is taught in other scriptures would not be nearly so plain and precious. (A Witness and a Warning, pp. 18–19.)

THE BOOK OF MORMON AS A LIAHONA

The Liahona in the Book of Mormon was more than just a compass; it was also a revelator, in that it gave Lehi's family "understanding concerning the ways of the Lord." (1 Nephi 16:29.) And like so many other spiritual gifts, it worked "according to the[ir] faith and diligence and heed." (1 Nephi 16:28.) Elder Robert E. Wells likened the Liahona to the manner in which the Book of Mormon operates in our lives:

"As I read the Book of Mormon, . . . something strange seems to happen to me. Passages of scriptures that I have read many times in one light seem to change—and suddenly there is a new meaning to that old and familiar scripture. I like to think that the Book of Mormon is truly like the Liahona of old. Not only does it point us in the way of the Lord and to the Lord according to the faith, diligence, and heed we give it, but *if we are interested enough to read it again and again, from cover to cover, there are times when a 'new writing'—plain to be read—seems to appear*." ("The Liahona Triad," in *Doctrines of the Book of Mormon*, p. 13; italics added.)

It is the purity of the text, not just in what is written, but the purity in which it has traveled from Moroni to Joseph to us, that allows such enlightening to happen. The family of Lehi could have traveled from Jerusalem to Bountiful in ninety days, but they tarried in the wilderness for about eight years, because "they were slothful, and forgot to exercise . . . faith and diligence." (Alma 37:41.) Notice that Elder Wells said that the Book of Mormon can only be a Liahona for those of us who exercise "faith," and "diligence" and "are interested enough to read it again and again."

Many years ago, as a seminary teacher in Arizona, I was giving one of the Brethren a ride to a fireside. I indicated to him that I would be back in the classroom tomorrow and I would like to give my students a message from him that would help them in their studies of the Book of Mormon. What he told me fit perfectly into the pattern identified by

Elder Wells about the price that must be paid in allowing the Book of Mormon to operate like a Liahona in our lives.

He encouraged me to share the following analogy with my students (I will take his teachings and put them into my own words): Have you ever noticed the rippling effect that occurs when you drop a pebble into a perfectly still pond? The ripples are small waves that travel out from the point where the pebble first entered the water. At first it looks like nine or ten ripples travel outward and then disappear into the pool. If you film this occurrence and then play it back at a very slow speed, however, you will witness an amazing thing. There are, indeed, nine or ten circular ripples, like small rings, bunched together, close to the point of entry. They travel quickly away from the center, like tiny tidal waves. If you look carefully, you will notice that they then begin to separate and break free from the other ripples that once were so close to them. Where they once seemed almost connected, they each now take on a life of their own, as they travel away from the point of entry. They seem to never end.

Now, imagine that reading the Book of Mormon is like standing over a still pond and dropping a pebble into the water. The rings we have already identified represent each time you read the Book of Mormon from cover to cover. We will call these "rings of understanding." Remember, there were about eight to ten rings within the water that were bunched very close together near the point of entry, until they began to break free, and expand wider and wider. As we begin reading the Book of Mormon, our "rings of understanding" may expand very little at first. But as we persist (just like the outer rings that broke free), we will eventually experience that ring of understanding that will open to us a window of knowledge that will expand and enlighten us in ways we could hardly have imagined when we began our study.

He admonished me to encourage my students to commit themselves to studying the Book of Mormon until they reached that "ring of understanding" that will break away and expand them in ways that will bless them forever. He said that the rings close to the point of entry represent our reading of the Book of Mormon for the purpose of finding the witness spoken of in Moroni 10:3–5. He indicated that too many people in the Church do not see the Book of Mormon as a Liahona, and when they reach the "ring of understanding" that allows them to say they know the book is true, they stop reading with any real intensity. He said this happens to far too many of our missionaries when they return home from their missions.

He encouraged me to tell my students to never lose their hunger for reading the Book of Mormon, and they would find the concept of "rings of understanding" to be true. He told me that faith in the Lord's timing as well as diligence is required in reading the Book of Mormon. What only took him a few minutes to share has had a great impact on my teaching of the power of the Book of Mormon.

If you recognize the fact that the Book of Mormon is a Liahona and hold fast to it throughout your life, it will seem to have a different writing from time to time. You'll also find that because of this quality of changeable revelation—based on the circumstances and needs of the person reading it at the time—you can say you know the Book of Mormon is true, but you can never say you *know* the Book of Mormon. There's always more. Indeed, the "rings of understanding" never end.

When we read it to gain a testimony, it will read a certain way. When we read it as missionaries it will be different still. As a newly-wed, as a father, and as a Sunday School teacher I have found this to be true. Just like the Liahona, the text will have a "new writing" or message based upon the circumstances we are in as we read the text. This does not allow the doctrine to change from individual to individual, but it does give the book the ability to communicate on an individual basis.

A number of years ago I was teaching this concept in a returned missionary Book of Mormon class at BYU. A student named Kristen

Hall sent me this letter that bears witness to the point. The following is a portion of that letter:

I had been in Portugal for two months, still with my first companion, and we were in the process of finding another area to proselyte. It seemed we had already worked the small city and we were absolutely stumped as to what to do. As we searched, we thought about a barrio (state funded apartments) of about fifteen buildings called Largateiro. The elders had told us never to go there because the last missionaries were driven out with rocks. We thought about working there, but were concerned because of this. It was the only place we hadn't gone. We went there and began to meet the people. They told us they knew who we were and they didn't believe in our teachings.

The next morning as I began my personal study I prayed that the Lord would teach me through the scriptures what He would have me do. I came to Alma 8:11 and I saw where Alma had had a similar experience with the people of Ammonihah, who said, "We know that thou are Alma . . . and we do not believe." (Alma 8:11.) We began to pray about the area and how we should work there. As I continued to read of Alma's experience I saw something I had never seen before. After Alma had been kicked out of the city he was met by an angel who comforted him and then encouraged him to go back to Ammonihah. In verse 18 it says, "he entered the city by another way."

That is when it came to us; we needed to enter that barrio a different way—to proselyte it in a way that hadn't been done before. So we decided to work through the inactive members. So we began contacting them, and they began to invite their friends.

I had read Alma 8:18 many times before but had never

thought of it in that way. I know that the Lord used that scripture to answer our prayer. Following this, we began to see success.

I'm confident that each person who has read the Book of Mormon with faith and diligence over the years can bear a similar testimony. Because of the reasons I have listed, and perhaps others I have not, the Book of Mormon truly has the power to act as a Liahona in our lives.

JUDGED FROM THE BOOK

As members of the Church, we have a solemn responsibility concerning this book, even as it relates to our own eternal welfare. Within the space of a few chapters Nephi bears witness to this fact numerous times. Speaking of the latter-day audience who shall receive the Book of Mormon, he wrote that its "words shall judge them at the last day." (2 Nephi 25:18.) In the same chapter he stated, "And the nations who shall possess them shall be judged of them." (2 Nephi 25:22.) A few verses later, he adds, "The words which I have spoken shall stand as a testimony against you." (2 Nephi 25:28.) Later he adds the Savior's witness, "Out of the books which shall be written I will judge the world." (2 Nephi 29:11.)

Elder Marion G. Romney added his testimony to that of Nephi and the Savior's: "For me there could be no more impelling reason for reading the Book of Mormon than this statement of the Lord that we shall be judged by what is written in it." (Conference Report, Apr. 1960, p. 110.)

Nephi concluded his record with a haunting farewell that leaves a warning to those of us who have been given the opportunity to read his words: "I bid you an everlasting farewell, for *these words shall condemn you at the last day.*" (2 Nephi 33:14; italics added.)

Nephi was no more bold than our latter-day prophets concerning our responsibility. President Joseph Fielding Smith said, "No member of this Church can stand approved in the presence of God who has not seriously and carefully read the Book of Mormon." (Conference Report, Oct. 1961, p. 18.)

President Ezra Taft Benson added his warning: "Do eternal consequences rest upon our response to this book? Yes, either to our blessing or our condemnation. Every Latter-day Saint should make the study of this book a lifetime pursuit. Otherwise he is placing his soul in jeopardy." (A Witness and a Warning, p. 7.)

We do not have to wait until the judgment day to reap the penalties of neglecting the Book of Mormon. President Benson said, "Social, ethical, cultural, or educational converts will not survive under the heat of the day unless their taproots go down to the fulness of the gospel which the Book of Mormon contains." (Ensign, May 1975, p. 65.)

These warnings should not be taken as negative motivation, but as a reminder of our sacred responsibility. It has been my experience that few people embrace the light fully because they are afraid of the dark. Our motivation for reading the Book of Mormon should be based upon our hunger for the text, not a fear of reprisal. Another worthy reason for reading the Book of Mormon comes from our willingness to allow it to bring us as well as others closer to Christ. But if we do not take our responsibility seriously, we cannot escape the consequences that fall upon us as guardians of this sacred text.

I do not believe that the method of accountability at the Judgment Day regarding this book will come in the form of an academic exam that will test our knowledge of the peoples, places, and events among the Nephites. However, the test may come in our willingness to expose ourselves to its pages and then to use the book to bless the lives of those around us.

Over the years I have come to understand that the real test for us personally goes beyond that of just obtaining a testimony. It does not come down to just knowing the Book of Mormon is true, but whether we are true to the Book of Mormon. In the final analysis it is not if we have digested the Book of Mormon, but if the Book of Mormon has digested us. Therein lies the test. The process becomes finalized when a person can stand before the Lord as a living witness to the power of the Book of Mormon in aiding an individual and attain "the measure of the stature of the fulness of Christ." (Ephesians 4:13.)

Elder Dallin H. Oaks said: "This process requires far more than acquiring knowledge. . . . We must act and think so that we are converted by it. . . . The Final Judgment . . . is an acknowledgement of the final effect of our acts and thoughts—what we have *become*." (Conference Report, Oct. 2000, pp. 40–41.)

It is in this goal to *become* Christlike that the power of the Book of Mormon is manifest. The book truly has the power to draw a person "nearer to God . . . than . . . any other book." (Joseph Smith, *History of the Church*, 4:461.) Of this I bear my witness.

WORKS CITED

1978 Devotional Speeches of the Year: BYU Devotional and Fireside Addresses. Provo: Brigham Young University Press, 1979.

1984–85 Devotional and Fireside Speeches. Provo: Brigham Young University Press, 1985.

1988–89 Devotional and Fireside Speeches. Provo: Brigham Young University Press, 1990.

Alma, the Testimony of the Word: Papers from the Sixth Annual Book of Mormon Symposium, 1991. Monte S. Nyman and Charles D. Tate Jr., eds. Provo, Utah: Religious Studies Center, Brigham Young University, 1992.

Ballard, Melvin J. Melvin J. Ballard—Crusader for Righteousness. Salt Lake City: Bookcraft, 1966.

Barlow, Ora H. The Israel Barlow Story and Mormon Mores. Salt Lake City: Ora H. Barlow, 1968.

Bassett, K. Douglas. Kisses at the Window, Salt Lake City: Hawkes Pub., 1985.

———. Latter-day Commentary on the Book of Mormon. American Fork, Utah: Covenant Communications, 1999.

Benson, Ezra Taft. A Witness and a Warning: A Modern-day Prophet Testifies of the Book of Mormon. Salt Lake City: Deseret Book, 1988.

———. Come unto Christ. Salt Lake City: Deseret Book, 1983.

———. Teachings of Ezra Taft Benson. Salt Lake City: Bookcraft, 1988.

Black, Susan Easton. Finding Christ through the Book of Mormon. Salt Lake City: Deseret Book, 1987.

The Book of Mormon: First Nephi, the Doctrinal Foundation: Papers from the Second Annual Book of Mormon Symposium. Monte S. Nyman and Charles D. Tate Jr., eds. Provo: Religious Studies Center, Brigham Young University, 1988.

Brigham Young Magazine. Provo: Brigham Young University, 1993–.

Brigham Young University 1996–97 Speeches. Provo: Brigham Young University, 1997.

Brown, James S. *Life of a Pioneer*. Salt Lake City: G. Q. Cannon & Sons, 1900.

BYU Speeches of the Year, 1963. Provo: Brigham Young University, 1964.

BYU Today. Provo: BYU Alumni Association, 1981–1992.

Cannon, George Q. *Gospel Truth: Discourses and Writings of President George Q. Cannon*, Classics in Mormon Literature Series, sel. Jerreld L. Newquist. Salt Lake City: Deseret Book, 1987.

Conference Reports of The Church of Jesus Christ of Latter-day Saints. The Church of Jesus Christ of Latter-day Saints, 1897–.

Cowley, Matthew. *Matthew Cowley Speaks*. Salt Lake City: Deseret Book, 1954.

Covey, Stephen R. *Spiritual Roots of Human Relations*. Salt Lake City: Deseret Book, 1970.

Curtis, Lindsay R. *Parables for Teaching*. Salt Lake City: Bookcraft, 1981.

Davis, Mac. *Sports Shorts*. New York: Bantam Books, 1963.

Doctrines of the Book of Mormon: The 1991 Sperry Symposium, Bruce A Van Orden and Brent L. Top, eds. Salt Lake City: Deseret Book, 1992.

Ensign. The Church of Jesus Christ of Latter-day Saints, 1971–.

Eyring, Henry B. *To Draw Closer to God: A Collection of Discourses*. Salt Lake City: Deseret Book, 1997.

"Family, The: A Proclamation to the World." *Ensign*, Nov. 1995, p. 102.

Faust, James E. *Finding Light in a Dark World*. Salt Lake City: Deseret Book, 1995.

Gore, Al. *Earth in the Balance: Ecology and the Human Spirit*. Boston: Houghton Mifflin, 1992.

Grant, Heber J. *Gospel Standards: Selections from the Sermons and Writings of Heber J. Grant*, comp. G. Homer Durham. Salt Lake City: Improvement Era, 1981.

Hinckley, Gordon B. *Standing for Something: Ten Neglected Virtues that Will Heal Our Hearts and Homes*. New York: Times Books, 2000.

———. *Teachings of Gordon B. Hinckley*. Salt Lake City: Deseret Book, 1997.

Holland, Jeffrey R. *Christ and the New Covenant: The Messianic Message of the Book of Mormon*. Salt Lake City: Deseret Book, 1997.

Hymns of The Church of Jesus Christ of Latter-day Saints. Salt Lake City: The Church of Jesus Christ of Latter-day Saints, 1985.

Jackson, Kent, ed. *Studies in Scripture, Vol. 7: 1 Nephi to Alma 29*. Salt Lake City: Deseret Book, 1987.

Journal of Discourses. 26 vols. London: Latter-day Saints' Book Depot, 1854–1886.

Kimball, Spencer W. *Faith Precedes the Miracle*. Salt Lake City: Deseret Book, 1972.

———. *The Teachings of Spencer W. Kimball*. Edward L. Kimball, ed. Salt Lake City: Bookcraft, 1982.

Lee, Harold B. *The Teachings of Harold B. Lee*. Clyde J. Williams, ed. Salt Lake City: Bookcraft, 1996.

Maxwell, Neal A. *A Wonderful Flood of Light*. Salt Lake City: Bookcraft, 1990.

———. *Not My Will, But Thine*. Salt Lake City: Bookcraft, 1988.

———. *Notwithstanding My Weakness*. Salt Lake City: Deseret Book, 1981.

McConkie, Bruce R. *A New Witness for the Articles of Faith*. Salt Lake City: Deseret Book, 1985.

———. *Doctrinal New Testament Commentary*. 3 vols. Salt Lake City: Bookcraft, 1965–1973.

———. *Mormon Doctrine*, 2d ed. Salt Lake City: Bookcraft, 1966.

———. *Sermons and Writings of Bruce R. McConkie*. Mark L. McConkie, ed. Salt Lake City: Bookcraft, 1998.

———. *The Millennial Messiah: The Second Coming of the Son of Man*. Salt Lake City: Deseret Book, 1982.

———. *The Promised Messiah: The First Coming of Christ*. Salt Lake City: Deseret Book, 1978.

McKay, David O. *Pathways to Happiness*. Llewelyn R. McKay, comp. Salt Lake City: Bookcraft, 1957.

Merriam-Webster's Collegiate Dictionary, 10th ed. Springfield, Mass.: Merriam-Webster, 1996.

Millet, Robert. *The Power of the Word: Saving Doctrines from the Book of Mormon*. Salt Lake City: Deseret Book, 1994.

———. *Selected Writings of Robert L. Millet: Gospel Scholars Series*. Salt Lake City: Deseret Book, 2000.

Oaks, Dallin H. *The Lord's Way*. Salt Lake City: Deseret Book, 1991.

Packer, Boyd K. *Our Father's Plan*. Salt Lake City: Deseret Book, 1984.

———. *The Shield of Faith*. Salt Lake City: Bookcraft, 1998.

———. *Teach Ye Diligently*. Salt Lake City: Deseret Book, 1975.

Pearsall, Paul. *The Heart's Code: Tapping the Wisdom and Power of Our Heart Energy*. New York: Broadway Books, 1998.

Pratt, Parley P., *Autobiography of Parley P. Pratt*. Rev. and enhanced by Scot Facer Proctor and Maurine Jensen Proctor. Salt Lake City: Deseret Book, 2000.

———. *Key to the Science of Theology*. Salt Lake City: Deseret Book, 1965.

Shakespeare, William. *Titus Andronicus*.

Simpson, Robert L. *Proven Paths*. Salt Lake City: Deseret Book, 1974.

Smith, Joseph F. *Gospel Doctrine: Selections from the Sermons and Writings of Joseph F. Smith*, John A. Widtsoe, comp. Salt Lake City: Deseret Book, 1939.

Smith, Joseph Fielding. *Church History and Modern Revelation*. 4 vols. Salt Lake City: The Church of Jesus Christ of Latter-day Saints, 1946–1949.

———. *Doctrines of Salvation*. 3 vols. Salt Lake City: Bookcraft, 1954–1956.

Smith, Joseph Jr. *History of The Church of Jesus Christ of Latter-day Saints*. 7 vols. 2d ed. rev. Edited by B. H. Roberts. Salt Lake City: The Church of Jesus Christ of Latter-day Saints, 1932–1951.

———. *Teachings of the Prophet Joseph Smith*, sel. Joseph Fielding Smith. Salt Lake City: Deseret Book, 1976.

Teachings of Presidents of the Church: Harold B. Lee. Salt Lake City: The Church of Jesus Christ of Latter-day Saints, 2000.

Teachings of Presidents of the Church: Joseph F. Smith. Salt Lake City: The Church of Jesus Christ of Latter-day Saints, 1998.

ten Boom, Corrie. "I'm Still Learning to Forgive," *Guideposts*, November 1972.

Thurman, Howard. *The Luminous Darkness: A Personal Interpretation of the Anatomy of Segregation and the Ground of Hope*. New York: Harper & Row, 1965.

Whitney, Orson F. *The Life of Heber C. Kimball*. Salt Lake City: Bookcraft, 1945.

Woodruff, Wilford. *The Discourses of Wilford Woodruff*. G. Homer Durham, ed. Salt Lake City: Bookcraft, 1969.

Young, Brigham. *Discourses of Brigham Young*. John A. Widtsoe, ed. Salt Lake City: Deseret Book, 1973.

INDEX